DECISION MAKING FOR STUDENT SUCCESS

"Using clear explanations and numerous examples, the authors present an array of innovative practices shown to improve the educational outcomes for students. Drawing from research in multiple fields, the authors provide a nuanced picture of the challenges students face when making college decisions to help us understand not only why these barriers are so formidable, but also very real ways to overcome them. This book is a great resource for anyone working to support college access and success in this complex world."
—Bridget Terry Long, Saris Professor of Education and Economics, Harvard Graduate School of Education, USA

"A terrific, accessible introduction to the power of 'nudges' in improving education. Researchers, educators, and anyone who wants to lend a hand to struggling students will find important insights in this volume."
—Susan Dynarski, Professor of Economics, Education and Public Policy, University of Michigan, USA

Each year, many students with affordable college options and the academic skills needed to succeed do not enroll at all, enroll at institutions where they are not well-positioned for success, or drop out of college before earning a credential. Efforts to address these challenges have included changes in financial aid policy, increased availability of information, and enhanced academic support. This volume argues that the efficacy of these strategies can be improved by taking account of contemporary research on how students make choices. In *Decision Making for Student Success*, scholars from the fields of behavioral economics, education, and public policy explore contemporary research on decision making and highlight behavioral insights that can improve postsecondary access and success. This exciting volume will provide scholars, researchers, and higher education administrators with valuable perspectives and low-cost strategies that they can employ to improve outcomes for underserved populations.

Benjamin L. Castleman is an Assistant Professor of Education and Public Policy at the University of Virginia, USA.

Saul Schwartz is a Professor of Public Policy and Administration at Carleton University, Canada.

Sandy Baum is a Research Professor of Education Policy at George Washington University and a Senior Fellow at the Urban Institute, USA.

DECISION MAKING FOR STUDENT SUCCESS

Behavioral Insights to Improve College Access and Persistence

Edited by Benjamin L. Castleman,
Saul Schwartz, and Sandy Baum

Routledge
Taylor & Francis Group

NEW YORK AND LONDON

First published 2015
by Routledge
711 Third Avenue, New York, NY 10017

and by Routledge
2 Park Square, Milton Park, Abingdon, Oxon, OX14 4RN

Routledge is an imprint of the Taylor & Francis Group, an informa business

Library of Congress Cataloging-in-Publication Data
Decision Making for Student Success–
Library of Congress Cataloging in Publication Control Number:
2014040949

ISBN: 978-1-138-78497-0 (hbk)
ISBN: 978-1-138-78498-7 (pbk)
ISBN: 978-1-315-76793-2 (ebk)

Typeset in Bembo
by Apex CoVantage, LLC

Printed and bound in the United States of America by Publishers Graphics,
LLC on sustainably sourced paper.

CONTENTS

PREFACE

Sandy Baum, Benjamin L. Castleman,
and Saul Schwartz

Efforts to increase the number of students who enroll and succeed   postsecondary education are rooted in concerns about both the labor ma·   c needs of the U.S. economy and the persistent disparities in college acces·   id completion. Over the decade from 2002 to 2012, when 80 percent tc   3 percent of recent high school graduates from families in the highest quint¹   of the income distribution enrolled in college, the postsecondary enrollment   e in the lowest quintile of the income distribution fluctuated between 51 perc..c and 58 percent. For middle-income students the range was 58 percent to 67 percent (National Center for Education [NCES], 2013).

Moreover, many students who enroll do not complete the credentials they are seeking. Of those who began their studies in 2007, 56 percent had earned degrees or certificates six years later; 15 percent were still enrolled; and the remaining 29 percent had not earned a credential and were no longer enrolled at any postsecondary institution (Shapiro, Dundar, Ziskin, Yuan, & Harrell, 2013).

Some of the barriers to greater educational attainment are clear. Education is expensive, and we have to be sure both that funds are available to support those who cannot independently afford to pay for college and that students earlier in their schooling know that financial assistance will continue to be available in the future so that they can confidently invest in preparing and planning for college. Another challenge to resolving inequalities in college access and success is the dramatic disparity in the quality of our elementary and secondary schools. Too many young people graduate from high school unprepared to do college-level work—if they graduate at all.

Diminishing financial barriers and improving academic preparation require both systemic change and significant ongoing investment. At the same time, there are many students each year who have the academic skills to succeed in college and have affordable college options, but who do not enroll at all, enroll at institutions where they are not as well-positioned for success as they might be elsewhere, or drop out of college before earning a credential. These are students whose postsecondary outcomes educators and policymakers could conceivably influence with targeted investments in the near term.

Designing effective strategies for improving student success requires in-depth understanding of how students make choices, how their behaviors and responses to opportunities and circumstances affect their educational outcomes, how they process available information, and how the structure of the student aid system and the classroom might either interfere with or support their aspirations. This is the focus of the chapters in this collection.

Increased understanding of human behavior and decision-making processes is contributing to a number of policy areas. For instance, strategies to simplify information about available choices or to provide people with prompts to follow through on intentions they have set for themselves have generated positive outcomes in a range of fields, from retirement planning to public health. The chapters in this volume represent an important step in extending these approaches into the area of postsecondary education. Taken as a whole, these chapters provide important insights into potential strategies for improving educational attainment. These strategies are not likely to provide the solutions to the problems of inadequate funding and inadequate academic preparation. But they may move the needle on efforts to support students in overcoming other hurdles to college success.

This volume grew out of a project supported by a grant from the Bill & Melinda Gates Foundation to the George Washington University Graduate School of Education and Human Development and led by Sandy Baum, Robert Shireman, and Patricia Steele. Earlier versions of some of the chapters included here were part of the project and others have been added.

Chapter 1 is a primer on behavioral concepts. It will help readers unfamiliar with behavioral principles to become familiar with the terminology used in this volume. The primer includes clear examples of how students facing complex and unfamiliar decisions and processes might end up missing out on opportunities that would help them to achieve their postsecondary goals. A glossary at the end of the book provides a quick reference for readers, with definitions and clarification of the concepts discussed in the eight chapters in this volume.

The Chapters

The insights of cognitive psychology and behavioral economics remind us that the standard economic models of rational, utility-maximizing individuals are not adequate for developing a comprehensive understanding of how people behave.

These insights suggest that there are ways to "nudge" people into making choices consistent with their long-run interests and goals.

While our focus in this volume is on postsecondary education outcomes, it is clear that we can learn from studies of the ways people behave in other environments. In Chapter 2, "Motivation, Behavior, and Performance in the Workplace: Insights for Student Success in Higher Education," Charles Kurose looks to the literature on motivation and its relationship to performance in the workplace. His goal is to find potential lessons for higher education in studies of effective strategies for improving workplace outcomes. Kurose emphasizes the importance of goal setting and the prevalent finding that specific, challenging goals elicit the best outcomes. However, because completing college is a complex task that spans multiple years, these goals should focus on learning processes rather than on final performance outcomes. The goals should direct attention and effort toward development of the skills and abilities that one needs in order to succeed in college, rather than toward general goals students are unlikely to know how to achieve.

In Chapter 3, "Student Aid, Student Behavior, and Educational Attainment," Sandy Baum and Saul Schwartz examine the financial aid system's impact on student choices and behaviors. They discuss the importance of simple incentives like giving students more money when they enroll in more courses and make more academic progress; they focus primarily on insights from behavioral economics and cognitive psychology, which suggest that responses are less straightforward. For example, in the face of complexity, students, like anyone else, are likely to take the path of least resistance, going with the most salient option or the one that requires the least action, and they weigh potential losses more than potential gains of the same magnitude. The authors suggest ways in which the current system of grants and loans may exacerbate these tendencies, rather than counteracting them. They discuss the tendency for people to over-estimate their ability to beat the odds, leading to choices that may be self-defeating, such as excessive borrowing for college. Rather than advocating a specific set of policy changes, Baum and Schwartz focus on increasing our understanding of how the student aid system shapes student behaviors and how modifications might facilitate the goals of improved access and success.

In Chapter 4, "How Can Financial Incentives Improve the Success of Disadvantaged College Students? Insights from the Social Sciences," Nicole M. Stephens and Sarah S. M. Townsend emphasize the role of incentives and how a better understanding of the complexities of human decision making can strengthen our ability to provide an environment in which students adopt behaviors more likely to further their goals. The authors examine the potential effectiveness of financial incentives in modifying student behaviors. Their analysis is in the context of key barriers facing disadvantaged students seeking a college education. They argue that properly designed financial incentives have the potential to help students overcome financial barriers and develop necessary academic skills. While specifically targeted supplementary subsidies might make it easier for disadvantaged students to overcome some environmental barriers resulting from prevalent negative stereotypes and prejudices, money alone will not solve these problems. Moreover, the fundamental issue that some students lack the "cultural capital"—the understanding of the rules of the game—necessary to succeed in an academic environment, is not amenable to such a straightforward solution

Benjamin L. Castleman's "Prompts, Personalization, and Pay-Offs: Strategies to Improve the Design and Delivery of College and Financial Aid Information" (Chapter 5) asks how we can communicate more effectively with students. The lack of adequate information about the costs and benefits of college and about how to navigate the complex processes associated with applying for admission and for financial aid is frequently cited. Recent efforts on the part of the federal government and others are generating college search websites, net price calculators, and new ways of estimating the pay off to specific college credentials. But Castleman asks whether the *availability* of simpler and more personalized information will be sufficient to mitigate the informational obstacles that prevent low-income students from attending colleges and universities that are well-matched to their abilities and interests. He looks to recent work in a range of behavioral sciences to examine how information is presented and delivered and whether students and their families can access individualized assistance when they need it. He points to evidence that low-cost interventions providing students with prompts and reminders to complete important tasks in both the college and financial aid processes can increase college enrollment. Castleman's chapter provides an important reminder that we should stop to think about how potential students are likely to access and process information before we rush simply to provide even more sources of information.

In "The Shapeless River: Does a Lack of Structure Inhibit Students' Progress at Community Colleges?" (Chapter 6), Judith Scott-Clayton describes the complexity and confusion students often face in their attempts to navigate college, and draws upon recent research from behavioral economics and psychology to examine how the structure of the decision-making process may influence students' ultimate outcomes. She suggests that community college students will be more likely to succeed in programs that are tightly structured, with limited bureaucratic obstacles and little room to unintentionally stray from paths toward completion. The author concludes that a lack of a deliberate "choice architecture" in many institutions may result in suboptimal outcomes for students. While there is no silver-bullet intervention to address the problem, several promising approaches and directions for future research are highlighted.

In "Prepare for Class, Attend, and Participate! Incentives and Student Success in College" (Chapter 7), Robert M. Shireman and Joshua A. Price focus on some of the specific goals Kurose (Chapter 2) argues are likely to be most effective. Recognizing the role of cognitive biases like time-inconsistent preferences, which cause people to make immediate decisions inconsistent with long-run goals they have previously established, the authors discuss potential strategies for encouraging more constructive decisions and behaviors. These strategies build upon practices that are currently being used, but attempt to use behavioral economic tools to improve their effectiveness. For example, making the benefits of going to class more salient by providing monetary incentives to attend. In all, the goal is to use effective teaching to empower students to succeed in college.

In the final chapter of the volume, "Behavioral Nudges for College Success: Research, Impact, and Possibilities," Jill Frankfort, Ross E. O'Hara, and Kenneth Salim describe examples of relatively simple strategies that appear to be successful in increasing the frequency with which students engage in the behaviors known to improve academic outcomes. Minor interventions can have a measurable impact on how at-home students feel at their institutions, on their perception of socially acceptable behavior, and on their decisions about how much to study and attend class. The authors focus on low-cost strategies, frequently relying on modern communications technology, and are optimistic that increased understanding of how people actually make decisions and choose modes of behavior can have a significant impact on student outcomes.

All of the chapters in this volume highlight the contributions the behavioral social sciences have made to our understanding of human decision making. Behavioral insights do not negate the importance of money or of people's responses to financial incentives, but they enrich and complicate the picture. Particularly in complex situations where there are not obvious and manageable steps to follow to achieve a goal, people tend to make choices based on what is presented as the option that requires the least active decision, to respond to information that is hard to ignore, and to avoid paths that risk losses from the status quo. The issue is not that students—or adults in other environments—are lacking in ability. It is that human beings naturally respond in ways that do not always lead to the best outcomes.

To further the goal of increasing educational attainment, we should take these realities into consideration when we provide information about postsecondary education and its risks and benefits, when we design the system of subsidies intended to diminish financial barriers to education, and when we design the educational environments in which more students will thrive. Giving people more money, especially more money attached to desirable outcomes, matters. But money alone will not close the gaps in college access and success. We need to better understand the hurdles students face in taking advantage of educational opportunities, and we must modify the learning environments, the incentive systems, and the subsidy programs to better support the human beings navigating those systems.

References

National Center for Education Statistics Digest of Education Statistics. (2013). Percentage of recent high school completers enrolled in 2-year and 4-year colleges, by income level: 1975 through 2012. [Table 302.30]. Retrieved from http://nces.ed.gov/programs/digest/d13/tables/dt13_302.30.asp

Shapiro, D., Dundar, A., Ziskin, M., Yuan, X., & Harrell, A. (2013, December). *Completing College: A National View of Student Attainment Rates-Fall 2007 Cohort* (Signature Report No. 6). Herndon, VA: National Student Clearinghouse Research Center.

1

BEHAVIORAL ECONOMICS AND POSTSECONDARY ACCESS

A Primer

Benjamin L. Castleman, Sandy Baum, and Saul Schwartz

The disparities in college access and success by socioeconomic status are well-documented. In 2012, just over half of 18- to 24-year-olds from the lowest family income quintile who had earned a high school diploma or GED in the past year enrolled in college, compared with 81 percent of students from the highest family income quintile (Digest of Education Statistics, 2013). What is less apparent is *why* these disparities have persisted. After all, the federal and state governments have invested hundreds of billions of dollars in need-based financial aid over the last several decades (College Board, 2014). Over the same time period, secondary schools serving low-income communities have received large federal supplements to their per-pupil funding to address long-standing achievement gaps by race and income. Why, then, with such substantial investments in need-based financial assistance and instructional spending at the secondary level, do we still see so much inequality in who goes to and succeeds in college? In order to further probe this question we need to first pose two others: how do students decide whether to enroll in college? And once they are in college, how do they decide whether to continue with their studies?

Policy makers and researchers have historically thought of student decision making about postsecondary education as a cost-benefit analysis (Becker, 1964). The crux of this theory is that students map out various options they are considering after high school. These might include enrolling at a residential four-year college, commuting from home to a community college, or getting an apartment and working full-time. Students then weigh the costs associated with each option, including out-of-pocket expenses like tuition but also foregone earnings if they were to enroll in college full-time, against benefits, such as the annual earnings premium they would gain if they had a postsecondary degree rather than just a high school diploma, or the enrichment they would experience from pursuing courses and subjects aligned with their intellectual interests. The prevailing assumption for many years was that the vast majority of students would choose the option that maximized the benefits relative to the costs. One implication of this basic model is that, in the absence of financial aid, students from low-income families may be more likely to conclude that the costs of going to college exceed the benefits, and therefore choose not to enroll in college.

Moving Beyond the Traditional Decision-Making Model

Extensions from this core cost-benefit model provide additional insights into why students may decide that the costs of pursuing college exceed the benefits they would realize. One reason may be that students' families depend heavily on them for the wages they can earn or for the childcare they can provide for younger siblings. The responsibility that students feel to provide for their families may add to the costs they feel they are incurring by going off to college. If the student goes to college, she imposes a real cost on her household, particularly if her family is also having to contribute towards tuition and living expenses.

The belief that cost and credit constraints may prevent college-ready low-income students from pursuing college has motivated the need-based financial aid policies in the United States. If the costs of college are prohibitively high for low-income students, the government can give them need-based grants that lower costs to the point where students decide the benefits of matriculating exceed the expense and therefore enroll. If, after receiving grant aid, students and their families are willing to pay the balance of what they owe but face credit constraints, the government can guarantee access to loans, subsidize students' loan interest rates, or defer students' repayments until after they finish college.

A large body of research literature has demonstrated that offering low-income students need-based financial aid has a substantial impact on their college outcomes—improving the rates at which they enter and graduate from college. For instance, a need-based grant program in California increased college enrollment by 3–4 percentage points among financial aid applicants, while a need-based award in Florida increased the share of students who earned a bachelor's degree from a public university by six percentage points (Castleman & Long, 2013; Kane, 2003). These results are particularly impressive because the aid students received under these programs provided incremental increases in financial assistance on top of already substantial federal aid. And yet, the offer of need-based financial aid hasn't been sufficient to eliminate income inequalities in college outcomes for students with the same academic achievement (Long & Mabel, 2012). Why?

Over time researchers have learned that, in important ways, student decision-making is not quite so straightforward as the simple benefit-cost model would suggest. One assumption built into the model, for instance, is that students have access to complete information about the various options that are available to them, as well as a comprehensive understanding of the benefits and costs associated with each option. How, though, would we expect low-income students—who are often the first in their families to go to college—to have a good idea of what each postsecondary option has to offer? And given the high student-to-counselor ratios in high schools and that most school counselors have little experience with financial aid issues, is it realistic to think that students can accurately estimate the net costs and benefits of going to college? In fact, the opposite is often true. Low-income students and their parents tend to substantially overestimate how much college would cost them net of the financial aid they would be eligible to receive (Avery & Kane, 2004; Grodsky & Jones, 2007; Horn, Chen, & Chapman, 2003).

Just as financial aid policies were designed to address cost barriers to college for low-income students, a whole host of informational interventions have arisen to account for the assumption that students may not know enough about their postsecondary options or about the benefits and costs associated with each of these opportunities. In the 1980s and 1990s these initiatives took the form of publications, thick as a phonebook, which provided extensive information about many colleges and universities. By the 2000s, these books had evolved to publicly- and privately-funded websites that provide even more detail about an even broader range of institutions. In recent years, a new set of informational tools has proliferated to help students estimate both the net price of and average earnings associated with colleges they might be considering.[1]

Presumably access to such comprehensive information, in conjunction with generous financial aid, should allow all students, regardless of their financial circumstances, to find and attend affordable colleges that are well-matched to their academic ability. Students' actual postsecondary decisions, however, suggest a very different story. Many qualified low-income high school graduates never apply to college at all. A substantial share of academically-accomplished high school graduates who have applied and been accepted to college and who intend to enroll as of high school graduation do not matriculate anywhere in the following year (Castleman & Page, 2014). Even among academically-talented low-income students who do matriculate, as many as half do not even apply to, let alone enroll at, selective colleges and universities that they appear to have the academic credentials to attend (Bowen, Chingos, & McPherson, 2009; Hoxby & Avery, 2012; Smith, Pender, & Howell, 2013). As a consequence, students can wind up attending institutions that are more expensive, have fewer resources to support them, and from which they are substantially less likely to graduate. And despite concerted efforts to convey to students the availability of federal and state financial aid, over 13 percent of students who enroll in college and who *would have been* eligible for need-based aid do not apply (King, 2004; Kofoed, 2013).

Behavioral Insights Into Decision Making

The focus of the chapters that follow is to explore how insights from various behavioral sciences—behavioral economics, social and cognitive psychology, even neuroscience—can inform the way that policy makers, researchers, and educators think about how students approach decision making about whether and where to enroll, how to obtain financial aid, and how to succeed in college once they have matriculated. The purpose of this chapter is to provide readers with a conceptual understanding of behavioral sciences—a behavioral primer—upon which the subsequent chapters can build. The primer is organized with two primary groups of readers in mind—those who want an intuitive and easy-to-grasp understanding of behavioral ideas, and those who want to explore the concepts in greater depth. For the first groups, we bring the concepts to life through an in-depth vignette of a student confronting typical behavioral challenges on his path to college. We focus on the behavioral concepts that are most relevant to understanding student decision making about postsecondary education.

One of the core behavioral issues we illustrate in the vignette is the disconnect between the goals people have for their futures and the investments they are willing to make in the present to realize these goals. Even students who believe that they stand to realize substantial returns to a college education may be reluctant to absorb seemingly small upfront costs to finance their education. We also discuss how simple differences in the channels through which information is communicated about college and financial aid can affect students' postsecondary decisions. Students face complex decisions along the path to college and our vignette describes common behavioral responses in the face of such complexity, including the tendency to procrastinate on important but confusing tasks. We explore how the many competing factors for students' time and attention, both before and during college, may interfere with meeting important deadlines. And we investigate how students' pre-existing beliefs, or anchoring, about the costs of college can affect whether they believe postsecondary options are available to them and their families.

The chapters that follow this primer draw on these concepts both to illuminate the challenges that may impede students' enrollment and success in college and to identify possible behavioral solutions to support improved student outcomes. For instance, in Chapter 7, Price and Shireman discuss how students' bias towards the present may contribute to them skipping class in favor of a more pressing activity or commitment even if they recognize that attending class is important for their academic success in college and even if they had planned to attend. In Chapter 6, Scott-Clayton discusses how the volume and complexity of course choices students face at community colleges can interfere with their ability to make progress towards a degree.

For readers who want a deeper understanding of the concepts we illustrate through these vignettes, we have interspersed callout boxes that explain several of these behavioral ideas—individual preferences that are not consistent over time, how people respond to complexity, framing and channel factors, and cognitive challenges adolescents face in decision making—in greater detail. These call-out boxes also highlight the core psychological and economic theories upon which these ideas are based. For readers who are curious to learn still more about the behavioral sciences after reading this primer, and particularly readers who would like to delve into the technical papers that explore this work, we provide a glossary with brief definitions of a broad range of behavioral concepts as well as a list of suggested readings at the end of the volume.

Our vignette centers around Kevin, a college-intending high school senior who has not completed the FAFSA by the end of high school. A lack of awareness about the availability of financial support may prevent Kevin from matriculating at a well-matched college—or from actually making it to college at all. The vignette that follows does not correspond to an actual student; rather, it is a composite profile of the types of issues that many low-income and first-generation students encounter as they attempt to navigate the path to college.

A final word before we profile Kevin: helping students and their families to navigate complex postsecondary decisions will not on its own eliminate disparities in college participation and success among students, even among students with similar academic achievement. We are cognizant that the cultural and environmental influences that surround students exert a strong influence on their aspirations and on their perceptions of the types of higher education institutions they can access, long before they begin exploring specific college options. Although well-designed behavioral interventions cannot substitute for the social capital that helps more affluent students travel the road to and through college, we believe these strategies can guide students towards more informed postsecondary pathways, and therefore take a meaningful step toward reducing the inequalities in who goes to and succeeds in college.

Kevin

Kevin worked hard throughout high school to be where he is now: at the end of his senior year, several college acceptance letters in hand and a promising future ahead of him. The journey wasn't easy. Kevin attends an under-resourced high school in a rough section of a large Midwestern city. His mother encouraged him to work hard in school but had few resources and limited schooling experience to offer him. She had graduated from high school but did not go to college, and currently works two part-time retail jobs. This brings in just enough income to make ends meet, but leaves little to spare for anything else.

From an early age, Kevin knew he wanted something different from his life than what he saw most people in his neighborhood experiencing, and he believed school would be his ticket to brighter horizons. When kids on his block were ditching school or skipping class, Kevin was soaking up everything his teachers had to offer. He took part in enrichment programs after school and spent several hours of each weekend at the library, waiting for his turn to get online and read about the places to which he would some day travel.

Kevin's hard work and passion for learning paid off. By the start of senior year he had a strong GPA and was determined to apply to college. Kevin had a million questions about college and the application process that he wanted to ask someone, but had to compress his curiosity into one thirty-minute meeting with a school counselor. The counselor was impressed by Kevin's record and academic interests and suggested several colleges that he might apply to, including the state public flagship university, a less selective public four-year university located near his city, and the nearby community college as a safety school.

Kevin spent the next few months working on his applications. Several of his teachers offered to write recommendation letters and his junior year English teacher helped him with his essay. Just before the Christmas vacation Kevin put his applications in the mail, cautiously optimistic about his postsecondary options.

During their brief meeting, his counselor had encouraged him to apply for financial aid to help pay for college. Kevin had asked the counselor if he had a copy of the application to complete; the counselor told him, "you can apply on the FAFSA website after the New Year." Kevin didn't have reliable internet access at home, but during the first weekend in January he was able to get online at the library and logged on to the FAFSA website. Getting started was straightforward enough, but beyond that Kevin couldn't make much progress. The FAFSA asked for all kinds of information about his family's income and assets, little of which Kevin knew with any precision. One thing was immediately clear: to do the FAFSA he would need his mom's tax returns, and even with the tax returns he would need his mom to help him answer many of the questions.

That night he asked his mother if she had done her taxes yet. She seemed confused by the question.

> "It's not even the middle of January. My taxes aren't due for months, and I haven't even gotten any forms from my job yet. Why?"
> "Because I need them to apply for financial aid for college. The application asks about your taxes," Kevin replied.
> "You mean taking out loans?" his mother asked.
> "Maybe some, but I think there's free money too," Kevin said.

Kevin asked his mother if she would come to the library to look at the FAFSA with him. She was working the next two weekends but they were able to go together at the end of January. Kevin's mom knew a bit more than Kevin did but was also confused by several of the questions.

> "Why do they need to know so much?" she asked.
> "I don't know mom," Kevin replied.
> "Isn't there someone at school you can ask?" she wondered.

The next week Kevin saw his counselor in passing and asked if he could help with the FAFSA. "I had to do it twenty years ago when I was applying for college, but haven't helped students with it," the counselor replied. "I think there might be times at the library when you can get help with the FAFSA?" By now it was February. Kevin meant to find out from the library if they had FAFSA help, but the librarian who had helped organize the event in the past didn't work on the weekends when Kevin was there, and he had a hard time remembering to call her during the week. He was also busy with his classes and friends, and though he meant to devote time to figuring out the FAFSA, the weeks kept passing by. Even though it bothered him on some level that he hadn't completed the application, Kevin figured he could always apply for financial aid when he found out which colleges had accepted him.

Kevin was also pretty sure that, even if he got into all of the colleges to which he had applied, he would only be able to afford the community college or nearby public institution. Between what his mom had set aside over the years and what he figured he could earn from a summer job, Kevin was pretty confident he'd be able to scrape together enough to pay for the first year, either at the community college or by enrolling as a commuter student at the nearby public four-year university. But he figured the cost of living on campus at the public flagship was probably more than he could handle.

Spring progressed, and sure enough, Kevin received acceptances from the three colleges to which he had applied. He was incredibly excited to have gotten into all three of the schools, and his mother was very proud of him, bragging to all her friends about how her son was going off to school. His acceptances had come with a bunch of other information, but in his excitement at seeing the acceptance letter Kevin had only skimmed these other documents. He figured he would get to all that information later, but he got busy with various end of senior year activities, and before he knew it high school graduation had arrived.

Shortly after graduation Kevin started working at a local electronics store. He liked interacting with customers, helping them choose which computer or TV to buy, and he really liked his boss, who was just a few years older than he was and who had graduated from college a year or two earlier. On one slow day, a few weeks into the summer, his boss asked him what he was going to do in the fall. Kevin told him that he could definitely afford the community college, but was hoping to earn enough over the summer to enroll at the nearby four-year institution instead.

> "That's great," said his boss. "But you're a really smart kid—did you apply anywhere else?"
> "Yeah," Kevin replied. "I got into the flagship, but I can't afford that."
> "Really?" said his boss. "Even with financial aid?"

> "My mom and I couldn't figure out those forms," said Kevin. "Anyway, I make good money here and this way I can live at home while I'm in school."
>
> "Man, there's like thousands of dollars in free money you can get once you get those forms done. I can help you and your mom if you want."

Kevin took his boss up on the offer; a few evenings later he and his mom brought all their paperwork in, and his boss helped them complete their FAFSA. Several weeks later, Kevin got financial aid packages from all three institutions. He had applied too late to qualify for additional state aid or institutional grants from the flagship, and the cost was more than his family could afford. But at least he and his mother would have to pay much less out of pocket with the federal grant aid applied to the cost of tuition at the local four-year.

By now, the start of the fall semester was just weeks away. He was beginning to have cold feet about starting school. He had made a lot of money over the summer, and was hesitant to give up his hours so that he could enroll full-time in school. After thinking about this for a while, he approached his boss.

> "Do you think I could stay on during the year?" he asked.
>
> "You mean, like work nights when you're not in school?" asked his boss.
>
> "No, I was thinking I could stay on full-time and then maybe take classes at the community college at night," said Kevin.
>
> "No way man," replied his boss. "I know the money's nice now, but that's peanuts compared to what you can make with a college degree. Think about how long it's going to take you to earn your degree if you only take 1–2 classes a semester."

Kevin pushed to keep working in the fall but his boss was adamant. "Listen, man, it's your choice whether to go to school, but it's my choice whether to let this job be your reason not to go, and I'm not going to do that."

Next to his mom, there wasn't anyone Kevin respected more than his boss. He still had a hard time giving up his job, but what his boss said about how much he'd earn with a degree made a big impact on him. The beginning of September rolled around, and after a going-to-college party his mom had organized, Kevin left for the first day of classes. The college plans he had dreamed about for so long were finally a reality.

Interpreting Kevin's Experience Through a Behavioral Lens

Kevin's story highlights many of the challenges that academically-accomplished, low-income students encounter on the road to higher education. Take, for instance, Kevin's analysis at the end of senior year that he could afford to pay for the first year of college with his mom's savings and his summer earnings.

While this analysis may be correct, it is also incomplete. Even if he is able to pay tuition for the first year, will he be able to afford tuition in future years? After all, his ability to pay for college in the first year stems in part from his mother having saved some money for his college education. How likely is it that she would be able to contribute the same amount in subsequent years? Kevin also overlooks the fact that a college's sticker price—what is published as the cost of tuition, room and board, and additional fees—is often dramatically different from the actual price students pay net of financial aid they receive. Given Kevin's income level it is quite possible that the public flagship would be *cheaper* than the nearby university had he applied for financial aid earlier in senior year, in advance of state and institutional priority deadlines.

To illustrate the magnitude of the savings Kevin realized by completing the FAFSA, let's assume he was planning to enroll at the University of Wisconsin–Milwaukee. According to the College Board, the sticker price of attending UW–Milwaukee as a commuter student would have been approximately $14,000 for the 2013–2014 academic year. With financial aid, the cost to Kevin of attending UW–Milwaukee as a commuter student would have been $6,000.[2]

Such a large price differential begs the question of why a student as hard working and determined as Kevin wouldn't follow through and complete the FAFSA before high school graduation, even given some initial difficulty. Kevin's story illustrates several common behavioral responses that can often lead people to make decisions that may not be in their best interest. The first challenge Kevin encountered was the complexity of the FAFSA application. Had the FAFSA been straightforward, Kevin would probably have completed it on the first try, or perhaps when he sat down to review it with his mom. A large body of research, however, has drawn attention to the complexity of the FAFSA, and the difficulty that many families have completing the application (Bettinger, Long, Oreopoulos, & Sanbonmatsu, 2012; Dynarski & Scott-Clayton, 2006). Economists have long recognized the investments that people like Kevin have to put into the FAFSA—time, energy, perseverance—as real and meaningful costs. Conceivably the costs of completing the FAFSA could be high enough to outweigh the benefits that come from doing so, but for most people this is unlikely. After all, Kevin gained thousands of dollars in federal Pell Grant aid once he completed the FAFSA.

WHY IS DECISION MAKING PARTICULARLY CHALLENGING FOR ADOLESCENTS?

The behavioral responses we describe in this primer—and apply in the chapters that follow—affect people of all ages. For instance, faced with a complex array of choices, many of us can probably think of a time when we used a simplifying strategy to make a decision, like buying a car because we had heard from friends that it was a reliable model. Given their stage of cognitive development, however, adolescents are particularly prone to certain behavioral responses that can lead them to forego activities that appear to be in their long-term interest.

For each of us, the process of making decisions is largely governed by two primary systems within our brains (Kahneman, 2011). Think of one system as your brain's accelerator (Casey, Jones, & Somerville, 2011). This system generates our immediate responses, impulses, and emotional reactions. When the dessert tray rolls by in a restaurant, the accelerator hits the floor and tells us that we want something sweet to eat. Think of the other system as your brain's brake. This system is responsible for logical analysis, careful deliberations, and conscious reflection. This is the part of our brains that says, "But aren't you trying to watch what you eat?" in response to our immediate desire for chocolate cake.

Among adults, both systems are well developed and are typically able to operate in balance. While there are still circumstances in which the fast-response system governs our decision making, we are also frequently able to moderate our impulses thanks to the slow-and-thoughtful system. For adolescents, on the other hand, these two systems are in very different stages of development. The fast-response system is firing at full throttle, while the slow-and-thoughtful system is just beginning to come online. As a result, adolescents are highly responsive to immediate and enticing stimuli, like video games, and cognitively less capable of undertaking the type of careful reasoning that is often essential to get to and through college (Casey, Jones, & Somerville, 2011; Keating, 2004). This cognitive imbalance can be magnified for students from disadvantaged backgrounds who often have to devote their time and energy to addressing immediate stressors, like financially supporting their families or dealing with neighborhood violence (Mullainathan & Shafir, 2013).

The dominance of the fast-response system helps explain why adolescents are particularly likely to procrastinate on complicated decisions like choosing a college or field of study, and particularly likely to be swayed by more tangible factors like the quality of a dorm room or which classes their friends are taking. Helping more economically-disadvantaged youth to pursue and succeed in quality college options will therefore likely require expanding their access to caring adults who can help guide them through these decisions.

What behavioral economists have demonstrated is that people are theoretically willing to absorb the costs that accompany a task like completing the FAFSA—they're just not always actually willing to do so in the present. This stems from the fact that people's preferences for how to spend their time (and more broadly, resources) vary depending on when they have to make the investment. For instance, many people will say that they would be willing to put in eight hours of work in six months to earn $100. Ask the same people, however, if they would put in eight hours today to earn $100 tomorrow, and a substantial number will decline.

The behavioral insight here is that individuals are often unwilling to incur near-term costs even if they stand to realize a considerable return on this investment down the road. Because the costs appear more bearable in the future, people often put off an investment of their time or resources until another day. The challenge is that when the next day arrives, people again find that the costs today loom larger than the costs in the future, so the cycle of procrastination continues. In subsequent chapters we refer to individuals who display this behavior as having "time inconsistent preferences." In Chapter 3, Baum and Schwartz discuss time-inconsistent preferences in the context of student financial aid, and investigate how student aid can be optimally structured to overcome students' tendency to place substantial weight on upfront and immediate costs associated with financial aid applications and college attendance. In Chapter 7, Price and Shireman investigate how students' bias towards the present influences whether they engage in important aspects of the collegiate academic experience and explore strategies to improve student engagement that address this present bias. An important point to reiterate is that people often see these costs as worthwhile—they often just struggle to absorb them in the present. In Kevin's case, he was clearly motivated to apply for financial aid. Yet the complexity of the process imposed a variety of costs on him: time costs to try to make sense of the form and devote several weekend days to get online to try to complete the application; relational costs to enlist his mother and school counselor for help; psychological and emotional costs from navigating a complicated and confusing bureaucratic process. Kevin's deferral of completing the FAFSA can be interpreted therefore, as a common behavioral response that people have in the face of complex or arduous tasks.

WHAT ARE TIME-INCONSISTENT PREFERENCES AND HOW DO THEY AFFECT DECISION MAKING?

The concept of time-inconsistent preferences is one to which many of us can probably relate. For instance, how many readers have had the experience of committing to a meeting or conference in the future, only to find that when the date arrives it is very inconvenient to actually attend (Zauberman & Lynch, 2005)? Or, how many readers aspire to watch more enriching television (think PBS), only to find that when you sit down with the controller in hand, you're invariably drawn to more tantalizing shows (think *Real Housewives of Beverly Hills*) (Read, Loewenstein, & Kalyanaraman, 1999)?

This experience of finding that our preferences change in a systematic way over time runs counter to the way that economists have traditionally thought about decision making. In standard economic models, individuals' preferences are thought to be time-consistent. That is, if people are willing to set aside a day of work to attend a professional development workshop or conference, that preference should hold whether the workshop or conference is in a few days or in six months. In fact, however, experimental research consistently demonstrates that the trade-offs we are willing to make differ depending on the point in time when the decision occurs. Continuing with the conference example, the same people who are willing to register for a conference several months into the future may be considerably less willing to commit to giving up a day to attend the same conference next week.

The time-inconsistency of people's preferences is frequently accompanied by a strong bias towards the present. We are typically more protective of our time and resources in the short term than we think we will be further down the road. This present-bias often arises in students' decisions about whether to pursue postsecondary education. On the one hand, the considerable majority of high school students aspire to go to college and recognize the long-term financial benefits of higher education. Yet when it comes time to assume costs associated with applying to and attending college, even small cost obstacles can deter students from completing key stages of the application process (Pallais, 2015).

The Psychological Foundation for Time-Inconsistent Preferences

Psychologist George Ainslie coined the phrase "picoeconomics" to refer to the tendency of individuals to prefer a smaller reward when it is immediately available over a larger reward for which they would have to wait (Ainslie, 1992). Ainslie observed, however, that when individuals have to wait for the smaller reward their preferences will shift for the larger pay-off, even when the time between the small and large rewards remains constant. Ainslie interpreted this phenomenon in terms of intrapersonal conflict, where people have to weigh their future desires against the sacrifices that obtaining these later outcomes would require from their present selves. Behavioral economists Richard Thaler and Shlomo Benartzi built on Ainslie's work by investigating the tension between individuals' desire to save for retirement in the future with their actual spending and investment allocations in the present (Thaler & Benartzi, 2004). Thaler and Benartzi found that people want to save in the future but often struggle to commit themselves to setting aside money to achieve these goals. In Thaler and Benartzi's model of decision making, individuals have to balance the impulses of their present selves with the intentions of their future selves. Present bias often leads people to privilege the present over the future self, making it challenging to achieve longer-term goals. The authors also find that providing people with a way of committing to their future selves, for instance by allocating a portion of future salary increases to retirement savings, can overcome the impulses of the present self.

Another behavioral explanation for why Kevin did not complete the FAFSA could be that information about how to complete the FAFSA was not delivered through media that effectively reached Kevin or inspired him to take action. Psychologists have demonstrated that small but important details, or channel factors, about how decisions are presented can often exert a strong influence on the actions that people take. An early study exploring the importance of channel factors focused on how to get more Yale students to get tetanus vaccinations (Leventhal, Singer, & Jones, 1965). Seemingly sensible strategies, like providing a booklet about how tetanus is transmitted or showing students graphic photos of patients suffering with tetanus, were ineffective at boosting vaccination rates. Providing students with a map of the Yale campus showing where the health center was located along with hours of operation, on the other hand, increased vaccination rates significantly. Whereas the first two strategies focused on persuading students of the importance of getting a tetanus vaccination, what the third strategy revealed was that students already understood the importance of getting vaccinated—they just didn't know where or when to go for the shot.[3]

The Yale tetanus study is analogous in many ways to Kevin's experience with the FAFSA. Kevin was motivated to apply for financial aid and was willing to invest time to complete the application. He just didn't know where to go for help. Kevin's school did not offer FAFSA completion support and it was unclear whether or when the library offered help with financial aid applications. Unbeknownst to Kevin, there is a toll-free FAFSA hotline operated by the United States Department of Education that students and their families can call with questions, but the hotline was not publicized in a way that made Kevin aware of it. It's also quite possible that one, if not all, of the colleges to which Kevin applied would have offered him individualized help completing the FAFSA. In fact, several of the colleges may have sent Kevin information about applying for financial aid with his acceptance, along with follow-up reminders about aid applications. But Kevin did not read all of the materials accompanying his acceptance letters and if Kevin was like many of his peers, and checked email only sporadically, it is quite likely these messages passed by unnoticed. In Kevin's case, making FAFSA assistance available at his school or better publicizing existing support resources probably would have been sufficient to help him and his mother complete the application on time. Castleman's chapter (Chapter 5) in this volume investigates how the current design and delivery of college and financial aid information may unintentionally create obstacles to students attending institutions that are well-matched to their interests and abilities. Castleman's essay also explores how college and financial aid information can be better communicated to students and their families, in part by taking into consideration the medium through which information is distributed.

HOW DO PEOPLE RESPOND TO COMPLEX INFORMATION?

In the classic movie *Flight of the Navigator*, a boy returns to Earth after eight years in outer space. Asked what he would like, he responds, "How about a Big Mac, large fries and a Coke? They're still around, I hope." The response: "Well, now, that all depends. Do you want New Coke, Classic Coke, Cherry Coke, Diet Coke or caffeine-free Coke?" He is, not surprisingly, immobilized by all these options.[4]

Like the little space traveler, many of us find it impossible to make any choice at all when faced with too many options. Navigating complicated processes to get to a desired outcome can also interfere with reaching our goals. Several concepts from the behavioral sciences provide insight into how complexity interferes with people realizing their goals.

Cognitive overload: When faced with important, complicated decisions, people have trouble gathering all of the relevant information, defining their goals, and weighing the costs and benefits of different options. Financial decisions like choosing a college and figuring out how to pay for it epitomize this type of difficult analysis. A common response is to *procrastinate*. For example, prospective students may put filling out the financial aid application in the "tomorrow pile," and never get around to completing it.

The path of least resistance: When faced with too many choices or with a process that is perplexing, people frequently go with the path of least resistance, which is often the *default option*. There are many alternative plans for federal student loan repayment but the many borrowers who don't make an active choice are put in the standard 10-year fixed payment plan. If lack of action instead put people into a plan that limited payments based on earnings, many more would end up having the advantage of that protection.

Channel factors: People are more likely to reach their goals when there is an easy and obvious path to a desired outcome. Adding or removing seemingly insignificant barriers to behaviors makes a disproportionate difference in outcomes. Sending prospective students a link to a form they should complete will work better than just reminding them to fill out the form.

Simplifying strategies: When faced with complex decisions, people are likely to rely on a number of simplifying strategies. The *availability* bias is one example. If a prospective student doesn't know how to choose among colleges, he may opt for the school that sends him email ads or the place where someone from his high school went. Increasing the *salience* of an option or information about that option may affect choices. Price and Shireman (this volume) point to the posting of calorie counts for foods as an example of consciously modifying the salience of important information.

An additional behavioral explanation for why Kevin did not invest the time to apply for financial aid has to do with people's tendency to base decisions on the first piece of information with which they are presented about the various options from which they are choosing and about which they know very little. Psychologists refer to this tendency as anchoring, and numbers often serve as particularly weighty anchors. In one of the seminal studies on anchoring, study participants were prompted to state the last two digits of their social security numbers and were then asked how much they would bid on various items, such as wine and chocolate. The amount that participants with higher social security numbers bid on these items was often twice as high as what participants with lower social security numbers bid, simply because they had been primed to think of a higher number in advance of making a bid (Ariely, 2008). A related concept is the availability bias: people tend to base their judgments on highly-publicized and recent information, which can lead to erroneous conclusions. For instance, people may be more concerned about dying from a lightning strike than from excessive heat exposure, despite the fact that the latter claims sixteen times as many lives each year (National Safety Council, 2014). Lightning strikes, however, are widely covered in the media when they happen. The availability of this information generates an inaccurate perception of the frequency with which they occur.

In the realm of college financing and postsecondary success, families like Kevin's frequently anchor their estimates of how much they'll have to pay for college to the frequent media reports about the soaring cost of tuition. The "sticker" price of elite private institutions, like Harvard, is often quoted in these stories, leading families to believe that attending college costs all families in excess of $60,000 per year. The sticker price of course obscures two important facts: First, very few people go to colleges and universities with sticker prices as high as Harvard's. Second, schools like Harvard also provide generous financial aid, particularly to low-income students, so the net price is much lower. Yet with this anchor in place, low-income families often substantially overestimate what college will cost them, and may preemptively conclude that private colleges and universities would be outside their reach.

Kevin was likely correct in his conclusion that the local community college and nearby university offered the lower sticker prices, but possibly misinformed about which institution would offer the lowest *net* price. Availability bias may have influenced the college recommendations that Kevin's school counselor offered. If those were the institutions where most students from Kevin's high school attended—and perhaps where Kevin's counselor or his colleagues went—they might appear at the top of the list of colleges the counselor recommends, even if there were less familiar institutions that were a better fit for Kevin. Baum and Schwartz, Castleman, and Scott-Clayton's essays all explore how information is currently communicated to students and their families about the cost of college attendance, including financial aid for which they might qualify, and how students' perceptions of this information may influence the types of post-secondary pathways they pursue, if any. Each author also explores strategies to help students and their families obtain more realistic estimates of the net price of pursuing higher education.

Finally, the behavioral concept of loss aversion can help explain why Kevin almost faltered in the weeks before the fall semester on following through on his college intentions. Loss aversion refers to people's tendency to prefer avoiding losses more than they prefer gaining something new. When asked, for instance, how much they'd have to win in a coin toss to take the risk of losing $10, most people want at least a $20 pay-out if the coin comes up in their favor to accept the 50 percent chance that they would have to give up $10 of their own money.

In education, researchers have leveraged loss aversion in the design of financial incentives for teachers. One study showed that when teachers were paid an upfront bonus that they had to give back if their students' learning did not improve sufficiently, students' test scores went up by a substantial margin. Students whose teachers were randomly assigned to receive a more standard bonus, paid *after* students' progress was measured experienced smaller and statistically insignificant gains (Fryer et al., 2012). For Kevin, loss aversion may have contributed to his reluctance to give up a steady paycheck at the electronics store, particularly when the potential benefits associated with college were less-defined and primarily accrued years into the future.

It is worth emphasizing that the behavioral obstacles we describe Kevin encountering are by no means limited to the process of students getting to college. Once they are on campus, students continue to face complex information and complicated processes, such as choosing a course sequence that leads to a major in which the student is interested, or remembering to complete tasks like re-filing for financial aid in the face of many pressing academic and social commitments. And while Kevin intends to follow the traditional path of pursuing college full-time directly after high school, adult learners comprise an increasing share of students in higher education. For these students the behavioral obstacles of succeeding in college can be even more daunting, particularly since they typically lack access to quality information or counseling about their college options. It is therefore imperative that we consider the challenges that a diverse array of students encounter throughout their postsecondary paths, and explore how concepts and ideas from the behavioral sciences can be leveraged to support these students' success.

Kevin's experience also highlights the importance that caring and involved adults play in many students' lives. As Kevin's story illustrates, these adults need not be parents, teachers or school counselors; employers, sports coaches, clergy members, and family friends often play important mentoring roles in helping students access and succeed in college. While behavioral strategies hold considerable promise for improving students' college outcomes, we view these as helpful complements to, but certainly not substitutes for, existing financial aid programs or for individualized advising and support from a caring mentor.

Notes

1. At the federal level, examples of these tools include the White House Scorecard and the FAFSA 4Caster.
2. We obtained this estimate using the net price calculator on the UW–Milwaukee website, and assuming that Kevin's mother made less than $30,000 per year. We also make the simplifying assumption that Kevin did not lose out on aid he would have received from UW–Milwaukee by completing his FAFSA during the summer, rather than earlier in senior year.
3. One limitation of the Yale study is that it was conducted with a small sample size, so there is some question about the generalizability of these findings. We include the description of the Yale study not because of the rigor of the evidence generated, but rather to illustrate the importance of channel factors, given that the Yale study is viewed as seminal in identifying this concept. For a more recent and larger-scale illustration of similar concepts, see Milkman et al., 2011.
4. www.imdb.com/title/tt0091059/

References

Ainslie, G. (1992). *Picoeconomics: The strategic interaction of successive motivational states within the person.* New York: Cambridge University Press.

Ariely, D. (2008). *Predictably irrational: The hidden forces that shape our decisions.* New York: Harper Perennial.

Avery, C., & Kane, T. J. (2004). Student perceptions of college opportunities. The Boston COACH program. In C. Hoxby (ed.). *College choices: The economics of where to go, when to go, and how to pay for it.* Chicago: University of Chicago Press.

Becker, G. S. (1964). *Human capital: A theoretical and empirical analysis, with special reference to education.* Chicago: University of Chicago Press.

Bettinger, E., Long, B. T., Oreopoulos, P., & Sanbonmatsu, L. (2012). The role of application assistance and information in college decisions: Results from the H&R Block FAFSA experiment. *Quarterly Journal of Economics, 127*(3), 1205–1242.

Bowen, W. G., Chingos, M. M., & McPherson, M. S. (2009). *Crossing the finish line: Completing college at America's public universities.* Princeton, NJ: Princeton University Press.

Casey, B., Jones, R. M., & Somerville., L. H. (2011). Braking and accelerating of the adolescent brain. *Journal of Research on Adolescence, 21*(1), 21–33.

Castleman, B. L., & Long, B. T. (2013). Looking beyond enrollment: The causal effect of need-based grants on college access, persistence, and graduation. (No. 19306). NBER Working Paper. Retrieved from www.nber.org/papers/w19306

Castleman, B. L., & Page, L. C. (2014). A trickle or a torrent? Understanding the extent of summer "melt" among college-intending high school graduates. *Social Sciences Quarterly, 95*(1), 202–220.

The College Board (2014). *Trends in student aid 2014.* New York, NY: The College Board.

Digest of Education Statistics (2013). Table 302.30: Percentage of recent high school completers enrolled in 2-year and 4-year colleges, by income level: 1975 through 2012. Retrieved from http://nces.ed.gov/programs/digest/d13/tables/dt13_302.30.asp

Dynarski, S. M., & Scott-Clayton, J. E. (2006). The cost of complexity in federal student aid: Lessons from optimal tax theory and behavioral economics. *National Tax Journal 59*(2), 319–356.

Fryer, R. G., Levitt, S. D., List, J., & Sadoff, S. (2012). Enhancing the efficacy of teacher incentives through loss aversion: A field experiment (No. 18237). NBER Working Paper. Retrieved from www.nber.org/papers/w18237

Grodsky, E., & Jones, M. T. (2007). Real and imagined barriers to college entry: Perceptions of cost. *Social Science Research 36*(2), 745–766.

Horn, L., Chen, X., & Chapman, C. (2003). *Getting ready to pay for college: What students and their parents know about the cost of college tuition and what they are doing to find out.* U.S. Department of Education, National Center for Education Statistics: Washington, D.C.

Hoxby, C., & Avery, C. (2012). The missing "one-offs": The hidden supply of high-achieving, low-income students (No. 18586). NBER Working Paper. Retrieved from www.nber.org/papers/w18586

Kahneman, D. (2011). *Thinking, fast and slow.* New York: MacMillan.

Kane, T. J. (2003). A quasi-experimental estimate of the impact of financial aid on college-going (No. 9703). NBER Working Paper. Retrieved from www.nber.org/papers/w9703

Keating, D. P. (2004). Cognitive and brain development. In R. M. Lerner & L. Steinberg (Eds.), *Handbook of adolescent psychology* (2nd ed., pp. 45–84). New York: Wiley.

King, J. E. (2004). Missed opportunities: Students who do not apply for financial aid. American Council on Education Issue Brief. Retrieved from www.soe.vt.edu/highered/files/Perspectives_PolicyNews/10-04/2004FAFSA.pdf

Kofoed, M. S. (2013). To apply or not apply: FAFSA completion and financial aid gaps. Working paper Available at SSRN: http://ssrn.com/abstract=2353846 or http://dx.doi.org/10.2139/ssrn.2353846

Leventhal, H., Singer, R., & Jones, S. (1965). Effects of fear and specificity of recommendation upon attitudes and behavior. *Journal of Personality and Social Psychology, 2*(1), 20–29.

Long, B. T., & Mabel, Z. (2012) "Barriers to College Success: Income Disparities in Progress to Completion." Unpublished manuscript, Harvard University.

Milkman, K. L., Beshears, J., Choi, J. J., Laibson, D., & Madrian, B. C. (2011). Using implementation intentions prompts to enhance influenza vaccination rates. *Proceedings of the National Academy of Sciences, 108*(26), 10415–10420. doi:10.1073/pnas.1103170108

Mullainathan, S., & Shafir, E. (2013). *Scarcity: Why having too little means so much.* New York: Time Books.

National Safety Council. (2014). *What are the odds of dying from…* Retrieved from www.nsc.org/news_resources/injury_and_death_statistics/Pages/TheOddsofDyingFrom.aspx

Pallais A. (2015). Small differences that matter: mistakes in applying to college. Forthcoming, *Journal of Labor Economics, 33*(2).

Read, D., Loewenstein, G., & Kalyanaraman, S. (1999). Mixing virtue and vice: Combining the immediacy effect and the diversification heuristic. *Journal of Behavioral Decision Making, 12*(4), 257–273.

Smith, J., Pender, M., & Howell, J. (2013). The full extent of student-college academic undermatch. *Economics of Education Review, 32*, 247–261.

Thaler, R. H., & Benartzi, S. (2004). Save more tomorrow: Using behavioral economics to increase employee saving. *Journal of Political Economy, 112*(1), 164–187.

Zauberman, G., & Lynch, J. G. (2005). Resource slack and propensity to discount delayed investments of time versus money. *Journal of Experimental Psychology, 132*(1), 23–37.

2

MOTIVATION, BEHAVIOR, AND PERFORMANCE IN THE WORKPLACE

Insights for Student Success in Higher Education

Charles Kurose

Student success in higher education is becoming an increasingly important issue for policy-makers, educators, business leaders, parents, students, and anyone else concerned about the ability of the higher education system to deliver on promises of individual prosperity and a secure economic and civic future for the country. Over the past several decades, efforts to broaden access to college have dramatically expanded the opportunities individuals have to pursue higher education. But unless the students who enroll in college are successful and move on to become productive members of society, much of this progress will be squandered. Finding ways to ensure that students succeed in college is thus a vital objective for higher education policy-makers and practitioners.

To promote student success in higher education, it is important to develop strategies to motivate students and incentivize the behaviors that produce better performance in college. One promising place to look for these types of strategies is the workplace, where industrial and organizational psychologists have long been studying worker motivation and the behaviors that lead to higher levels of performance on the job. Knowledge of how the complex relationships among motivation, behavior, and performance operate in workplace settings is crucial for managers tasked with getting the most out of their employees; this knowledge can also help educators charged with supporting student success. This chapter aims to illuminate these issues by discussing the insights from research about workplace motivation and behavior that may be transferrable to other contexts such as higher education. Considerable potential exists for this research to inform efforts to improve student success in higher education.

The rest of this chapter is divided into four sections. The first section discusses goal setting, which is one of the most extensively researched topics related to workplace motivation, and how goal setting strategies can be used to improve student success in higher education. The second section deals with a concept called self-efficacy, which captures the beliefs people hold about what they're capable of achieving. Fostering self-efficacy beliefs can improve individual performance. The third and fourth sections then discuss two relatively new but promising areas of research—personality traits and affect—and suggest how these emerging topics may bear on student success in college. Throughout the chapter, the discussion draws on what we've learned from research conducted in workplace settings, but the focus is always on illustrating how these insights might be used to help design efforts to improve student success in higher education.

Achieving Better Performance Through Goal Setting

Goals can be powerful tools for the improvement of individual performance in any number of settings. Conceptually, goals are the means by which people translate their motivations into actual behaviors and actions. In other words, people set goals as a way of bridging the gap between simply wanting to do things (motivation) and actually doing them (behavior). For example, if a student is motivated to excel in college, she may have the goal of getting straight As. The goal provides a tangible objective for her to work toward. In pursuit of her goal, the student displays goal-oriented behaviors such as attentiveness in class and diligent completion of assignments. Importantly, different types of goals will incentivize different types of behaviors. A student whose goal is to get Bs, for example, is unlikely to exhibit exactly the same behaviors as the student whose goal is to get straight As—the student who is satisfied with Bs may skip class on occasion or put less overall effort into the assigned coursework.

The key insight here is that because of the connection between goals and behavior, goal setting can be used strategically to incentivize and promote the behaviors that lead to higher levels of performance. What are the most effective types of goals? Decades worth of research examining this question in workplace contexts has determined that setting *specific, high goals* tends to produce better performance outcomes than does setting vague and unchallenging goals such as "do your best." The first field work to document this important finding looked at worker productivity at a logging company in the early 1970s. The researchers compared the performance of logging crews—some of whom were assigned specific high goals for how many cords of wood to produce while others were simply told to do their best—and found that both productivity and attendance were significantly higher among the logging crews that had been assigned specific, high goals (Latham & Kinne, 1974). In the forty years since this early research, motivation researchers have documented the efficacy of specific, high goals in relation to more than 100 different work-related tasks performed by over 40,000 participants in eight different countries (Locke & Latham, 2005).

This powerful finding from goal setting research could inform policies and practices aimed at improving student success in higher education. It may seem like an obvious point that students would perform better in college if only they would do things like pay more attention in class and put higher levels of effort into assignments, but does setting specific high goals actually lead to these types of behaviors? Research suggests that the pursuit of goals encourages attention, effort, persistence, and cognition—all things that are essential for success in higher education—and that specific high goals are the best facilitators of these behaviors (Latham, 2007). Colleges and universities may want to consider implementing advising programs through which students would perform goal setting exercises and map out specific objectives for each of their upcoming courses. It also might be helpful to have entering students develop goals for their entire course of study—for example, goals about how many credits to have completed by a given point in time. The basic function of this type of goal-focused counseling would be to get students thinking explicitly about what they hope to achieve and to encourage them to set the bar appropriately high.

It is important to acknowledge that the usefulness of specific high goals has limits. Although higher performance might result from nudging students to aim higher than they naturally would, setting impossibly difficult goals might not be constructive for students. Challenging oneself is good, but might not seeking to do the impossible simply lead to frustration and discouragement? Setting a difficult goal could motivate someone to try especially hard to achieve it, but might not an easier goal sometimes be better, as when someone's confidence is down and any type of win—large or small—is much needed? Likewise, it makes sense that defining a goal very specifically could help direct attention toward the goal and away from distractions, but in certain situations, couldn't defining a goal too precisely induce tunnel vision, stifling creativity and ultimately lowering the odds of achieving the goal?

These questions illustrate the need to avoid putting too much faith in the efficacy of specific high goals. An enormous amount of research has shown that specific high goals lead to better performance on average and over time, but this doesn't mean that setting a specific high goal will always be the best course of action in every situation. Motivation researchers have identified a number of factors that can influence the effectiveness of setting specific high goals, and it is crucial that efforts to use goal setting for the improvement of performance—in the workplace, the college classroom, or elsewhere—be mindful of these considerations. The following sections discuss three particularly salient factors: goal commitment, feedback, and task complexity.

Goal Commitment

Goal commitment is one factor that influences the effectiveness of specific high goals. This notion has clear intuitive appeal—if someone feels no commitment to a goal, then it makes no difference whether it's a vague and unchallenging goal or a specific and difficult goal because it might as well not exist. The natural question, then, is what can be done to increase people's commitment to the goals they have set or have been assigned? Research suggests that there are two broad ways to enhance goal commitment: increasing the attractiveness of the goal and increasing the expectation of achieving the goal (Klein, Wesson, Hollenbeck, & Agle, 1999).

To ensure the attractiveness of goals, ideally individuals would be intrinsically interested in their goals and the activities associated with pursuing those goals, rather than having only an extrinsic interest in them. The distinction between intrinsic and extrinsic incentives is an important concept in motivational psychology—people are intrinsically motivated to do something when they value or enjoy the activity itself, and they are extrinsically motivated when their reason for partaking is to obtain some external reward or benefit (e.g., money) that is attached to but distinct from the activity itself. Scholars continue to debate the merits of intrinsic versus extrinsic incentives, with particular controversy surrounding the question of whether extrinsic incentives might actually "crowd out" feelings of intrinsic interest in some situations (Frey & Jegen, 2001). Few would disagree, however, that when possible, measures should be taken to enhance intrinsic interest in pursuing a goal.

Research suggests that goals may be more intrinsically motivating (and in that sense more attractive) when they activate feelings of autonomy within the individual (Ryan & Deci, 2000). When people feel autonomous, meaning that they have control over their goals and how to go about pursuing them, they tend to feel more intrinsically motivated and will be more committed to their goals. If, for example, colleges provided advisory goal setting services, it might be wise to allow students to set their own goals rather than assigning goals to them. It would still be important to encourage students to make their goals challenging and to define them clearly. Autonomy might also be promoted by giving students more choice in how to go about pursuing their goals. For instance, autonomy might be enhanced if students are allowed to choose from a variety of potential assignments (e.g., more choices for paper topics). In general, efforts to promote autonomy in relation to goals can engender a greater degree of intrinsic motivation, which in turn can increase the attractiveness of the goals and the individual's commitment to them.

The expectation of goal attainment is a second avenue through which goal commitment can be influenced. When people think they won't end up achieving their goals—either because they doubt their abilities or because they believe that factors beyond their control will interfere—goal commitment suffers. This suggests that finding ways to increase self-efficacy, which captures the beliefs an individual holds about his or her capabilities (further discussed in the next section), would be a worthwhile strategy for improving goal commitment. It also suggests that efforts should be made to remove uncertainty surrounding the environmental factors that can either enable or obstruct someone's opportunity to pursue goals to the best of his or her ability. In the context of higher education, for example, a first-year student will be less committed to the goal of completing a four-year degree if she isn't sure that the financial resources will be available to cover tuition, fees, and living expenses in future years. Financial aid programs that provide long-term rather than short-term assurances of financial support create the conditions in which students can commit to ambitious goals and achieve their greatest potential.

Feedback

In addition to goal commitment, another factor that influences the relationship between specific, high goals and performance is whether people receive feedback about their progress towards reaching the goal. In the absence of feedback, people may struggle to assess progress on their own, which can diminish the usefulness of the goal. At a minimum, some form of feedback is necessary for people to even determine whether goals have been reached. But more importantly, regular feedback allows people to evaluate and adjust their behavior as they work toward achieving their goals.

Not all feedback is helpful. In order for feedback to facilitate rather than undermine someone's progress toward a goal, it needs to account for the way the individual is mentally framing his or her efforts to reach the goal. For any given goal, someone could be framing the purpose of his or her goal-directed efforts either positively or negatively. For example, a student may be studying hard for an upcoming midterm because she takes pride in her grades and wants to do well (positive frame), or she may be studying hard for the upcoming midterm because she is trying to avoid getting a bad grade (negative frame). Note that the student's observable behavior (studying hard) and her goal (doing well on the midterm) are unambiguous—the uncertainty lies in how she herself is view-ing the purpose of her goal-directed efforts. Maybe she primarily sees herself as striving to obtain a reward (getting a good grade), or maybe she primarily sees herself as striving to avoid a punishment (getting a bad grade). Although this may seem like a trivial semantic point, it actually carries important implications for the effectiveness of different types of feedback.

Researchers have found that positive feedback is a motivating force when it is received in relation to positively framed behavior, and that negative feedback is a motivating force when it is received in relation to a negatively framed behavior (Van Dijk & Kluger, 2004, 2011; Kluger & Van Dijk, 2010). The psychology behind this finding is complex,[1] but what it basically means is that feedback needs to be personalized to the person's outlook in order for it to be effective. While it would unrealistic to expect that the people providing feedback in higher education (e.g., faculty members, graduate student teaching assistants, etc.) should undertake a detailed psychological profiling of each of their students to allow for the precise tailoring of feedback, it would require minimal effort for graders to be cognizant of the impact of different feedback types and, when possible, to try to deliver feedback that will have the most productive influence on each individual student. To ensure that everyone is taking these simple measures, it may be worthwhile to incorporate workshops about the psychology of feedback into professional development programs for teachers in higher education.

Task Complexity

Research shows that the complexity of the task being performed is another factor that can significantly influence the effectiveness of specific, high goals.[2] When the task at hand is particularly complex, and especially when it is an unfamiliar task that requires knowledge, skills, and abilities that have yet to be acquired, setting a vague goal such as "do your best" may actually produce better performance on the task than setting a specific, high goal does—a finding that appears to directly contradict the other research documenting the effectiveness of specific high goals.

The explanation for this important finding lies in the behaviors that different types of goals tend to promote under conditions of task complexity. When faced with a complex and novel task, people sit at the bottom of a learning curve, and effective performance on the task often requires that they first develop certain task-specific skills and abilities. (For example, imagine trying to do virtually anything on a computer without ever having typed on a keyboard before.) In these circumstances, setting a specific high goal for task performance can actually have the adverse effect of fixating one's attention on a distant performance outcome (i.e., the goal) rather than directing it toward engagement in the all-important learning process. Preoccupied with the faraway performance standard, people tend to switch haphazardly between task strategies, panicking to find something that will work, rather than adopting a more systematic approach to acquiring important task-related knowledge and skills. In contrast, setting a vague goal doesn't offer the distraction of a distant performance objective, and people whose goal is simply to "do their best" have an easier time focusing on developing the capabilities that ultimately lead to higher levels of performance on complex and novel tasks.

Understanding how to set effective goals for complex and novel tasks is crucial for the successful use of goal setting in higher education. The tasks and activities that students encounter at college (e.g., writing research papers, conducting experiments in science labs, navigating the course selection process, or securing financial aid) are complex by anyone's standard. For many students, and especially for first-generation students, the world of higher education is an unfamiliar place and much of what is expected of them will seem novel and will take time to learn and adapt to. Very few students—even among those coming from the most privileged backgrounds—arrive at college with all of the knowledge, skills, and abilities they need in order to excel in this complex and novel environment right away. Almost by definition, students are there to learn. In order for goal setting strategies to effectively promote student success in higher education, they must recognize and reflect the complexity and novelty of these circumstances.

One promising strategy for making specific high goals work under conditions of complexity and novelty is to set a sequence of proximate goals that guide the individual down the path toward achieving a more distant goal.[3] For example, consider the worthy but unworkably distant goal of completing a bachelor's degree within four years. This is a specific and challenging goal, but it provides the student with none of the guidance needed to successfully work toward it. To promote the timely completion of credentials, at the beginning of students' first years, colleges might have them outline plans for how many and which credits (e.g., meeting targets within a major or concentration) they're aiming to have taken by the end of each successive year. The usefulness of setting a sequence of proximate goals is also a rationale for stacking credentials—in addition to the fact that students can obtain certificates and sub-baccalaureate degrees even in the event that they don't complete a bachelor's degree, stacking credentials divides the pursuit of a bachelor's degree into more manageable segments. Sequences of proximate goals might also be useful at the level of individual courses. Syllabi that detail the specific knowledge and skills students are expected to have obtained by various points in the semester are more conducive to student success than those that only provide a schedule of assignments because they highlight for the student the process of acquiring the knowledge and abilities needed to perform at a high level in the course.

A second strategy for goal setting under conditions of complexity and novelty is to articulate "learning" goals rather than "performance" goals. Studies have found that specific high goals are still more effective than vague goals in these circumstances provided that the goals direct attention toward the learning process itself.[4] For example, if a student is studying for an oral exam, it would be more productive for her to set the goal of improving her oral communication skills (a learning goal), which she could pursue by giving and getting feedback on a practice version of the oral exam, rather than simply setting the goal of getting an A on the oral exam (a performance goal). Recall that when the task is complex, the potential pitfall of a specific high goal is that it can counterproductively direct attention toward some distant performance outcome instead of focusing it on the learning process. This risk can be mitigated by setting specific high learning goals as opposed to specific high performance goals because learning goals direct attention and effort toward the acquisition of the knowledge, skills, and abilities that one must have in order to perform well on complex and novel tasks.

Building Self-Efficacy for Improved Performance

Self-efficacy, which captures the beliefs someone holds about what he or she is capable of achieving, has a powerful influence on motivation, behavior, and performance. Self-efficacy is an important determinant of the goals that people set, their expectations of achieving those goals, and their ability to see opportunities rather than obstacles in the world around them. Self-efficacy also affects the behaviors people exhibit as they pursue their goals and aspirations by influencing how much effort they exert and their resilience in the face of challenges and setbacks.

People with higher self-efficacy tend to set higher goals, expect to achieve more, try harder, and persist longer in their endeavors, with the result that higher self-efficacy tends to produce higher levels of performance. This notion—that strong self-held beliefs about what one is capable of doing would improve one's ability to do those things well—has clear intuitive appeal, but it also has empirical support (Stajkovic & Luthans, 1998). Research conducted in workplace contexts has examined whether employees' job performance improves when supervisors convey that they have greater belief in the employees' ability to perform at a high level, which leads the employees to strengthen their own self-efficacy beliefs. Researchers have used this strategy to artificially induce higher self-efficacy in study subjects in environments ranging from the military to factory settings, finding that higher self-efficacy regularly leads to better performance at work.[5]

Higher self-efficacy, however, may not always be a good thing. Although there is significant evidence of a positive relationship between self-efficacy and performance, some researchers have found that when self-efficacy beliefs amount to overconfidence, they can have a detrimental impact on performance as people start to commit logic errors (Vancouver, Thompson, Tischner, & Putka, 2002). Researchers have also documented that high self-efficacy and the associated high degree of persistence may induce people to stick with failed courses of action in certain scenarios.[6] These warnings about the potential drawbacks of high self-efficacy should be kept in mind, but it must also be stressed that the vast majority of research about self-efficacy and performance in the workplace indicates that performance benefits when self-efficacy beliefs are higher. Moreover, even if there are limits beyond which strong self-efficacy beliefs may become counterproductive, this doesn't necessarily amount to a rationale for not seeking to bolster people's self-efficacy. It just means that people should also be trained to recognize when they're overconfident and may need to adjust their outlook accordingly (Latham, 2007).

Developing Self-Efficacy

Given that performance tends to benefit from higher self-efficacy, what measures can be taken to improve people's self-efficacy? Writing for managers interested in improving employee performance, Bandura (2009) addresses this question directly. Self-efficacy beliefs can be developed in four ways: through one's own experiences, through observing other people's experiences, through persuasion, and through the interpretation of physical and emotional states. Self-efficacy beliefs are most commonly formed through the interpretation of one's own experiences of success and failure. But self-efficacy can also be influenced vicariously through the observation of other people's experiences—when you see a similar person succeed (or fail) on some task, this affects your own beliefs about your capacity to succeed in the same endeavor. Self-efficacy beliefs can also be formed through social persuasion, as when a professor signals an appreciation for a student's intelligence and ideas and, as a result, that student's self-efficacy rises. Finally, physical and emotional states can influence one's self-efficacy—for instance, nervousness and fatigue can be interpreted as indictors of personal deficiency. These four avenues, alone or in combination, are the ways in which self-efficacy beliefs develop.

Bandura (2009) advocates an approach to cultivating high self-efficacy called "enablement through guided mastery" that engages the multiple channels through which self-efficacy can be developed. A guided mastery intervention has three phrases—enabling modeling, guided skill perfection, and transfer training by self-directed success. In the first phase, skills, abilities, and habits are modeled as a way of communicating basic information about rules, strategies, and execution. In the guided skill perfection phase, learners practice these new competencies in a simulated environment in which stakes are low, allowing them to focus on developing familiarity, fluency, and proficiency. The third and final phase then involves the application of these newly acquired competencies in a real-life environment. Crucially, this transfer phase doesn't entail simply dumping people back into their natural environment in a trial by fire. The transfer phase should be purposefully structured to allow people to experience small (but not trivial) successes as they gradually solidify self-efficacy beliefs and become comfortable with using their new competencies in a self-directed and self-regulated fashion.

Enablement through guided mastery was developed in the business world, but it has the potential to improve student success in college as well. In fact, this type of self-efficacy intervention may be particularly well suited for college students because many people enroll in higher education at a point in their lives when they are still discovering themselves and developing their self-concepts.[7] In a higher education setting, the application of enablement through guided mastery might take the form of single seminars or entire courses designed for incoming students. These courses would focus specifically on communicating expectations about college-level coursework and then teaching and practicing studying, writing, and testing skills and habits in an ungraded, low-stakes environment. These skills and habits could then be gradually transferred into higher-stakes classroom environments with assignments deliberately structured to reinforce self-efficacy beliefs relating to these essential competencies.

The strength of enablement through guided mastery as an approach to building self-efficacy and improving individual performance is its integration of behavioral and cognitive dimensions. Enablement through guided mastery focuses on developing important skills, abilities, and habits (i.e., behaviors) through a process that fortifies them with strong self-efficacy beliefs (i.e., cognition). This type of program could be helpful for all college students, but may be especially beneficial for underprepared students who are struggling to adapt to the demands of college. Many of the current efforts to prepare these students for college have a distinctly cognitive theme—they focus on activities like remedial education that are designed to fill in gaps in students' academic backgrounds. But to effectively promote student success in higher education, more behaviorally-focused efforts are needed to teach students the skills and habits they need to thrive at college. Enablement through guided mastery is an approach that could be used to develop these types of behaviors while backing them up with strong and resilient self-efficacy beliefs.

The Connection Between Personality Traits and Performance

Goal setting and self-efficacy are among the most heavily researched topics in the literature on motivation, behavior, and performance in the workplace. More recently, personality traits have been garnering an increasing amount of attention. Personality traits are stable, dispositional characteristics of individuals. Personality traits are thought to be connected to the behaviors people display, so researchers have been studying personality traits as a way of understanding how to explain and predict the way people behave (and consequently how they perform) in different situations. The hope is that by understanding personality traits better, it may be possible to design situations and environments in ways that bring out the best in people and improve their performance.

There are five major personality traits—conscientiousness, emotional stability, extroversion, agreeableness, and openness to experiences—that together are thought to capture the relevant dimensions of an individual's personality.[8] Research conducted in workplace settings suggests that conscientiousness and (to a lesser extent) emotional stability are associated with higher levels of performance across a range of different occupations and performance measures (Barrick, Mount, & Judge, 2001).[9] The other three personality traits (extroversion, agreeableness, and openness to experiences), however, do not appear to be associated with higher performance in a generalized sense. Instead, these personality traits appear to be related to performance in certain contexts, but not in others. Altogether, what the research suggests is that some personality traits appear to matter quite a lot, while others seem to matter only sometimes. How can this be explained? Researchers have concluded that personality traits do indeed predict the way people behave, but only in relevant situations (Stewart & Barrick, 2004). In the right context, personality traits can find expression in behavior and, as a result, influence performance, but this does not happen for all personality traits in all scenarios.

To illustrate this, imagine a student who scores high on a measure of extroversion, which is a trait that appears to be associated with higher performance only in some contexts. If she's working on a group project, her extroversion is likely to manifest in her behavior and ultimately benefit her performance—she'll interact more with the other group members and share more of her thoughts and ideas than she would have if she were less extroverted. But if she's studying for a final exam, it seems unlikely that her extroversion is going to directly affect her behavior, since studying for an exam is a largely solitary experience. Her extroversion might indirectly influence her performance on the exam—for instance, by compelling her to seek out a study group—but it could also go in the other direction by drawing her to a party rather than to the library on the night before the exam. The point is that the behavioral effect of this student's extroversion is unclear in some scenarios (e.g., studying for a test) but straightforward in others (e.g., working on a group project). Note, however, that this is arguably not the case for a personality trait like conscientiousness. There are few if any scenarios in which conscientiousness doesn't help (or at least not hurt) the level of one's performance. It makes sense then that certain traits (i.e., conscientiousness and emotional stability) are associated with higher performance across contexts, but that other traits (i.e., extroversion, agreeableness, and openness to experiences) are associated with better performance only in some scenarios—namely, the scenarios that allow for their expression in people's behavior.

The research on workplace motivation suggests that personality traits combine with contextual factors to influence behavior and performance. But how can this knowledge be applied to improve student success in higher education? Since personality traits are stable dispositions, it isn't possible to actually change students' personalities in ways that would facilitate desirable behavior and improve performance in college. Instead, strategies need to focus on creating environments that encourage the productive expression of the traits that students have. Conscientiousness and emotional stability, when present, don't appear to need much help in this regard. But there are steps colleges can take to increase the chances that the other primary personality traits will be channeled into productive and rewarding behaviors. The assignment of group work, for example, creates an outlet for extroverted students to channel that facet of their personalities into their schoolwork. Providing ample opportunities for students to partake in extracurricular activities on campus and in the surrounding community creates a supportive atmosphere for students who exhibit a high degree of openness to new experiences.

These suggestions may be helpful at some schools but not at others—designing student activities and academic experiences in ways that elicit the best aspects of students' personalities is a delicate task, and successful strategies are likely to vary across institutions. Given the crucial role of context in shaping the expression of personality traits in behaviors, it would be unwise to generalize to higher education from studies that have been conducted in very specific workplace settings. The reliable and generalizable insight that does emerge from the research about personality in the workplace is that personality traits are important predictors of behavior, but their influence on performance is highly dependent on contextual factors.

The Power of Positive Feelings

Along with personality traits, affect is a subject that has recently begun to attract significant attention from researchers of workplace motivation. Affect is a concept that captures someone's feelings, such as moods, emotions, and attitudes. It should come as no surprise that affect can have an important influence on motivation and behavior—anyone who has had a bad day knows this from personal experience. When someone is in a lousy mood, or when someone is experiencing an unpleasant emotion such as anger or disappointment, it shows in the way he acts, often with regrettable consequences.

Research conducted in workplace settings indicates that positive affect is associated with better performance on the job, and that this positive relationship between affect and performance exists for a variety of performance measures, including supervisory evaluations and sales performance (Lyubomirsky, King, & Diener, 2005). Exactly how this relationship works, however, isn't totally straightforward. Intuitively, it seems reasonable that positive feelings would be motivating and would encourage behaviors that result in better performance, but is this always the case? Feelings of happiness and excitement about work could motivate some people to be diligent and conscientious, but couldn't they also lead other people to be overconfident and careless?

This highlights the importance of understanding the relationship between affective states (e.g., emotions and moods) and specific behaviors, rather than simply noting the overall connection between positive affect and better performance outcomes. Many researchers think of affect as playing an intermediary role between the experiences people have and the behaviors they display in response to those experiences (Weiss & Cropanzano, 1996). Emotions and moods arise as reactions to external events (e.g., stress may result when a quick deadline is set for a report) and they shape the translation of these events into observable behaviors (e.g., stress may cause one to be more careless when writing the report). Importantly, affective reactions can happen in a split-second, bypassing the more reasoned and careful mental processes that people use to interpret events when they have more time. This means that affect can play a unique role in determining behavior—unlike the setting of a goal, which is often a deliberate cognitive process, affect can influence someone's behavior without that person even realizing that it is happening. Affect doesn't always (or even usually) influence behavior this quickly, but the fact that it can underscores the need to better understand the relationship between affect and behavior.

This is a relatively new area of research, but the existing research largely suggests that in the workplace, positive moods are associated with a set of desirable behaviors, and negative moods are associated with a number of undesirable behaviors. For example, studies have shown that positive moods may lead to more efficient and thorough decision making, higher levels of creativity, cooperative and pro-social behavior, lower levels of absenteeism and turnover, and sustained effort.[10] Some questions do remain, however, about the universality of these findings. Other research suggests that under certain circumstances, a negative mood may actually produce better decision making, perhaps through a "depressive realism effect" (Barsade & Gibson, 2007). Similarly, some studies have found that negative mood may be more conducive to creativity (George & Zhou, 2002). These exceptions are few, however, and they do little to undermine the emerging consensus that positive moods tend to lead to any number of desirable workplace behaviors.

If positive affect can encourage desirable behaviors and, in turn, better performance, colleges and universities may be able to develop affect-based strategies for improving student success. Research about "emotional contagion" in groups suggests a promising approach to this endeavor. Emotional contagion, which is not the nasty disease that it sounds like, is a phenomenon in which a group leader's affect essentially rubs off on the other members of the group. This phenomenon has been documented in group-based work settings (Barsade, 2002), and it seems likely that it would occur in classrooms as well. In other words, if the professor is in a positive mood, to at least some extent this lifts the moods of the students in the room. This leads to the obvious but nevertheless compelling notion that if postsecondary teachers could be made happier, their students might benefit. Given the dramatic shift over the last few decades in the composition of the faculty workforce, which has seen the balance of faculty (especially instructional faculty) switch from primarily tenured/tenure-line faculty to primarily non-tenure-track and adjunct faculty, the affective well-being of faculty members may be an increasingly salient issue. Many adjunct faculty members are underpaid, lack job security, and have few opportunities for upward professional mobility (AFT, 2010)—these are not circumstances that make for a happy teacher. If colleges are serious about promoting student success, a reasonable step to take would be to improve the working conditions of the people who teach them.

Conclusion

Research about motivation, behavior, and performance in the workplace has considerable potential to inform policies and practices aimed at improving student success in higher education. In particular, findings from research on goal setting and self-efficacy, which are by far the most extensively studied topics in the field, suggest a number of promising strategies for improving student success. In addition, research on personality traits and affect, which have been understudied but which are now gaining much more scholarly attention, has turned up useful insights that are potentially relevant to higher education. These latter two areas of research are also worth keeping an eye on moving forward, as researchers are regularly producing important new findings.

Goal setting is a useful strategy for the improvement of performance in almost any setting. A vast literature on goal setting documents that setting specific high goals tends to produce higher levels of performance than does setting vague or otherwise unchallenging goals such as "do your best." It is crucial, however, to acknowledge the exceptions to this powerful finding about the efficacy of specific high goals. Three factors in particular—goal commitment, feedback, and task complexity—appear to influence the effectiveness of setting specific high goals. Initiatives aimed at improving student success by using goal setting strategies must incorporate ways to ensure goal commitment, deliver productive feedback, and design goals that will work in environments as complex and novel as the world of higher education.

Along with goals, people's self-held beliefs about what they are capable of achieving have an important influence on their motivation, the behaviors they display, and, ultimately, the level of their performance. Self-efficacy beliefs are formed in a number of different ways and efforts to increase people's self-efficacy beliefs should leverage these multiple channels. A promising approach to building high self-efficacy through these many avenues is called enablement through guided mastery. Enablement through guided mastery is a program that combines behavioral and cognitive features—it focuses on modeling, acquiring, and transferring essential skills and abilities in a process that backs them up with strong and resilient self-efficacy beliefs. Enablement through guided mastery is a program that has been used with success in the business world, and it could do the same in higher education.

Finally, although researchers' understanding of personality traits and affect remains at an early stage, these areas of research highlight important considerations for anyone seeking ways to improve student success in higher education. It is well established that personality traits combine with contextual factors to influence behavior and individual performance. Although personality traits are stable and cannot be manipulated, the research suggests that situations and environments could be designed in ways that elicit the productive expression of personality in behavior. Affect also appears to play an important role in motivation and behavior, and positive affective states have been linked to a number of desirable behaviors as well as overall performance on the job. Affect thus provides a further potential angle for efforts aiming at improving student success in higher education by incorporating knowledge about motivation in the workplace.

Notes

1. The logic behind this finding centers on identifying the type of behavioral framing (positive/promotion or negative/prevention) for which a given feedback type (positive or negative) is likely to induce the "aroused" psychological state that encourages higher levels of subsequent activity and effort. When someone has a promotion focus toward a task, positive feedback induces high arousal because it signals that more rewards could be within reach, but negative feedback is simply discouraging, which is a low-arousal psychological state. The result is that when people receive positive feedback (but not negative feedback) under a promotion focus, they tend to either maintain or increase subsequent effort so that they'll obtain the reward they're on track for. In contrast,

when someone has a prevention focus toward a task, positive feedback induces a sense of relaxation (low arousal) because it signals "mission accomplished," but negative feedback produces stress—a high arousal state—which drives the person to try harder. It is important, however, not to interpret all of this too categorically. For the scenario in which negative feedback is received in relation to prevention-focused behavior, some questions do remain about the overall effect on subsequent motivation and effort. Under a prevention focus, negative feedback induces feelings of stress that motivate people to try harder to prevent the looming unwanted outcome, whereas positive feedback induces relaxation since the focus on avoiding threat has been satisfied. In this sense, negative feedback is more motivating than positive feedback under a prevention focus. But in other ways, negative feedback can be damaging—most notably in its potential to lessen someone's self-efficacy beliefs, thus resulting in a reduction of subsequent effort. The net result of these conflicting effects on motivation is likely to hinge on characteristics of the individual, such as the resiliency of his or her self-efficacy beliefs.

2. This finding was first reported by Kanfer and Ackerman (1989) in their seminal study of air traffic controllers performing a complex and novel flight simulation task, and it has since been replicated in many other studies of goal setting under conditions of task complexity (Kanfer, Ackerman, Murtha, Dugdale, & Nelson, 1994; Mitchell, Hopper, Daniels, George-Falvy, & James, 1994; Mone & Shalley, 1995; Winters & Latham, 1996).

3. Latham and Seijts (1999) studied young adults who were paid to build toys under a complex scheme of fluctuating input materials prices. Some were given a distal profit goal, others were given a "do your best" goal, and others were given a distal profit goal coupled with a series of more proximal goals designed to lead them toward better long-run performance. Consistent with Kanfer and Ackerman (1989), the researchers found that those in the "do your best" goal condition outperformed those in the distal profit goal condition, but they also found that those in the proximal goals condition had the highest performance of all.

4. Winters and Latham (1996) reported this finding in a study of college students who were asked to perform a complex scheduling task. The finding has also been replicated in subsequent studies (Seijts & Latham, 2005; Latham & Brown, 2006).

5. The work of Dov Eden and his colleagues accounts for a large share of the existing research on using this approach to improving self-efficacy in organizational settings, and their work focuses heavily on studying members of the Israeli Defense Forces (Eden & Ravid, 1982; Eden & Shani, 1982; Eden, 1993; Oz & Eden, 1994; Dvir, Eden, & Banjo, 1995; Davidson & Eden, 2000). This is not to say, however, that their work accounts for all of the existing research. For example, studies about Pygmalion effects have been conducted in factories (King, 1971) and retail settings (Sutton & Woodman, 1989). McNatt (2000) conducted a meta-analysis of the existing research that used Pygmalion effects to study the relationship between self-efficacy and performance, and found a significant effect size, but also noted that the effect size can vary across contexts.

6. Studies indicate that in scenarios called "escalation situations," people with higher levels of self-efficacy are more likely to persist with or even escalate their commitment to failing ventures than are people with lower levels of self-efficacy (Whyte, Saks, & Hook, 1997; Whyte & Saks, 2007). This form of counterproductive behavior may arise when the individual in question feels personally responsible for the decision to undertake the venture in the first place—seeking to justify or cover up that mistake, the individual will stay the course even as it becomes clear that the venture is going to fail.

7. Although adult students now account for a considerably larger proportion of postsecondary enrollment than they did once upon a time—43 percent of students enrolled in 2010 were aged 25 or older, compared to 28 percent in 1970 (NCES, 2012)—the majority of college students today are still under the age of 25.

8. Researchers have identified a number of other, more narrowly defined personality traits, but these five, which together are known as the Five Factor Model (FFM), provide a reasonable picture of an individual's personality and are by far the most extensively studied personality traits.

9. Examples of the types of performance measures for which a conscientiousness-performance link has been found include supervisor performance appraisal ratings (Dunn, Mount, Barrick, & Ones, 1995), training performance (Martocchio & Judge, 1997), sales levels (Barrick, Stewart, & Piotrowski, 2002; Vinchur, Shippmann, Switzer, & Roth, 1998), and group task performance (Neuman & Wright, 1999).

10. Studies have shown that positive mood states, but not negative mood states, lead to more effective decision making (Isen, 2001), higher levels of creativity (James, Brodersen, & Eisenberg, 2004; Amabile, Barsade, Mueller, & Staw, 2005), cooperative and prosocial behavior (George, 1991), lower levels of absenteeism and turnover (Pelled & Xin, 1999), and sustained effort (Foo, Uy, & Baron, 2009).

References

Amabile, T. M., Barsade, S. G., Mueller, J. S., & Staw, B. M. (2005). Affect and creativity at work. *Administrative Science Quarterly, 50,* 367–403.

American Federation of Teachers (AFT). (2010). *American academic: A national survey of part-time/adjunct faculty.* Washington, DC: American Federation of Teachers, AFL-CIO.

Bandura, A. (2009). Cultivate self-efficacy for personal and organizational effectiveness. In E. A. Locke (Ed.), *Handbook of principles of organizational behavior: Indispensable knowledge for evidence-based management* (pp. 179–200). West Sussex, UK: John Wiley & Sons.

Barrick, M. R., Mount, M. K., & Judge, T. A. (2001). Personality and performance at the beginning of the new millennium: What do we know and where do we go next? *Personality and Performance, 9,* 9–30.

Barrick, M. R., Stewart, G. L., & Piotrowski, M. (2002). Personality and job performance: Test of the mediating effects of motivation among sales representatives. *Journal of Applied Psychology, 87,* 43–51.

Barsade, S. G. (2002). The ripple effect: Emotional contagion and its influence on group behavior. *Administrative Science Quarterly, 47,* 644–675.

Barsade, S. G., & Gibson, D. E. (2007). Why does affect matter in organizations? *Academy of Management Perspectives, 21,* 36–59.

Davidson, O. B., & Eden, D. (2000). Remedial self-fulfilling prophecy: Two field experiments to prevent Golem effects among disadvantaged women. *Journal of Applied Psychology, 85,* 386–398.

Dunn, W. S., Mount, M. K., Barrick, M. R., & Ones, D. S. (1995). Relative importance of personality and general mental ability in managers' judgments of applicant qualifications. *Journal of Applied Psychology, 80,* 500–509.

Dvir, T., Eden, D., & Banjo, M. L. (1995). Self-fulfilling prophecy and gender: Can women be Pygmalion and Galatea? *Journal of Applied Psychology, 80,* 253–270.

Eden, D. (1993). Leadership and expectations: Pygmalion effects and other self-fulfilling prophecies in organizations. *Leadership Quarterly, 3,* 271–305.

Eden, D., & Ravid, G. (1982). Pygmalion versus self-expectancy: Effects of instructor- and self-expectancy on trainee performance. *Organizational Behavior and Human Performance, 30,* 351–364.

Eden, D., & Shani, A. B. (1982). Pygmalion goes to boot camp: Expectancy, leadership, and trainee performance. *Journal of Applied Psychology, 67,* 194–199.

Foo, M. D., Uy, M. A., & Baron, R. A. (2009). How do feelings influence effort? An empirical study of entrepreneurs' affect and venture effort. *Journal of Applied Psychology, 94,* 1086–1094.

Frey, B. S., & Jegen, R. (2001). Motivation crowing theory. *Journal of Economic Surveys, 15,* 589–611.

George, J. M. (1991). State or trait: Effects of positive mood on prosocial behaviors at work. *Journal of Applied Psychology, 76,* 299–307.

George, J. M., & Zhou, J. (2002). Understanding when bad moods foster creativity and good ones don't: The role of context and clarity of feelings. *Journal of Applied Psychology, 87,* 687–697.

Isen, A. M. (2001). An influence of positive affect on decision making in complex situations: Theoretical issues with practical implications. *Journal of Consumer Psychology, 11,* 75–85.

James, K., Brodersen, M., & Eisenberg, J. (2004). Workplace affect and workplace creativity: A review and preliminary model. *Human Performance, 17,* 169–194.

Kanfer, R., & Ackerman, P. L. (1989). Motivation and cognitive abilities: An integrative/aptitude-treatment interaction approach to skill acquisition. *Journal of Applied Psychology, 74,* 657–690.

Kanfer, R., Ackerman, P. L., Murtha, T. C., Dugdale, B., & Nelson, L. (1994). Goal setting, conditions of practice and task performance: A resource allocation perspective. *Journal of Applied Psychology, 79,* 826–835.

King, A. S. (1971). Self-fulfilling prophecies in training the hard-core: Supervisors' expectations and the underprivileged workers' performance. *Social Science Quarterly, 52,* 369–378.

Klein, H. J., Wesson, M. J., Hollenbeck, J. R., & Agle, B. J. (1999). Goal commitment and the goal setting process: Conceptual clarification and empirical synthesis. *Journal of Applied Psychology, 84,* 885–896.

Kluger, A. N., & Van Dijk, D. (2010). Feedback, the various tasks of the doctor, and the feedforward alternative. *Medical Education, 44,* 1166–1174.

Latham, G. P. (2007). *Work motivation: History, theory, research, and practice.* Thousand Oaks, CA: Sage Publications.

Latham, G. P., & Brown, T. C. (2006). The effect of learning vs. outcome goals on self-efficacy, satisfaction and performance in an MBA program. *Applied Psychology: An International Review, 55,* 606–623.

Latham, G. P., & Kinne, S. B. (1974). Improving job performance through training in goal setting. *Journal of Applied Psychology, 59,* 187–191.

Latham, G. P., & Seijts, G. H. (1999). The effects of proximal and distal goals on performance on a moderately complex task. *Journal of Organizational Behavior, 20,* 421–429.

Locke, E. A., & Latham, G. P. (2005). Goal setting theory: Theory building by induction. In K. G. Smith & M. A. Hitt (Eds.), *Great minds in management: The process of theory development* (pp. 128–150). New York, NY: Oxford University Press.

Lyubomirsky, S., King, L., & Diener, E. (2005). The benefits of frequent positive affect: Does happiness lead to success? *Psychological Bulletin, 131,* 803–855.

Martocchio, J. J., & Judge, T. A. (1997). Relationship between conscientiousness and learning in employee training: Mediating influences of self-deception and self-efficacy. *Journal of Applied Psychology, 82,* 764–773.

McNatt, D. B. (2000). Ancient Pygmalion joins contemporary management: A meta-analysis of the result. *Journal of Applied Psychology, 85,* 314–322.

Mitchell, T. R., Hopper, H., Daniels, D., George-Falvy, J., & James, L. R. (1994). Predicting self-efficacy and performance during skill acquisition. *Journal of Applied Psychology, 79,* 506–517.

Mone, M. A., & Shalley, C. E. (1995). Effects of task complexity and goal specificity on change in strategy and performance over time. *Human Performance, 8,* 243–262.

National Center for Education Statistics. (2012). Digest of education statistics, 2011 (NCES Publication No. 2012001). Washington, DC: U.S. Department of Education. Available from http://nces.ed.gov/programs/digest/d11/tables/dt11_200.asp

Neuman, G. A., & Wright, J. (1999). Team effectiveness: Beyond skills and cognitive ability. *Journal of Applied Psychology, 84,* 376–389.

Oz, S., & Eden, D. (1994). Restraining the Golem: Boosting performance by changing the interpretation of low scores. *Journal of Applied Psychology, 79,* 744–754.

Pelled, L. H., & Xin, K. R. (1999). Down and out: An investigation of the relationship between mood and employee withdrawal behavior. *Journal of Management, 25,* 875–895.

Ryan, R. M., & Deci, E. L. (2000). Intrinsic and extrinsic motivations: Classic definitions and new directions. *Contemporary Educational Psychology, 25,* 54–67.

Seijts, G. H., & Latham, G. P. (2005). Learning versus performance goals: When should each be used? *The Academy of Management Executive, 19,* 124–131.

Stajkovic, A. D., & Luthans, F. (1998). Self-efficacy and work-related performance: A meta-analysis. *Psychological Bulletin, 124,* 240–261.

Stewart, G. L., & Barrick, M. R. (2004). Four lessons learned from the person-situation debate: A review and research agenda. In B. Schneider & D. B. Smith (Eds.), *Personality and Organizations* (pp. 61–86). Mahwah, NJ: Lawrence Erlbaum Associates.

Sutton, C. D., & Woodman, R. W. (1989). Pygmalion goes to work: The effects of supervisor expectations in a retail setting. *Journal of Applied Psychology, 74,* 943–950.

Van Dijk, D., & Kluger, A. N. (2004). Feedback sign effect on motivation: Is it moderated by regulatory focus? *Applied Psychology: An International Review, 53,* 113–135.

Van Dijk, D., & Kluger, A. N. (2011). Task type as a moderator of positive/negative feedback effects on motivation and performance: A regulatory focus perspective. *Journal of Organizational Behavior, 32,* 1084–1105.

Vancouver, J. B., Thompson, C. M., Tischner, E. C., & Putka, D. J. (2002). Two studies examining the negative effect of self-efficacy on performance. *Journal of Applied Psychology, 87,* 506–518.

Vinchur, A. J., Schippmann, J. S., Switzer III, F. S., & Roth, P. L. (1998). A meta-analytic review of predictors of job performance for salespeople. *Journal of Applied Psychology, 83,* 586–597.

Weiss, H. M., & Cropanzano, R. (1996). Affective Events Theory: A theoretical discussion of the structure, causes and consequences of affective experiences at work. In B. M. Staw & L. L. Cummings (Eds.), *Research in organizational behavior: An annual series of analytical essays and critical reviews, Vol. 18* (pp. 1–74). Greenwich, CT: Elsevier.

Whyte, G., & Saks, A. M. (2007). The effects of self-efficacy on behavior in escalation situations. *Human Performance, 20,* 23–42.

Whyte, G., Saks, A. M., & Hook, S. (1997). When success breeds failure: The role of self-efficacy in escalating commitment to a losing course of action. *Journal of Organizational Behavior, 18,* 415–432.

Winters, D., & Latham, G. P. (1996). The effect of learning versus outcome goals on a simple versus a complex task. *Group and Organization Management, 21,* 236–250.

3

STUDENT AID, STUDENT BEHAVIOR, AND EDUCATIONAL ATTAINMENT

Sandy Baum and Saul Schwartz

Introduction

Forty years ago, when the federal system of student loans and grants was born, about half of all recent high school graduates enrolled in college. While significant differences persist across demographic groups, we have made considerable progress in improving access to higher education. Today, two-thirds of those who complete high school enroll in two-year or four-year colleges within a year (NCES, 2013, Table 302.10). Since 1972, the percentage of adults ages 25 or older who have completed at least four years of college has increased from 12 percent to 32 percent (U.S. Census Bureau, 2014, Table A-2).[1]

Despite this progress, many of those who start college never earn degrees. Among Americans ages 25 and older, 17 percent have some college but no degree (U.S. Census Bureau, 2014, Table A-4). Among students who first enrolled in college in fall 2007, less than 60 percent had completed a degree or certificate after six years. While some were still enrolled, just under one-third had left without a credential (Shapiro & Dundar, 2013). The rising price of college, increasing reliance on student debt, and the significant earnings gap between those with only some college and those who completed degrees have led to an increasing focus on improving completion rates.[2]

Increasing the number of adults with postsecondary credentials depends both on removing barriers to college access and on finding ways to improve completion rates. In addition to the social and economic factors shaping the lives of young people long before they reach the age when they might begin postsecondary study, the quality of postsecondary pedagogy and academic support systems, the mechanisms available for financing college, and the attitudes and behaviors of students all influence the rate at which individuals successfully complete programs of study.

The financial aid system is only one part of this story. But the availability of financial subsidies, the extent to which students understand and can access the system, and the enrollment patterns it encourages all contribute to educational attainment. The issue is not just whether the money is there, but whether financial aid programs and processes are structured to maximize the impact of the available funds on student enrollment and success.

This chapter examines the U.S. financial aid system from the perspective of its influence on behaviors likely to affect postsecondary enrollment and success. The federal student aid system was designed to diminish financial barriers for students without sufficient resources to pay for college. The idea that its design might affect whether or not students achieve their goals in a timely manner was not an evident concern.

Financial aid programs are too often built around the assumption that students and their families can easily weigh the costs and benefits of their postsecondary choices. A basic assumption is that if students don't have enough money to pay for college, giving them more money will make it possible for them to enroll. But if students do not know the price of college, if they do not know how much financial aid they will receive, or if they do not know what long-term benefits they can expect to receive from going to college, they will not be able to make informed decisions.

Moreover, information is not the only problem. Evidence from the fields of cognitive psychology and behavioral economics suggests that in addition to having limited information, students, like anyone else, respond to how things are framed, to complexity, to default options, and to the anecdotes that are freshest in their minds. As a result, people frequently act in ways that do not maximize their long-run welfare.

While all human beings are subject to these "cognitive biases," some potential students may be more susceptible than others, and the students at whom need-based financial aid is aimed are particularly vulnerable. For example, students whose parents did not go to college and who attend high schools where relatively few people go on to postsecondary education may not know how to approach the complex decisions they have to make. They are unlikely to have access to college-preparation resources, and tend to have less information about applying to college, accessing financial aid, and choosing appropriate institutions and programs than young people growing up in affluent, college-going cultures. For a variety of reasons, it is also likely that the cognitive biases leading to suboptimal decisions and outcomes are stronger in this group. For example, affluent young people who have grown up with the expectation that they will go to college easily slide into that decision as their default, often taking the necessary steps to prepare academically and complete the application process without considering other options. Those who have grown up thinking of college as an unrealistic option and assuming they will go to work as soon as they finish high school face a different "default option." For them, the most obvious path is likely to be moving straight into the labor market.

To explain why and how many people make choices that do not serve them well, behaviorists have defined two broad categories of decision-making processes—relatively slow, careful reasoning and fast, intuitive judgment. The fast system, now often called System 1, is automatic, is based on emotions and instincts, works quickly with little or no effort and no sense of voluntary control, and can process many things simultaneously. The slow system, now often called System 2, is based on reflection and logic and requires effort and concentration. As we explain below, many decisions about higher education are likely to utilize the "fast" side of the ledger, despite the fact that to be made well, they require considerable deliberation and preparation. The short cuts tend to take over when decisions are complex, involve uncertainty and long-term benefits, and do not allow people to learn from prior experience (Kahneman, 2011).

In this chapter, we give particular attention to concepts from behavioral economics and cognitive psychology, but also address rational responses to the monetary incentives built into the system. Our main concern is directly changing student behaviors, although we briefly address institutional behaviors as well. Our goal is not to describe the optimal aid system and the ideas included do not involve a fundamental overhaul of the system. The policy reforms we discuss are those that best illustrate the role of cognitive and behavioral issues. The idea is not that modifications of the type discussed would solve the college completion and educational attainment problems, but that they could engender significant steps in the right direction.

In the sections that follow, we focus on several key components of the student aid system and how behavioral insights, a number of which are introduced in Chapter 1 of this volume, relate to the effectiveness of current and potential policies. In the first section of this chapter, we discuss the aid application process, which governs access to these funds. The next sections focus on grant aid and on student loans. Before the concluding section, we address institutional responses to the student aid system.

Applying for Financial Aid

Over time, the components of the student financial aid system have multiplied, the rules and regulations associated with these programs have become more elaborate, and the eligibility criteria and application processes have become more complex. Despite recent steps to simplify the federal aid application process, students and families have great difficulty navigating it (Dynarski & Scott-Clayton, 2006; Baum, McPherson, & Steele, 2008; Dynarski & Wiederspan, 2012). Because of its complexity, the structure of the system may negatively affect access and persistence and create avoidable problems with education debt.

In order to apply for federal financial aid, or for need-based aid from states and institutions, students (and parents) must complete the Free Application for Student Financial Aid (FAFSA). This application is long and confusing and asks detailed financial questions that require information from tax forms and other sources. While the application process has been simplified in recent years, with the advent of computer technologies allowing filers to skip irrelevant questions and with the cooperation of the IRS in transferring some data from tax forms to the FAFSA, complexity remains a barrier preventing a significant number of qualified students from applying for aid.[3]

It might seem that these hurdles should be insignificant when weighed against the thousands of dollars of aid for which students may be eligible if they successfully navigate the application process. But as discussed in Chapter 1 of this volume, responses to complexity are a core component of behavioral analysis. Given the complexity of the decision about what kind of education to undertake after high school and how to finance that education, we should not be surprised that confusing processes such as applying for aid can create disproportionate barriers and that intuitive rules of thumb can play an important role.

People who are faced with a complex or difficult choice often *procrastinate* rather than going through the challenging task of making the choice before them. People may procrastinate either because the choice itself is difficult or because the action required to implement the choice is complicated. As a result, missed deadlines and other minor hurdles interfere with the educational progress of many low-income students (Avery & Kane, 2004).

Convincing evidence of the barrier posed by the FAFSA is provided by an experiment conducted by Bettinger et al. (2012). In this study, the offer to low-income individuals of immediate in-person assistance in filling out the FAFSA for themselves (or for their children) plus an estimate of the aid for which each individual was eligible significantly increased college enrollment rates.

Research shows that while additional information about aid may benefit students, information alone is not sufficient to eliminate the barriers they and their parents face in the aid application process. Simplifying the application process and finding ways to prevent time-inconsistent preferences and procrastination from deterring students from achieving their goals may increase the ability of students to successfully apply for aid.

More Than Information

The complexity of the FAFSA and of the student financial aid system more generally have led to calls for better information. For example, student aid calculators are now required on the websites of all colleges and universities; however, the evidence provided by the Bettinger et al. (2012) study suggests that while disadvantaged students are more likely to enroll in college when they are given personalized assistance, the provision of information alone is not likely to have the same impact. This finding indicates that efforts to provide better high school counseling to disadvantaged students, whether by trained guidance counselors or by peer mentors, should involve individual-specific support and assistance, not just the provision of general information that presents students with a wide array of complicated choices.[4] The same is true of efforts to guide adult students into appropriate postsecondary paths.[5]

The findings from a 2010 British study raise additional questions about the effectiveness of just providing more information about financial aid or other aspects of the college decision. In this study, between a quarter and half of students who rated hypothetical items of information as very useful reported that they had not actually tried to find the information they rated as very helpful (Oakleigh, 2010). Similarly, Grubb (2006) found that U.S. students make little effort to search for information about educational options.

Simplifying the Application Process

Students would require less information and less guidance if the system for accessing student aid were simpler. Recommendations to move in this direction are now widespread, with a particular emphasis on relying on financial data available from the IRS to eliminate the need for students and families to complete a complex application (College Board, 2008; Rethinking Pell Grants, 2013; NCAN, 2013; Baum & Scott-Clayton, 2013). The arguments for this approach are compelling, but implementation should not ignore the finding from behavioral science that the effectiveness of information depends on the source of the information. The wrong messenger can make the right information ineffective. Some students and families, particularly those in precarious financial circumstances, might be hesitant to engage in any process that involves the IRS (College Board, 2010). This potential problem should not prevent moving forward with simplifying the application process, but it should be recognized and accommodated in the program design.

Other relevant suggestions include requiring that students complete the FAFSA before graduating from high school and simplifying the formula for aid eligibility to minimize the amount of information required.[6]

Commitment Devices

Even if people have clear preferences about the future, when the future arrives, those preferences may weaken in the face of the immediate actions required to realize the desired outcomes. They make choices today that their past selves would have rejected—a phenomenon known as *time-inconsistent preferences* (DellaVigna, 2009). This concept is relevant to the financial aid application process because an individual may have decided that she wants to go to college and will do whatever it takes to get there—in the future. But when the time actually arrives to fill out the application for aid, the immediate cost seems large and the vague benefits, still far in the future, are less compelling. It is therefore not surprising that people who think they want to go to college might resist incurring the costs—both the effort required to apply for college and the actual tuition payments—when the time to incur those costs arrives.

Time-inconsistent preferences strengthen the argument for eliminating the barriers created by the financial aid application process. Dynarski and Scott-Clayton (2006) mention the overweighting of immediate costs as one possible explanation for the relatively low postsecondary participation of low-income students, pointing out that higher-income students are less vulnerable to this problem because they go to high schools that reduce the cost of meeting these requirements by preparing them for the SAT, guiding them through the college and financial aid application processes, and reminding them of deadlines.

Some of those with time-inconsistent preferences are "sophisticates," aware of their own lack of self-control and thus aware that their future selves may not take the actions that they, at the current moment, think best. Others are "myopes," and appear unaware of the lack of self-control that their future selves will exhibit. Sophisticates may seek out commitment devices that constrain the behavior of their future selves. In a study by Ariely and Wertenbroch (2002), students were allowed to choose their own deadlines for a series of assignments. We might think people would prefer the latest possible deadline, giving themselves as much flexibility as possible. In the experiment, however, two-thirds of the subjects chose deadlines earlier than the last possible date, presumably in order to commit their future selves to work more quickly on the assignments than they otherwise would have.

Grant Aid

Simplifying the Grant System

Just as complexity discourages potential students from applying for financial aid, diminishing the probability that they will enroll in college, complexity in the structure of available grant aid reduces its effectiveness. Students may receive grants from a combination of federal, state, institutional, and private sources. The rules and processes for receiving these funds vary widely, and students rarely have reliable information about the funding that will be available to them until just before they actually begin classes.

The lessons discussed above suggest that grant aid should be simpler and more predictable in order to allow students to respond to the incentives it is intended to provide. One change consistent with this idea would be constructing internet-based look-up tables that allow students to better estimate their awards in advance. Because requiring students to reapply for aid every year generates uncertainty about continuing funding, a related idea is to award grant aid for the entire length of the program of study. Promising students aid for future years also has the advantage that it creates a sense of loss if they leave school without taking advantage of the funds they have been awarded.

Increasing the consistency of the information provided by different institutions would also be in line with evidence from the behavioral literature. Currently, many award letters are unclear about what grant aid the student is receiving, from which sources the aid is coming, and how much the student and family will have to pay. Requiring a common format for award letters could mitigate this problem. The Obama administration proposed standardization in 2011 under the rubric "smart disclosure," which meant "providing information in a straightforward common format."[7] The idea is that in a wide variety of decisions—including those concerning cell phone contracts and mortgages as well as postsecondary institutions—having standardized information facilitates comparison by consumers or by their advisors.

Encouraging Full-Time Enrollment

While many students have family and work responsibilities that make full-time enrollment unrealistic, completion rates for students who consistently enroll part-time are very low (Shapiro & Dundar, 2013; Complete College America, 2011; Clotfelter, 1991). Moreover, the definition of "full-time" enrollment that has evolved does students a disservice, because it implies slower credit accumulation than is required by most programs to complete an associate degree in two years or a bachelor's degree in four years. While these outcomes require that students earn an average of 15 credit hours per semester, the federal Pell Grant program and many state grant programs consider students full time if they are registered for 12 credit hours or more per semester.[8]

It might seem that the benefits of progressing as rapidly as possible through college would provide adequate motivation to students. Paying tuition for an extra year or two, being unable to work full time during an extended period of study, and postponing the financial benefits of being in the labor market with a college degree carry significant financial penalties. But these costs may not be sufficiently immediate, visible, and concrete to affect the choices many students make.

Defining full time as 12 credit hours makes this enrollment pattern the norm. Not surprisingly, in 2007–2008, 30 percent of students in semester-based schools receiving full-time Pell awards were registered for just 12 credit hours, and 56 percent of the "full-time" students were registered for fewer than 15 hours (NCES, 2008). Students can receive only one full Pell Grant in the course of a year, so if they enroll in the summer to complete the additional needed credits, they will not be eligible for Pell funding to support this work.

A simple change could provide encouragement for students to enroll full time. One example is provided by recent proposals that would link grant amounts to number of credits. Under this system students would receive larger grants if they enrolled for more credits.[9] They would receive additional funding if they enrolled for three terms over the course of a year rather than two (Baum &

Scott-Clayton, 2013; College Board, *Rethinking Pell Grants,* 2013). The Super Pell and Pell Well proposals recently put forward by NASFAA would have a similar effect (NASFAA, 2013).

Performance-Based Grants

The desire to give grants to the students who need them most has led policy makers to avoid tying need-based aid to academic performance, which is negatively correlated with socioeconomic status. Although a growing portion of state grant aid ignores financial circumstances all together and simply rewards high school grades or test scores, Pell Grants and need-based state aid rarely require more than minimal "satisfactory academic progress."

A focus on postsecondary academic progress, as opposed to past achievement, has the potential to increase student success.[10] Standard economic analysis suggests that if students are given more money for specific behaviors, those behaviors will become more common and there is evidence to support the idea that tying funding to credit completion can improve academic outcomes.

Examination of the impact of a West Virginia program tying scholarships to academic progress found that when students were granted free tuition conditional on accumulating a specified number of credits with a minimum GPA, graduation rates increased significantly. The findings suggest that the program worked by establishing clear academic goals and incentives to meet them, rather than simply reducing the cost of college (Scott-Clayton, 2011).

A series of randomized trials with a variety of high-need populations in different locations carried out by MDRC under their Performance Based Scholarship Demonstration tests the idea that students will progress more quickly if provided with clear and immediate incentives (MDRC, 2013). The evidence from these experiments suggests that students make more progress if they are given extra dollars to do so—but the effects are not large.

A number of studies have shown that not all students respond similarly to financial incentives. In particular, lower-income students are more price-sensitive than students with sufficient resources, whose choices are less dependent on financial subsidies (Kane, 1995; Bowen et al., 2009; Heller, 1997).

Of particular importance for the design of performance-based funding schemes is the evidence that for high-need students, dollars alone may not be enough to generate significant improvements in college success. Experimental evidence indicates that the combination of financial incentives with mentoring and educational services is most effective (Angrist, 2009).

This outcome suggests the possibility that combining grant aid with the provision of academic support services might be the most productive use of additional funding.[11] Another issue relevant to the successful design of performance-based funding schemes is that the most successful approaches provide incentives for actions over which students have control, such as enrolling full time or taking advantage of academic support systems. In contrast, they may not know how to accomplish outcomes such as higher grade point averages (Fryer, 2011).

Some efforts to encourage completion involve converting loans to grants or refunding a portion of tuition for students who complete their degrees on time (THECB, 2013). This framework is based on the idea that students will respond in a rational way to financial incentives. Any program that rewards student success should incorporate the reality that academic success is highly correlated with student characteristics and that broad-based programs of this nature are likely to transfer funds to students from more privileged backgrounds. This problem suggests that performance-based grant aid might be most effective if used in a targeted way, supplementing grants to high-risk students in specific environments.

Early Commitment of Grant Aid

One decision-making shortcut involves not making an active decision at all but defaulting to the status quo. Complexity is one reason people gravitate towards the "default option" when faced with choices. If a decision is challenging or if complicated actions are required to reach one outcome but not another, people are likely to choose the path of least resistance, opting for the passive choice (Kahneman et al., 1991). Rather than accepting default options as given, policies can be designed to modify the dominant choice, or to consciously create a path of least resistance for the decision-maker.

An often-cited by study Madrian and Shea (2001) documents the power of the default option by reporting on the impact of a small change in the pension plan enrollment procedures prevailing at a large U.S. firm. The switch from requiring new employees to make a choice and take active steps to enroll in a pension plan to automatic enrollment (with the opportunity to opt out) led to nearly double the pension plan enrollment rate among newly hired employees compared to for those hired just before the change.

Many young people from low-income backgrounds who have few role models for continuing their education after high school may just assume they will not go to college, at least in part because of the expense. Early commitment of grant aid has the potential to change what these students see as the default option. Federal and state grant aid could be awarded well in advance of enrollment and students could have that information when they are making their choices.[12] Currently, most potential students receive financial aid information only after they have decided to go to college and taken most of the required steps to make that a reality. The early awarding of funds might change the norms and expectations of low-income and first-generation students, bringing them more in line with those of young people from more privileged backgrounds.

The Future to Discover experiment in Canada found that an early promise of financial aid significantly increased college enrollment and graduation rates of traditionally under-represented groups (SRDC, 2014). Future to Discover was a randomized trial that offered low-income high school students in the Canadian province of New Brunswick either an early commitment of $8,000 in grants, or a series of after-school postsecondary education workshops or both. The grants were contingent on high school graduation and enrollment in a two- or four-year college. The impacts of the financial incentive on enrollment were quite large, on the order of 7 to 8 percent (p. 4).

Recent proposals for early aid commitment systems include providing education accounts for middle school and high school students from low-income families (Rethinking Pell Grants, 2013; Huelsmann & Cunningham, 2013). Under such a system, low-income students would receive regular notification that they have money available only if they enroll in postsecondary education. Not taking advantage of this opportunity would involve a loss of funds, rather than just the avoidance of a major expense.

The early commitment of financial aid would be much more feasible if the aid application process was simpler and eligibility could be determined earlier.

Addressing Unexpected Changes in Circumstances

A promising accommodation to the reality that students are likely to overreact to immediate costs is to provide some aid at the moment that students face unexpected financial problems. Need-based grant aid is almost always based on measures of financial resources at a point in time many months before the student enrolls in school. But for students, immediate circumstances are most salient. A student whose car breaks down or whose babysitter quits in the middle of the semester is likely to see the situation as hopeless. The idea that students would estimate the long-term costs and benefits of borrowing money to solve immediate problems of this nature is unrealistic, given our understanding of how people make judgments. The salience of their immediate problems is likely to make money awarded at the moment of need more powerful than the same dollars awarded as part of a basic financial aid package. Such a program of emergency grant aid must be designed to minimize moral hazard—the tendency of people to create the circumstances for which they are insured. But recognizing the disproportionate interference with student success that can be created by relatively small immediate problems is critical to the design of effective student aid programs.

The overweighting of immediate costs affects persistence as well as the original enrollment decision. Students may decide that grappling with a difficult course, overcoming short-term financial problems, or facing the other challenges involved in getting through college just don't seem worth it at the moment, without giving sufficient weight to the long-run losses generated by leaving school.

Student Loans

Simplifying the Loan System

The primary purpose of student loans is to influence decisions about enrollment and persistence in postsecondary education. Over time, in an effort to facilitate college access, the federal government has ended up with an array of loan programs and repayment plans that significantly increase the complexity of the student financing system and arguably create real hardship for students at the same time that they increase access.

Students and families make multiple decisions about borrowing for college. They decide whether to borrow, whether to take federal loans or private loans or both, whether the student or the parent should take the loans and, of course, how much to borrow. More decisions come when it is time to repay the loans. Students have multiple options for federal loan repayment plans. They also make decisions about prioritizing their debt. Should they repay private loans before federal loans; auto loans before student loans?

One way of simplifying the student loan system would be to diminish the number of available loan programs and the number of repayment plan options. The standard economic rationale for providing multiple choices is that consumers have a wide range of circumstances and preferences. As Bar-Gill (2011) points out in the context of credit cards, a multiplicity of choices can be both efficient and beneficial. Just as some credit card users would prefer a higher interest rate but no annual fee, while others would make the opposite choice, some student borrowers might prefer to bear the higher interest costs involved in stretching their payments out over a longer time, while others prefer to pay as quickly as possible.

On the other side of this issue, however, is the *"paradox of choice,"* with expanding options leading to more difficult decision processes (Schwartz, 2004). For example, students presented with a long list of student loan options may be less likely to make well-considered choices than those who are presented with one option for parental borrowing and one for student borrowing. Despite a variety of good options for repayment plans, most borrowers stay in the standard ten-year repayment plan in which they are placed if they make no active choice.[13]

Proposals to eliminate the distinction between subsidized student loans, for which the federal government pays the interest while the student is in school, and unsubsidized loans, on which interest accrues continuously, would diminish the complexity of the student loan system. Moreover, eliminating the in-school subsidy would end the need for students to submit to a complicated financial need determination in order to access federal student loans.

Another simplification strategy would be to take steps to eliminate the confusion between federal and private student loans. It is not uncommon for students to take private loans without taking federal loans at all, or without exhausting their eligibility for federal student loans. Potential explanations for this choice, all based in behavioral economics, include the reality that federal loans require the FAFSA and private loans do not and that private lenders advertise in a way that makes their loans salient. Private loans may also have teaser introductory interest rates or may advertise the lowest available rates, although most borrowers will not be eligible for those rates. Moreover, many potential borrowers simply do not know the difference between the two forms of borrowing (CFPB, 2012).

A straightforward solution to this problem would be to eliminate any special treatment or provisions for "private student loans," such as the current law that makes it almost impossible to discharge these loans in bankruptcy. A private student loan is simply an unsecured consumer loan. Students could still choose this form of credit, but they would not be subject to the current confusion—and these loans would be dischargeable in bankruptcy like any other consumer loans.

Debt Aversion

Reluctance to incur debt is a critical issue in designing the most effective student aid system. The term "debt aversion" is used to refer to the idea that being in debt carries a psychic cost, apart from any of the explicit costs associated with the loan. Because people fear losses more than they value equivalent gains, they may hesitate to take risks, even if the actions perceived as risky have a high probability of improving their situations. While debt financing does not necessarily increase the total cost of attending college, the prospect of being left with unmanageable debt might deter people from making investments they would judge wise if the downside were simply wasted expenditures as opposed to debt.

Of particular concern is the idea that low-income students, who have no alternative means of financing postsecondary education, may be overly hesitant to borrow because of the fear that they will not be able to repay their debts. If ending their education with high school is the reference point for many low-income students, they will not perceive the absence of postsecondary education as a loss. Because they fear losses more than they value equivalent gains, there is a tendency to avoid risks. They undervalue uncertain potential future income gains, and they fear the loss of financial security associated with incurring significant debt. In contrast, for students from more affluent families and for those whose parents are college graduates, not going to college is likely to be perceived as a loss—a failure to meet expectations.

The empirical results about the existence of debt aversion among potential college students are mixed, and as discussed below, there may be countervailing psychological forces leading some students to borrow excessively for college. But the possibility of debt aversion is real enough to merit attention. One convincing analysis involves the borrowing decisions of law students.

Acknowledging the wide and rising gap in earnings between public-interest jobs and private sector jobs, some law schools have instituted loan repayment assistance programs (LRAP), which pay off the loans of graduates who work in public-interest jobs by, for example, forgiving the loans for graduates who work in such jobs for ten years after graduating. In 1997, the NYU law school announced a variant of their LRAP that would pay two-thirds of the tuition of students planning to go into public-interest jobs after graduation. If they chose other career paths, the tuition subsidy would be converted to a loan.

NYU set up an experiment, randomly assigning students who agreed to participate to either receive upfront loans that could be forgiven or tuition subsidies that could later turn into loans. The two programs were designed to be financially equivalent, taking into account all interest on the loans. Only if borrowing carried a psychic cost, apart from any financial or risk-related considerations, would the enrollment rates of the accepted students offered the two programs differ. In her analysis of the data arising from the experiment, Erica Field (2009) reports that among applicants for the 1999 class, 42 percent of the applicants offered the tuition subsidy enrolled, compared to only 32 percent of those offered forgivable loans. Among the applicants for the class of 2000, the gap was even larger, 20 percentage points in favor of the subsidies (Field, 2009). These effects are as close as researchers have gotten to documenting educational debt aversion in high-stakes decisions.

The post-law school choices of the two groups illustrate the importance of *reference points* and the related concept of *loss aversion*. People tend to judge options based on the changes they are likely to bring, rather than actually comparing end states. If the end state reflects a loss from the starting point, it seems worse than if the same situation involves the continuation of existing circumstances. In the NYU Law School experiment, those who had been given a tuition subsidy and who were considering a job in the private sector would have to take out an extra $30,000 in loans to repay their subsidy. Those who had not been given the subsidy would have already borrowed that $30,000 prior to considering the private option. Field argues that the reference point of the two groups would be different (even though the total amount borrowed would be the same) and the new $30,000 in borrowing would act as a disincentive to private employment for the subsidy group. In the experiment, those with the subsidy were significantly more likely to take on public-service jobs after law school.

Income-Based Repayment (IBR)

Income-based repayment systems provide assurance that excessive debt is unlikely to be a problem and should thus work to counter debt aversion. To date, however, relatively few borrowers have taken advantage of the existing U.S. programs in this category.

The power of the default option in situations where decisions are complex lies behind recent proposals to make income-based repayment automatic when students leave school and begin repaying their student loans. Currently, there is a long list of repayment plans from which to choose, but if borrowers do not actively choose an alternative plan, they are placed in the standard plan—a mortgage-style repayment plan involving regular payments over 10 years. Income-based repayment (IBR) allows borrowers to make payments as a function of their incomes so that those struggling to find a job or with low earnings can make little or no payment until their situations improve. If their hardship continues, the loans are eventually forgiven.

Making IBR the default option would lead more students to enroll in a repayment plan that eases the burden on them and might significantly reduce the frequency of student loan default. It would also make IBR more visible and salient, increasing the likelihood that students would actively choose it. In terms of enrollment and persistence, the goal would be to diminish the extent to which debt aversion discourages students from making the investment in postsecondary education.

Minimizing Risks

The student loan arena is receiving increasing attention because of the significant problems a visible minority of former students are experiencing repaying their loans. While debt aversion appears to lead some students to make sub-optimal postsecondary choices in order to avoid debt, other students may be led by other cognitive biases to borrow too much. A common finding of behavioral economists is that *overconfidence* leads people to take questionable risks because their subjective estimates of the probability of success are higher than the objective reality.[14]

Students considering courses of study in which the likelihood of success is objectively low may enroll anyway because they believe that they will succeed where others have failed. Where debt aversion might lead students to borrow too little, overconfidence can lead them to borrow too much. Inflated expectations of the probabilities of educational and occupational success leave some students with debt obligations that are disproportionate to their earnings.

Suggestions are emerging that would offer less favorable terms on loans for students embarking on educational paths with relatively low chances of success (NASFAA, 2013; Simkovic, 2013). But an alternative to modifying the terms or availability of loans based on repayment risk is to provide better disclosure to potential borrowers about the risks they face. An option emerging from the insights of the behavioral sciences literature is to provide "psychology-guided" information to potential borrowers.[15] For example, a risk index could be developed and then constructed for each borrower. Instead of altering interest rates on the basis of the index, the estimated risk of default could be communicated to the borrower with a simple visual device: The notice sent to students to inform them of the loan could have a hyperlinked red, green, or yellow light. The red light would indicate a program/school combination for which the probability of default was high. If any borrower chose to click on the link, the nature of the index and its application in the situation faced by that particular borrower could be explained.[16]

Bertrand and Morse (2011) employed this type of visual representation of important information in their study of payday lending. One of their interventions was to put on the envelope containing a newly-issued payday loan a picture showing how often payday loans are repaid without the borrowers having to take out another payday loan. For example, the fact that only two out of ten borrowers repay the payday loan without taking out another one is illustrated by two small human figures.[17] The most effective approach tested by Bertrand and Morse compared the dollar cost of borrowing a fixed amount ($300) from a payday lender to the cost of borrowing the same amount for the same length of time using a credit card. This intervention was based both on the idea of increasing the ease with which the payday loan could be evaluated and on the idea that payday borrowers might be thinking of their borrowing in too narrow a frame of reference.[18] That is, they see the $15 cost of a single transaction as too small to worry about instead of thinking about the larger cost of consistently borrowing from a payday lender.

This approach could have a bigger impact than simply publishing information about, for example, the default rates of graduates of specific programs and institutions. The cost of providing simple psychology-guided information is quite small and if the result is to reduce inappropriate borrowing by any significant amount, the benefits might easily exceed the costs. The assumption is not that all borrowing is inappropriate or irrational, but that the riskiest borrowing will be diminished by information designed with behavioral responses in mind.

Allowing the Discharge of Student Loans in Bankruptcy

The idea that overconfidence can lead to excessive borrowing might lead to the suggestion that the terms of student loans should be harsher or that access to those loans should be restricted. However, the reality is that any loan system designed to increase educational opportunities for at-risk students is likely to lead to some over-borrowing. The recognition that overconfidence leads people to borrow more than they are likely to be able to repay is one of the motivations for the "fresh start" principle that is so important to the general framework of personal bankruptcy. Student loans are much more difficult to discharge in bankruptcy than other forms of consumer debt, and that fact goes against the "fresh start" principle.

Before 1976, the bankruptcy rules for student loans were similar to those for other consumer debt. However, Congress made federal student loans very difficult to discharge in the late 1970s and since then has gradually imposed more restrictions. Beginning in 2005, for example, non-dischargeability was extended to private student loans. The rationale for making student loans almost impossible to discharge through bankruptcy seems to be rooted in the idea of "soft fraud," that students leaving school with heavy debts and promising careers will file for bankruptcy because they simply do not want to pay their debts (Pottow, 2007). No systematic evidence of such behavior has been produced.

The restrictions on discharging student debt in bankruptcy should push borrowers to move in the direction of other forms of consumer debt, such as credit cards. Few would argue that this is a desirable outcome. But those who are overconfident about their educational and career outcomes are not likely to be discouraged. Not believing that they are likely to end up with repayment difficulties, they will not be deterred from borrowing by the bankruptcy restrictions. In other words, the current policy is likely to discourage borrowers who should take student loans, while not reducing excessive borrowing by those who under-estimate their risks. Allowing discharge and improving IBR are better alternatives than the current inescapable hardship that faces too many people struggling to repay their student loans.

The Supply Side: Institutional Behavior

The primary focus of this chapter is on students, who represent the demand side of the market for postsecondary education. The current federal funding system is essentially a voucher system, providing funds to students depending on their circumstances and allowing them to use those funds at the institutions and programs of their choice. Institutions must simply meet administrative requirements and be accredited by an organization recognized by the federal government. But institutional behaviors, which can play an important role in student success, may also be affected by the design of student aid programs.

The voucher system of student aid was developed under the assumption that colleges and universities exist to provide high-quality educational services, thus aligning their interests with those of students. But this is not always a reasonable assumption. The primary motive for some institutions (not all of which are in the for-profit sector) is to maximize enrollments or revenues net of expenses, and there may sometimes be misalignment between student and institutional interests. Institutions too often respond to incentives that are—often unintentionally— embodied in the student aid system.

The student aid system does not include strong incentives for institutions to support students through to graduation. Although recruitment costs may be substantial, institutions enjoy the same revenue from new first year students as from continuing students, who are frequently more expensive to educate because of the specialized classes they require. Colleges also have financial incentives to direct students into lower-cost programs of study, as opposed to paths that may lead to better labor market outcomes but cost more to offer. It should therefore be no surprise that at least some suppliers of postsecondary education focus on maximizing the number of students enrolled without paying enough attention to student success.

In addition to responding rationally to the incentives embodied in the student aid system, postsecondary institutions often exhibit more awareness than do public policy makers of the way students actually respond to student aid structures. For example institutions observe that students and parents, who have little basis for judging the actual value of the educational experience at a particular college, respond positively to the appearance of a "good deal." Parents are proud of their children who receive "merit" scholarships.[19] This observation contributes to the current complex pricing and discounting patterns at colleges and universities.

Institutional actions could change both the way students finance college and their success rates. For example, just providing students with clear guidance about the nature of private student loans before they commit to this source of funds can make a measurable difference (Jaschik, 2007). A number of recent policy proposals with the goal of increasing access and success for low-income students are directed at influencing institutional behavior through incentives rather than restrictions.[20] The approach of awarding subsidies to institutions based on the success of low-income students is rooted in the idea that if they have a greater incentive to help their students succeed, institutions will respond more constructively to all student behavioral patterns. Pilot projects of this type should be carefully designed and evaluated in order to avoid unintended consequences such as increased admission requirements and dilution of academic quality and requirements.

Conclusion

Student aid makes college possible for many students who could otherwise not afford to participate in postsecondary education. However, these dollars could be more effective in increasing educational attainment if programs were designed with a clearer understanding of student behaviors. Students respond to financial incentives, and the incentives built into the aid system often do not encourage enrollment patterns most likely to lead to timely degree completion. But like other people, students also systematically make decisions that do not maximize their own long run well-being. Incorporating the insights of behavioral economics and cognitive psychology into the development of student aid policies has the potential to increase student success.

Like anyone else, some potential students respond to complexity by taking the path of least resistance and accepting what appears to them to be the default option. For many low-income students, this is likely to be not going to college. Time-inconsistent preferences can lead some people to procrastinate and, in this context, to fail to even apply for financial aid, despite a desire to continue their education. On the other hand, potential students may be overly optimistic about their own chances for success, even choosing to enroll in institutions where very few people succeed. Some of these patterns pull in opposite directions in terms of postsecondary financing decisions. For example, some students may fail to enroll or may drop out of college to avoid incurring debt. Others may borrow more than they can reasonably hope to repay.

Student aid policy should be designed to minimize the extent to which student decision making and behavioral patterns lead them into paths they would not choose for themselves if they could objectively evaluate and act on their long-term prospects. Some argue that "nudges" are simply a new form of government coercion (Farrell & Shalizi, 2011). But it is important to recognize that the status quo also "nudges" people. For example, one could argue that the complexity of the current system nudges people *not* to take advantage of existing subsidies. It would be a mistake to assume that only *changes* to public policy can be thought of as manipulating behavior (Sunstein & Thaler, 2003).

Any agenda for changing behavior, however, should be predicated on evidence that these changes in behaviors would lead to desirable changes in outcomes. It's not just a question of, for example, whether more people completing the application process for federal student aid would increase college enrollments but whether there is good reason for public policy to be designed with the intent of inducing people to apply for aid and to enroll in postsecondary programs.

We believe that the persistent gaps in enrollment and attainment by racial and ethnic group and by socioeconomic status justify designing effective nudges.[21] While some may be inadequately prepared for college and face low probabilities of success, for others, alternative choices and behaviors might make the difference between life with a college credential and life with more limited opportunities. Potential students may have incomplete information; they may face insurmountable budget constraints; they may not understand the benefits associated with postsecondary education—or their decision-making processes may not reflect the rational calculus so frequently assumed. Students may not trust the available information, they may fear taking on debt more than is reasonable, or they may see the path of least resistance as following the example of those around them who did not go to college.

In addition to constraining their personal outcomes, the failure of these individuals to invest in themselves carries a high cost to society as a whole. Those who could benefit but do not enroll are less productive members of the labor force, pay lower taxes, and are more reliant on public subsidies than they would otherwise be. Those who enroll and do not achieve their goals are in similar circumstances, with the added problems of having paid in time and money for education and ending up with debts they may not be able to repay.

Whatever the optimal number of people with postsecondary credentials, policies that limit individuals' access to the opportunity to live up to their potential cannot be the best outcome for society.[22] Similarly, a system that creates strong incentives for institutions to lure students into programs not likely to serve them well is hardly desirable.

Active consideration of the impact of student aid policies on both institutional and student behavior has the potential to significantly improve student outcomes. The behavioral insights highlighted in this chapter do not replace our longstanding understanding of the importance of financial and other incentives. But these more nuanced perspectives can enrich our understanding of student responses and should lead to improved program design. Experiments that provide the opportunity for careful evaluation of the effectiveness of specific program modifications are an important next step. As innovative ideas are tested, we should ask not only whether they work in the specific circumstances studied but why they work and how best to extend them to different populations.

Notes

1. These figures are based only on the civilian, non-institutionalized population. The percentages of African Americans and Hispanics 25 years old or older with four years of college or more were 22 percent and 15 percent, respectively, in 2013 (U.S. Census Bureau, 2014, Table A-2).
2. In the 1940s and 1950s, before associate degrees and postsecondary certificates were widespread, just under half of all adults with some college education had completed bachelor's degrees. Since the mid-1960s, that percentage has almost always been just over half (U.S. Census Bureau, 2014, Table A-1).
3. Mark Kantrowitz (2009) estimated that in 2007–2008, before the recent FAFSA simplification efforts, 2.3 million enrolled students who would have been eligible for Pell Grants failed to apply for financial aid.
4. Hoxby and Turner (2013) find that providing very high-achieving low-income students with inexpensive semi-customized information on the application process and colleges' net costs, along with no-paperwork application fee waivers, causes a significant increase in the percentage of these students applying to, being admitted to, and enrolling in selective institutions.
5. *Rethinking Pell Grants* (2013) highlights the needs for better-personalized guidance for adult students.
6. After an aggressive FAFSA completion campaign in the Chicago Public Schools, the FAFSA completion rate among eligible high school graduates increased from 65 percent in 2006 to 86 percent in 2010 (Chicago Public Schools, 2013). Note that if the system involves a *requirement*, although it may change the default option and the reference point for students, it differs fundamentally from the "nudges" on which behavioral analysis focuses.
7. See www.whitehouse.gov/sites/default/files/omb/inforeg/for-agencies/informing-consumers-through-smart-disclosure.pdf
8. Students registered for 9 to 11 credit hours receive ¾ of the amount for which they would be eligible at 12 credits, and those registered for 6 to 8 credits receive half. Less than half-time students can also receive grant aid.
9. Overall, funding would be limited to 125 percent of the credits required for the program in which they were enrolled.
10. The distinction between rewarding past and future achievement and the potential impact on student success of rewarding academic progress are emphasized in Brookings Institution State Grant Aid Study Group (2012).
11. The Rethinking Pell Grants Study Group made this proposal for adult students in their recent report (2013).

12. This approach is less feasible with institutional grant aid, which cannot be determined before the student applies for admission.
13. Faced with complex choices, students may focus on a few salient characteristics rather than trying to understand all of the options. In the credit card context, complexity allows the issuers to make salient features (the annual fee, the rewards program) attractive and to make the less salient feature (the late fees and foreign exchange fees) far less attractive (Bar-Gill, 2011).
14. A classic example of the overconfidence effect can be found in Svenson (1981), who found that 93 percent of American drivers thought that their driving skills were above the median.
15. Drawing a clear line between the rational model's focus on complete information and the behavioral model's focus on how people access and process information is difficult. We develop the behavioral approach further later in the paper, but psychology-guided information falls in the gray area between the two.
16. The credit-scoring algorithm used by private lenders to determine the terms and conditions of private loans is proprietary and is not revealed to potential borrowers.
17. Bertrand and Morse (2011, p. 1872). The actual information illustrated that 2.5 people out of 10 repay without first renewing their payday loan.
18. See Barberis et al. (2006) for a discussion of narrow framing and its application to financial decisions.
19. See Clifford & Rampell (2012) for a discussion of consumer demand for discounts in a retail environment.
20. Examples of relevant proposals include the Rethinking Student Aid Study Group (College Board, 2008), the Rethinking Pell Grants Study Group (2013), and a number of the recent Redesigning Aid Design and Delivery (RADD) projects funded by the Bill and Melinda Gates Foundation.
21. In 2011, 69 percent of white high school graduates enrolled immediately in college, as did 65 percent of black and 64 percent of Hispanic high school graduates (National Center for Education Statistics, 2012b, Table 210). However, 35 percent of white 25- to 34-year-olds had bachelor's degrees, compared to 21 percent of blacks and 15 percent of Hispanics in this age range, indicating large gaps in completion rates (U.S. Census Bureau, 2012). In 2010, 52 percent of high school graduates from the lowest family income quartile enrolled immediately in college, compared to 82 percent of those from the highest income quartile (NCES, 2012a, Table A-34–1), http://nces.ed.gov/programs/coe/tables/table-trc-1.asp). Among dependent students beginning their studies in 2003–2004, by 2009 38 percent of those from the lowest family income quartile had left without a credential, compared to 19 percent of those from the highest quartile (NCES, 2012b).
22. A recent analysis of the British higher education financing system from a behavioral perspective includes strong warnings about assuming that participation is the right choice for students. The stated goal is to help people to overcome barriers to sound decision-making—not necessarily to significantly increase enrollment rates (Diamond, Vorley, Roberts, & Jones, 2012).

References

Angrist, J., Lang, D., & Oreopoulos, P. (2009). Incentives and services for college achievement: Evidence from a randomized trial. *American Economic Journal: Applied Economics, 1*(1), 136–163.

Ariely, D., & Wertenbroch, K. (2002). Procrastination, deadlines, and performance: Self-control by precommitment. *Psychological Science*, *13*(3), 219–224.

Avery, C., & Kane, T. J. (2004). Student perceptions of college opportunities: The Boston COACH Program. In C. M. Hoxby (Ed.), *College choices: The economics of where to go, when to go, and how to pay for it* (pp. 355–394). Chicago, IL: University of Chicago Press.

Barberis, N., Huang, M., & Thaler, R. (2006). Individual preferences, monetary gambles and stock market participation. *American Economic Review, 96*(4), 1069–1090.

Bar-Gill, O. (2011). *Seduction by contract: Law, economics and psychology in consumer markets.* Oxford, UK: Oxford University Press.

Baum, S., McPherson, M., & Steele, P. (Eds.). (2008). *The effectiveness of student aid: What the research tells us.* New York, NY: The College Board.

Baum, S., & Scott-Clayton, J. (2013). *Redesigning the Pell Grant Program for the twenty-first century.* The Hamilton Project. Washington: The Brookings Institution.

Bertrand M., & Morse, A. (2011). Information disclosure, cognitive biases, and payday borrowing. *The Journal of Finance, 66*(6),1 865–1893.

Bettinger, E. P., & Long, B., Oreopoulos, P., & Sanbonmatsu, L. (2012). *The role of simplification and information in college decisions: Results from the H&R Block FAFSA experiment* (No. 15361). NBER Working Paper. Retrieved from www.nber.org/papers/w15361

Bowen, W., Chingos, M., & McPherson, M. (2009). *Crossing the finish line.* Princeton, NJ: Princeton University Press.

Brookings Institution State Grant Aid Study Group. (2012). *Beyond need and merit: Strengthening state grant programs.* Brown Center on Education Policy at Brookings. Washington, DC: The Brookings Institution.

Chicago Public Schools. (2013). CPS students post record FAFSA completion rate. Press Release. Retrieved from www.cps.edu/News/Press_releases/Pages/02_28_2011_PR1. aspx.

Clifford, S., & Rampell, C. (2012). Sometimes we want prices to fool us. *New York Times.* April 13.

Clotfelter, C. (1991). Patterns of Enrollment and Completion. In C. Clotfelter et al. (Eds.), *Economic challenges in higher education* (pp. 28–58). Chicago, IL: University of Chicago Press.

College Board. (2008). *Fulfilling the commitment: Recommendations for reforming student aid. The Report from the Rethinking Student Aid Study Group.* New York, NY: The College Board.

College Board. (2010). *Cracking the student aid code.* New York, NY: The College Board.

Complete College America. (2011). *Time is the enemy.* Washington, DC. Retrieved from www.completecollege.org/docs/Time_Is_the_Enemy_Summary.pdf

Consumer Financial Protection Bureau (CFPB). (2012). *Private student loans.* Report to the Senate Committee on Banking, Housing, and Urban Affairs, the Senate Committee on Health, Education, Labor, and Pensions, the House of Representatives Committee on Financial Services, and the House of Representatives Committee on Education and the Workforce. Retrieved from files.consumerfinance.gov/f/201207_cfpb_Reports_ Private-Student-Loans.pdf

DellaVigna, S. 2009. Psychology and economics: Evidence from the field. *Journal of Economic Literature, 47*(2): 315–72.

Diamond, A., Vorley, T., Roberts, J., & Jones, S. (2012) *Behavioral approaches to understanding student choice.* Higher Education Academy and National Union of Students.

Dynarski, S. M., & Scott-Clayton, J. E. (2006). The cost of complexity in federal student aid: Lessons from optimal tax theory and behavioral economics. *National Tax Journal 54*(2), 319–356.

Dynarski, S., & Wiederspan, M. (2012). Student aid simplification: Looking back and looking ahead. *National Tax Journal, 65*(1), 211–234

Farrell, H., & Shalizi, C. (2011). "Nudge" policies are another name for coercion. *New Scientist*. November 9. Retrieved from www.newscientist.com/article/mg21228376.500-nudge-policies-are-another-name-for-coercion.html

Field, E. (2009). Educational debt burden and career choice: Evidence from a financial aid experiment at NYU Law School. *American Economic Journal: Applied Economics, 1*(1), 1–21.

Fryer, R. (2011). Financial incentives and student achievement: Evidence from randomized trials. *Quarterly Journal of Economics, 26*(4), 1755–1798.

Grubb, N. (2006) "Like, What Do I Do Now?": The dilemmas of guidance counseling. In T. Bailey and V. Smith Morest (Eds.), *Defending the community college equity agenda* (pp. 195–222). Baltimore: Johns Hopkins University Press.

Heller, D. (1997). Student price response in higher education: An update to Leslie and Brinkman. *Journal of Higher Education, 68*(6), 624–659.

Hoxby, C., & Turner, S. (2013). *Expanding college opportunities for high-achieving, low income students*. Stanford Institute for Economic Policy Research, Discussion Paper No. 12–014. Retrieved from siepr.stanford.edu/?q=/system/files/shared/pubs/papers/12–014paper.pdf

Huelsman, M., & Cunningham, A. (2013). *Making sense of the system: Financial aid reform for the 21st century student*. Washington, DC: Institute for Higher Education Policy.

Jaschik, S. (2007). Bucking the tide on private loan. *Inside Higher Ed*. July 16. Retrieved from www.insidehighered.com/news/2007/07/16/barnard

Kahneman, D. (2011). *Thinking, fast and slow*. New York, NY: Macmillan.

Kahneman, D., Knetsch, J., & Thaler, R. (1991). Anomalies: The endowment effect, loss aversion, and status quo bias. *Journal of Economic Perspectives, 5*(1), 193–206.

Kane, T. (1995). *Rising public college tuition and college entry: How well do public subsidies promote access to college?* (No. 5174). NBER Working Paper. Retrieved from www.nber.org/papers/w5164

Kantrowitz, M. (2009). Analysis of why some students do not apply for financial aid. Finaid.org. Retrieved from www.finaid.org/educators/20090427CharacteristicsOfNonApplicants.pdf

Madrian, B., & Shea, D. (2001). The power of suggestion: Inertia in 401(k) participation and savings behavior. *Quarterly Journal of Economics, 116*(4), 1149–1187.

MDRC. (2013). Performance-based scholarship demonstration. Retrieved from www.mdrc.org/project/performance-based-scholarship-demonstration#featured_content

National Association of Student Financial Aid Administrators (NASFAA). (2013). Reimagining financial aid to improve student access and outcomes. Washington, DC: NASFAA.

National Center for Education Statistics (NCES). (2008). *National Postsecondary Student Aid Study 2008*. Retrieved from http://nces.ed.gov/surveys/npsas/

National Center for Education Statistics (NCES). (2012a). *Condition of Education*. Washington, DC: U.S. Department of Education.

National Center for Education Statistics (NCES). (2012b). *Digest of Education Statistics 2011*. Washington, DC: U.S. Department of Education.

National Center for Education Statistics (NCES). (2013). *Digest of Education Statistics 2013*. Washington, DC: U.S. Department of Education.

National College Access Network (NCAN). (2013). *Increasing return on investment from federal student aid*. Retrieved from www.collegeaccess.org/roifromfsa

Oakleigh Consulting and Staffordshire University. (2010). *Understanding the information needs of users of public information about higher education*. London: Higher Education Funding Council for England.

Pottow, J. (2007). The nondischargeability of student loans in personal bankruptcy proceedings: The search for a theory. *Canadian Business Law Journal, 44*(2), 245–278.

Rethinking Pell Grants Study Group. (2013). *Rethinking Pell Grants.* New York: The College Board.

Schwartz, B. (2004) *The paradox of choice: Why more is less.* London: HarperCollins.

Scott-Clayton, J. (2011). On money and motivation: A quasi-experimental analysis of financial incentives for college achievement. *Journal of Human Resources, 46*(3), 614–646.

Shapiro, D., & Dundar, A. (2013). *Completing college: A national view of student attainment rates, Fall 2007 Cohort.* National Student Clearinghouse Research Center.

Simkovic, M. (2013). Risk-based student loans. *Washington and Lee Law Review, 70*(1), 527ff.

Social Research and Demonstration Corporation (SRDC). (2014). *Future to discover: Fourth Year Post-secondary Impacts Report.* Ottawa: Author.

Sunstein, C., & Thaler, R. (2003). Libertarian paternalism is not an oxymoron. *University of Chicago Law Review, 70*(4). Retrieved from faculty.chicagobooth.edu/richard.thaler/research/pdf/LIbpatLaw.pdf

Svenson, O. (1981). Are we less risky and more skillful than our fellow drivers? *Acta Psychologica, 47*, 143–151.

Texas Higher Education Coordinating Board (THECB). (2013). College for all Texans. Retrieved from www.collegeforalltexans.com/apps/financialaid/tofa2.cfm?ID=447

U.S. Census Bureau. (2014). Educational Attainment: CPS Historical Time Series Tables, Tables A-1, A-2. A-4. Retrieved from www.census.gov/hhes/socdemo/education/data/cps/historical/index.html

APPENDIX

Potential Policy Reforms

Simplify the Application Process and the Array of Financial Aid Programs

Require students to complete the FAFSA as they are finishing high school, making applying for financial aid the default options.

Reduce the complexity of the financial aid application so that students don't avoid it.

Simplify the array of loan programs, consolidating and strengthening the income-based repayment plan.

Eliminate the official category of private student loans to avoid the confusion it creates for students who need to borrow.

Award grant aid for the entire length of the program of study, rather than requiring students to reapply every year, generating uncertainty about continuing funding.

Make eligibility simple and predictable, constructing look-up tables allowing students to better estimate their awards in advance.

Attempt to Modify the Expectations of Low-Income and First-Generation Students so They Are Less Likely to Follow the Path of Least Resistance in Not Applying for Financial Aid and Not Going to College

Provide early information about college options, the payoff to college, and financial aid in order to change expectations and modify the default option of low-income and first-generation students.

Provide Better Information Based on Behavioral Insights— Not Just More Information

Provide "psychology guided" information to potential borrowers, using simple and striking illustrations to communicate the risks of available options.

Consider the implications of the names used to identify different forms of student aid. Deferred payments might be less frightening than loans. Scholarships might be more appealing than tuition discounts.

Require institutions to use standardized award letters to inform students of their financial aid and the costs they will be incurring by enrolling.

In simplifying the financial aid application process and moving in the important direction of obtaining financial data directly from the IRS, recognize that many students and families are likely to have negative associations with that agency and design communication strategies to mitigate this problem.

Acknowledge that Students Respond to Financial Incentives and Structure those Incentives to Generate Positive Outcomes

Structure Pell Grant funding to better encourage full-time enrollment, instead of funding only 12 credit hours per semester for two semesters a year.

Target performance-based grant aid on high-need students for whom small increases in funding make a measurable different and small improvements in academic progress can make the difference between success and dropping out.

Attach Support Services to Student Aid Funds So Students Don't Have to Choose to Take Advantage of Them

Supplement grant funds with required use of mentoring and academic support services to these constructive paths are not optional for students.

Make continued receipt of grant aid or receipt of supplemental grant conditional on behaviors over which student have control, such as enrolling full-time or taking advantage of academic support systems.

Design Programs to Incentivize Positive Institutional Behaviors

Develop programs that coordinate institutional funding with student aid in ways that provide incentives for colleges to support student success, not just enroll students who come with funding.

4

HOW CAN FINANCIAL INCENTIVES IMPROVE THE SUCCESS OF DISADVANTAGED COLLEGE STUDENTS?

Insights from the Social Sciences

Nicole M. Stephens and Sarah S. M. Townsend

Introduction

Achievement gaps among college students from different social class, racial, or ethnic backgrounds are a persistent, ubiquitous problem in the United States (Bowen, Kurzweil, & Tobin, 2005; Steele, 2010). Low-income, first-generation, or underrepresented racial or ethnic minority students receive lower grades, take longer to graduate, and drop out at higher rates than their high-income, continuing-generation, or White and Asian counterparts (Pascarella, Pierson, Wolniak, & Terenzini, 2004; Sirin, 2005).[1] Because these underperforming students face an additional set of obstacles on the path to academic success, we refer to them as *disadvantaged* and to their higher performing peers as *advantaged*. Specifically, disadvantaged students tend to enter college with fewer academic skills (Pascarella et al., 2004; Warburton, Bugarin, & Nuñez, 2001) and financial resources (Walpole, 2003). They are also more likely to confront prejudice or negative stereotypes about their group (Croizet & Claire, 1998; Steele & Aronson, 1995) and to lack the "rules of the game" for achieving success as a college student (Bourdieu & Passeron, 1977; Bourdieu & Wacquant, 1992; Carter, 2003; Lareau, 1987; Stephens, Fryberg, Markus, Johnson, & Covarrubias, 2012). These additional challenges often contribute to underperformance and can prevent students from fully realizing their potential (Stephens, Markus, & Fryberg, 2012; Steele, 2010). Efforts to reduce achievement gaps must therefore address these obstacles.

This chapter examines one increasingly popular strategy for reducing achievement gaps: the use of financial incentives. In particular, we focus on the question of how to structure and implement financial incentive programs to maximize chances of improving disadvantaged students' success in college. To answer this question, we integrate behavioral insights from the social sciences with research in psychology, organizational behavior, and education. While we focus on financial incentives, many of the principles we discuss here are also relevant to non-financial incentives.

This discussion of using financial incentives to reduce achievement gaps is consistent with standard economic analyses, which indicate that people change their behavior when the benefits associated with that behavior change. However, understanding how to best design financial incentives and the circumstances in which they are most likely to be effective also requires behavioral insights from the social sciences. For example, the way that an incentive program is framed or the particular rewards to which incentives are tied (e.g., a plane ticket to visit family versus cash) can alter the effectiveness of the program. In order for incentives to most effectively improve the performance of disadvantaged college students, they must not only meet the baseline preconditions we discuss below, but also address the particular obstacles that disadvantaged students frequently confront in school.

In the next section, we draw on previous literature to describe some general baseline preconditions that should be taken into account in order for incentives to have a chance of serving as effective tools for producing long-term, self-sustaining behavioral change. We next consider whether financial incentives have the potential to narrow achievement gaps by helping disadvantaged students improve their academic performance. Specifically, we describe each of the distinct challenges often faced by this population, and examine whether and how incentives might be used to help these students overcome them. In doing so, we acknowledge that financial incentives are well equipped to address some obstacles but fall short in remedying others. In the final section, we discuss open questions that future research should address.

Can Financial Incentives Effectively Change Behavior?

We define financial incentives as the offer of a monetary reward or an item that students would otherwise have to purchase themselves in exchange for engaging in a desired behavior or accomplishing a particular goal. For example, if taking an advanced placement (AP) test is the desired behavior, then a financial incentive could be paying students $50 to take the test, waiving the fee that students would normally pay to take the test, or purchasing study materials to help them master the test subjects. A common assumption is that financial incentives are a powerful motivating force, and that people work or study harder, faster, or smarter *because* they are rewarded for doing so. Following this logic, people should be more motivated and perform better academically when incentives are present compared to when they are absent.

The organizational behavior, psychology, and education literature on the effectiveness of incentives, however, is rife with controversy and mixed in its conclusions. What is clear is that incentives work to enhance performance under some conditions and not others (for reviews of this literature, see Akin-Little, Eckert, Lovett, & Little, 2004; Cameron & Pierce, 2002; Condly, Clark, & Stolovitch, 2003; Jenkins, Mitra, Gupta, & Shaw, 1998; Lepper & Greene, 1978; Lepper, Greene, & Nisbett, 1973). When deciding whether to use incentives and how to maximize their chances of changing behavior, practitioners should therefore consider a host of situational and individual factors that inform how the targeted audience is likely to understand and respond to the incentives. In the inset below, we outline these baseline preconditions that guide whether and to what degree incentives will be effective.

BASELINE PRECONDITIONS FOR INCENTIVES TO BE EFFECTIVE

People Must Have the Following

Skills or knowledge required to complete the incentivized behavior
Resources (e.g., financial) and opportunities to complete the incentivized behavior

Incentives Should Accomplish the Following

Target behaviors that would otherwise not occur (i.e., when students are not intrinsically motivated)
Focus on short-term and concrete behaviors
Take into account the level of quality at which the task is completed
Be used repeatedly over time (not just on one occasion)
Be delivered immediately after the incentivized behavior occurs and be concretely tied to that behavior
Be made meaningful to the intended population (e.g., appropriate for a given age, role, social class, culture, etc.)

These insights can be fruitfully applied to programs designed to improve the performance of disadvantaged college students. Indeed, many programs have achieved the desired behavioral changes or academic outcomes (e.g., Patel & Richburg-Hayes, 2012), which suggests their potential to be effective. For example, Brock and Richburg-Hayes (2006) found that performance-based scholarships increased community college students' GPAs and progress toward degree completion. Similarly, Pallais (2009) found that a large merit-based scholarship program in Tennessee improved high school achievement (i.e., higher test scores). Additionally, Jackson's (2010) assessment of the Advanced Placement Incentive Program

(APIP) found that providing financial incentives to high school students for high scores on AP exams improved not only their exam scores but also their rates of college attendance and college performance.

However, not all financial incentive programs have achieved this degree of success. For example, in a series of randomized experiments that paid students for academic achievement (e.g., money for a good grade on a test), Fryer (2011) found that short-term financial incentives did not reliably improve students' performance. Even in the context of a successful program, their effects may be short-lived. Scott-Clayton (2011) evaluated the success of a merit scholarship program in West Virginia, which provides free tuition and fees to college students who maintain a minimum GPA and course load. The scholarship program increased BA completion rates and the number of credits that students completed during their first three years of college. However, the effect on credits disappeared during the last year, when students no longer faced the minimum requirements to renew the scholarship

These mixed findings suggest that financial incentives have the *potential* to improve the academic performance of disadvantaged college students when they are used properly. In the section that follows, we discuss how to tailor incentives to address the particular obstacles that disadvantaged students are likely to face.

Academic Skills

One obstacle that many disadvantaged college students confront is a lack of necessary academic skills. Low-income students, who are frequently first-generation and racial or ethnic minorities, are more likely to attend lower-quality, less academically rigorous high schools than high-income students (Alon, 2009; Bastedo & Jaquette, 2011; Carnevale & Rose, 2004; Pascarella et al., 2004; Warburton et al., 2001). When we use the term *low-income*, we refer to students whose family incomes are below the U.S. poverty line (e.g., $22,350 for a family of four in 2011; Federal Register, 2011). Even if these disadvantaged students make full use of every opportunity to learn and develop skills at their high schools (e.g., AP classes), they still are likely to enter college lacking some academic skills needed to perform up to their potential (Credé & Kuncel, 2008; Robbins, Lauver, Le, Davis, Langley, & Carlstrom, 2004; Choy, 2001).

Whether students have the skills needed for academic success is an important factor that may help explain the variation in the effectiveness of previous incentive programs. For example, Jackson's (2010) study of APIP suggests that the program's success resulted not only from providing incentives for high scores on AP exams, but also ensuring that students had the academic skills necessary to master material in AP classes and subsequently pass their exams. This program began as early as the seventh grade and used teams of teachers spanning different grade levels. The teams designed and implemented curricula to prepare students to learn the relevant material before they were eligible to register for AP courses and exams.

In contrast, a lack of academic skills may be one reason why Fryer found that paying middle and high school students for earning better grades did not reliably improve their performance. Indeed, across the four major cities in which he conducted the studies, Fryer did not find significant differences between the performance of students who were paid and those who were not. Although the incentives were motivating and generated enthusiasm among students who wanted to receive money for strong academic performance, follow-up interviews demonstrated that many students simply did not understand how to improve their academic performance (e.g., studying more, asking teachers for help). In other words, the incentive program did not meet the precondition that people have the skills or knowledge required to complete the incentivized behavior.

Can incentives help disadvantaged students improve their academic performance? To achieve this goal, incentives must be tied to activities that will develop the academic skills students need to fulfill their potential (see Jenkins et al., 1998). For example, if an incentive program seeks to improve the grades of disadvantaged students who have poor math skills, then practitioners should first identify the concrete behaviors that will likely improve or undermine math skills in that particular educational setting (e.g., grade level). Then, incentives should encourage the specific behaviors needed to improve math skills and discourage those that inhibit their development. Perhaps students could be incentivized for short-term academic behaviors, such as meeting with a teacher outside of class for tutoring or paying attention in math class, rather than for the long-term goal of improving their math grades. When students lack the academic skills needed to improve their grades, incentives should encourage the types of academic activities that produce better grades.

Financial Resources

Many disadvantaged students, particularly those from low-income backgrounds, face the obstacle of limited access to the financial resources needed to succeed in college. This resource gap is important to address because financial aid can improve students' college persistence and completion rates (Dynarski, 2008; Brock & Richburg-Hayes, 2006; Scott-Clayton, 2011). Indeed, a lack of financial resources can undermine academic performance through different processes (Paulsen & St. John, 2002; Cabrera, Nora, & Castaneda, 1992). Students with fewer resources often need to work multiple jobs to pay for their college tuition and living expenses, and, as a result, have less time to devote to their academic studies and social activities (Stinebrickner & Stinebrickner, 2003; Walpole, 2003; Ehrenberg & Sherman, 1987). Having less time to spend on one's classes can lead to lower grades (Kuh, Cruce, Shoup, Kinzie, & Gonyea, 2008; George, Dixon, Stansal, Gelb, & Pheri, 2008) and spending less time with peers may hinder students' cognitive development (Pascarella et al., 2004). Resource constraints may also prevent students from fully participating in the college experience (e.g., extracurricular activities), which could detract from their sense of belonging (Bohnert, Aikins, & Edidin, 2007) and undermine their academic performance (cf., Walton & Cohen, 2007).

Can incentives bridge the gaps in financial resources between low- and high-income students? Existing need-based financial aid programs are often designed to do just that. We believe that additional incentive programs have the potential to help financially disadvantaged students in two ways. First, incentives could directly bridge the gap by providing disadvantaged students with additional financial resources beyond the usual need-based financial aid (Henry & Rubenstein, 2002). Students could earn additional financial aid, for instance, by engaging in behaviors that will improve their grades (e.g., attending class, getting extra tutoring). Alternatively, students who already have the necessary academic skills could be required to attain a certain GPA to maintain their current levels of financial aid.

Second, incentives could mitigate some of the *consequences* of the financial resource gap. Due to a lack of financial resources, many students are not able to fully participate in the social and extracurricular activities central to the learning, growth, and overall development that the college experience can initiate (e.g., student clubs, sororities/fraternities, meals with friends). As a result, students may have difficulty finding a group of friends or a sense of community, and question whether they belong. Targeted financial incentives (i.e., incentives tied to a particular purpose) could be far more effective than general financial aid. For example, targeted incentives could encourage students to prioritize participating in extracurricular activities that might otherwise be unavailable to them. Although such incentives would not directly improve academic performance, they could do so indirectly by enhancing students' psychological experience of belonging in college (cf., Ostrove & Long, 2007; Walton & Cohen, 2007).

Cultural Capital

Many disadvantaged students, particularly those who are first-generation, lack the middle-class cultural capital or "rules of the game" for effectively navigating college settings (Horvat, Weininger, & Lareau, 2003; Lareau, 1987). Without college-educated parents, first-generation students are unlikely to have had family discussions about what it means to attend college or what students need to do to be successful there. As a result, these students may be less certain than continuing-generation students about how to choose a major, plan their class schedules, interact with professors, and select a future career (cf., Calarco, 2011; Kim & Sax, 2009).

In addition, many first-generation students have less familiarity with the cultural norms institutionalized in university settings than their continuing-generation peers. Specifically, U.S. universities tend to promote largely middle-class cultural norms and expectations for students (Fryberg & Markus, 2007; Greenfield, 1994; Kim, 2002; Li, 2003; Stephens, Fryberg, & Markus, 2012). Universities often ask students to pave their own path, express themselves, work independently, and challenge the status quo. These messages are consistent with the norms held by many continuing-generation students, who have been socialized in mostly middle-class contexts. However, first-generation students, who have been socialized in mostly working-class contexts, often experience these unfamiliar cultural norms as a "cultural mismatch" or as a sign that they do not fit in college settings. This cultural mismatch often guides first-generation students' behavior and can diminish their sense of comfort, render academic tasks difficult, and undermine their academic performance (Stephens, Fryberg, Markus, Johnson, & Covarrubias, 2012; Stephens, Townsend, Markus, & Phillips, 2012).

Can incentives provide disadvantaged students with the experience of a "cultural match" that they need to improve their performance in college? Unfortunately, we believe that incentives are poorly equipped to address this obstacle. While it might be possible to incentivize first-generation students to learn how to enact the middle-class behaviors expected of them in college, doing so might only highlight the cultural mismatch between such behaviors and the norms common in their working-class backgrounds (see Stephens, Fryberg, Markus, Johnson, & Covarrubias, 2012). Although financial incentives are unlikely to directly reduce the cultural obstacles that students often experience, incentive programs can be improved if they take disadvantaged students' particular cultural backgrounds into account.

A growing body of research in social psychology indicates that tailoring incentives to students' cultures, selves, or identities will render the incentives more effective in producing the desired changes in behavior (Oyserman, 2009; Oyserman & Destin, 2010; Oyserman, Fryberg, & Yoder, 2007; Stephens, Markus, & Fryberg, 2012; Walton & Cohen, 2007). Incentives can be made relevant by considering how students understand who they are (e.g., racial or ethnic identity) and why they behave as they do (e.g., why they want a college degree). One strategy would be to offer targeted incentives that provide what students in a given cultural context care about the most, rather than offering an equivalent amount of money that is not tied to a particular purpose. For example, if students were concerned about whether they could afford to visit their families over the holidays, then buying them plane tickets as an incentive for completing a certain number of credits should be more motivating than cash or a check. Another strategy is to frame incentives in a way that reflects students' values, motives, and concerns. For example, if a group of students views a college degree as a tool to give back to family or community, then the incentives could take that motive into account. An incentive program might be named "Building Blocks for Better Communities," which frames education as a route to contributing to community, instead of "Building Blocks for Academic Excellence," which frames education as a route to academic accomplishments.

Framing incentive programs in a culture-specific way would certainly require additional time and attention on the part of program developers and administrators, but could well make an important difference in their effectiveness.[2]

Additionally, to avoid stereotyping the targeted student population, practitioners would need to learn more about the concerns, interests, and motives of the particular population with whom they are working.

Social Identity Threat, Prejudice, and Discrimination

Many first-generation, low-income, and racial/ethnic minority students also confront negative attitudes about their groups (i.e., prejudice/stereotypes) or negative group-based treatment (i.e., discrimination; Croizet & Claire, 1998; Johnson, Richeson, & Finkel, 2011; Steele & Aronson, 1995). Although many students learn how to cope with these experiences, research reveals that chronic exposure to stereotypes, prejudice, and discrimination detracts from students' identification with and sense of belonging in the context of higher education (see Steele, 2010). As mentioned above, practitioners could use incentives to indirectly enhance students' experience by encouraging behaviors that foster belonging (e.g., participating in extracurricular activities). Thus, while financial incentives may indirectly help disadvantaged students to overcome some of the downstream consequences of negative stereotyping, prejudice, and discrimination, they are poorly equipped to directly address the obstacles themselves.

Can financial incentives help reduce the prevalence of negative stereotypes, prejudice, and discrimination faced by disadvantaged students in college and university settings? One strategy might be to incentivize advantaged students to behave in nonprejudiced ways toward outgroup members. Student groups such as sororities or fraternities could be incentivized to take concrete steps toward building a culture of tolerance and inclusion (e.g., sponsor events that increase understanding of cultural differences). This approach, however, presents at least two key problems. First, incentivizing inclusion is unlikely to be effective against the most common forms of prejudice, which are implicit and operate outside individuals' awareness and control (Greenwald & Banaji, 1995; Dovidio, Kawakami, Johnson, Johnson, & Howard, 1997). Second, a strategy that is not properly framed as a positive step toward improving the campus climate, rather than as a "prejudice-reducing" incentive program, could backfire. For example, if such a program fuels the perception that prejudice is a major issue on campus, the program could have the paradoxical consequence of amplifying, rather than mitigating, prejudice's pernicious effects. To avoid some of these potential pitfalls, an effective alternative could incentivize behaviors that are known to reduce prejudice and thereby improve intergroup relations. Colleges and universities could incentivize students to participate in community centers or other activities on campus in which students from diverse social groups are likely to interact. Research shows that these types of intergroup interactions have potential to reduce prejudice when the right conditions are in place (i.e., members of different groups are of equal status and share a common goal; Allport, 1954; Page-Gould, Mendoza-Denton, & Tropp, 2008; Pettigrew & Tropp, 2006).

Motivation

In addition to the previously mentioned obstacles that face disadvantaged students, lack of motivation can prevent all students from reaching their full academic potential. For example, at certain times in college (e.g., the so-called "sophomore slump"), all students may lack the motivation to do the work required to perform well in their classes or to fulfill academic requirements needed to earn a degree and graduate on time. Although disadvantaged students may also lack motivation, this obstacle is no greater than that faced by advantaged students (Steele, 2010). If anything, disadvantaged students who have overcome additional hurdles to make it to college are likely to have demonstrated higher levels of motivation and persistence (cf., Chen & Miller, 2012).

Can incentives help to increase the motivation of disadvantaged students in college and university settings? Research suggests that financial incentives can be effective at increasing motivation if used in the right circumstances. They could be used when students are otherwise unable to focus on the long-term goal of obtaining good grades and do the work necessary to ensure their academic success (Cameron, 2001). Practitioners should design incentives to encourage activities that would not occur in the absence of incentives (Deci, 1975; Lepper, Greene, & Nisbett, 1973). For example, if attending office hours is known to improve exam performance, and teachers observe that students do not often take advantage of this opportunity, then incentive programs could encourage students to attend office hours on a regular basis. Incentives could also be used to increase performance-enhancing behaviors at key times, such as during the sophomore slump, when students are typically less engaged.

While incentives can be effective when used in the right circumstances, they also can backfire without careful consideration of *why* people behave as they do (Ariely, 2008; Bowles, 2009). If incentives encourage activities that people are motivated to do for other reasons (e.g., being a good student), they can undermine motivation and decrease the likelihood that people will engage in the incentivized behavior in the future (Greene & Lepper, 1974; Greene, Sternberg, & Lepper, 1976; Lepper, Greene, & Nisbett, 1973). For example, many people donate blood because they want to see themselves or to be seen by others as charitable people. Likewise, many parents pick up their children from school on time because they want to be responsible parents. As a result, paying people to donate blood or to pick up their children on time could lead people to believe that they engage in those activities *because* they are being paid to do so. Ultimately, this new understanding of the reason for one's behavior could undermine people's motivation and actually reduce blood donation rates (Mellström & Johannesson, 2008) and increase the number of late parents (Gneezy & Rustichini, 2000). Extending the same logic to academic performance, financial incentives could undermine students' motivation by leading them to believe that they engage in academic activities (e.g., read books) *because* they are rewarded for doing so, rather than for the intrinsic enjoyment or because they aspire to be hard-working students.

Along the same lines, it is important to consider what providing an incentive for academic performance might unintentionally communicate to disadvantaged students about how other people perceive them or their groups. Incentivizing disadvantaged students for earning better grades might promote the negative stereotype that disadvantaged students do not perform as well as other students because they are simply lazy or unmotivated. This understanding could increase social identity threat and further undermine, rather than enhance, the performance of disadvantaged groups (see Steele, 2010).

Open Questions

Several questions remain about the best ways to use incentives to reduce or eliminate achievement gaps between disadvantaged and advantaged students.

Incentivizing Professors and Teaching Assistants

Most of the strategies described above focus on improving disadvantaged students' academic performance by changing their behavior. Examining the problem with a broader view of the contextual factors that contribute to students' performance might include the teachers and mentors whose behavior also has a significant impact. Can providing incentives to professors or teaching assistants improve the performance of disadvantaged college students? Professors and teaching assistants are a good place to start because they typically have the resources and skills to help students to improve their academic performance. The literature examining the effects of incentivizing teachers is mixed in its conclusions. While some research suggests that teacher incentives are not effective (e.g., Fryer, 2011; Springer et al., 2011), other studies demonstrate that they can be effective if they incorporate behavioral insights. The studies that suggest teacher incentives are ineffective have offered teachers financial incentives for students' performance at the end of the school year. In contrast, incorporating the idea that losses are felt more deeply than equivalent gains, Fryer, Levitt, List, and Sadoff (2012) gave elementary school teachers in Chicago a cash incentive at the beginning of the school year and asked them to return the money at the end of the year if their students performed below average. They found that disadvantaged students significantly increased their average math scores. Such a program could also be effective among university professors.

Applying the principles outlined above for developing students' academic skills, we suggest that effective incentive programs for professors and teaching assistants might similarly reward them for concrete, specific behaviors that are known to improve students' performance rather than for students' performance itself. For example, incentivizing professors to mentor disadvantaged students may not only help improve students' academic skills, but also help students feel more connected to the academic community, increase their sense of belonging, and acquire important cultural capital. Such financial incentives may be particularly effective in large, research-focused universities where the current incentive structure is not fully aligned with helping disadvantaged students, who may require more time and effort than their advantaged peers. Institutions might consider allowing professors to reduce their teaching obligations in exchange for their participation in mentorship programs for disadvantaged students.

Additional Strategies for Reducing Achievement Gaps

In addition to the various forms of financial incentives we have discussed, non-financial incentives (i.e., rewards that cost little or no money) may also help reduce the achievement gap between advantaged and disadvantaged students. Providing students with public recognition, such as being on a dean's list for achieving a desired outcome, may increase motivation or bolster disadvantaged students' feelings of belonging in college. However, to be effective, such non-financial incentives would also need to address the specific obstacles faced by disadvantaged students.

Finally, it is important to acknowledge that financial incentives are poorly equipped to address some of the important psychological obstacles that many disadvantaged students face in college, including the experience of a cultural mismatch, a lack of belonging, and social identity threat, prejudice, or discrimination. We suggest that the best way to equip students to overcome these obstacles is a multistrategy approach that incorporates incentives along with other appropriate psychological tools. In particular, a growing intervention literature in social psychology provides a number of useful strategies (Wilson, 2011; Yeager & Walton, 2011). Some of these interventions improve students' academic outcomes and foster belonging by encouraging them to reinterpret their adversity or difficult experiences (e.g., Blackwell, Trzesniewski, & Dweck, 2007; Cohen, Garcia, Apfel, & Master, 2006; Harackiewicz, Rozek, Hulleman, & Hyde, 2012; Walton & Cohen, 2011), while others focus on increasing students' understanding of the source of their particular obstacles and equipping them with culture-specific strategies for success (Johns, Schmader, & Martens, 2005; Stephens, Hamedani, & Destin, 2014).

Conclusion

Financial incentives provide a useful tool that can be leveraged to improve the performance of disadvantaged groups and reduce achievement gaps. However, like any tool designed to change behavior, incentives will be far more effective if they fully and carefully consider the context in which they are delivered and the population that they seek to target. In order to produce the desired long-term, self-sustaining behavioral change, policy-makers and practitioners must first take into account the preconditions required for students to have the opportunity to change their behavior. They must ensure that students have the academic skills and financial resources necessary to complete the desired behaviors. Further, effective incentive programs must address the particular obstacles that disadvantaged students frequently confront in higher education. They should be designed to promote people's sense of belonging in academic contexts, include people's culture-specific understandings of their behavior, and highlight what is most meaningful and motivating to them.

Notes

1. The term "first-generation" refers to students who have neither parent with a four-year college degree. The term "continuing-generation" refers to students who have at least one parent with a four-year college degree. In college settings, "underrepresented racial minorities" include African-American, Latino, and Native-American students.
2. Framing incentives in a culture-specific way does not require taking into account every possible source of cultural variation but rather requires attention to broad, overarching differences that occur along the lines of independence—e.g., prioritizing the individual over relationships—and interdependence—e.g., prioritizing family, community, and relationships over the individual. Research suggests that this independent-interdependent divide is the primary driver of cultural clashes between groups or between individuals and institutions, and that taking this divide into account can go a long way toward making incentives meaningful to the targeted population (Markus & Conner, 2013).

References

Akin-Little, K. A., Eckert, T. L., Lovett, B. J., & Little, S. G. (2004). Extrinsic reinforcement in the classroom: Bribery of best practice. *School Psychology Review, 33*, 344–362.
Allport, G. W. (1954). *The nature of prejudice*. Reading, MA: Addison Wesley.
Alon, S. (2009). The evolution of class inequality in higher education competition, exclusion, and adaptation. *American Sociological Review, 74*, 731–755.
Ariely, D. (2008). *Predictably irrational: The hidden forces that shape our decisions*. New York, NY: HarperCollins Publishers.
Bastedo, M. N., & Jaquette, O. (2011). Running in place: Low-income students and the dynamics of higher education stratification. *Educational Evaluation and Policy Analysis, 33*, 318–339.
Blackwell, L. S., Trzesniewski, K. H., & Dweck, C. S. (2007). Implicit theories of intelligence predict achievement across an adolescent transition: A longitudinal study and an intervention. *Child Development, 78*, 246–263.
Bohnert, A. M., Aikins, J. W., & Edidin, J. (2007). The role of organized activities in facilitating social adaptation across the transition to college. *Journal of Adolescent Research, 22*, 189–208.
Bourdieu, P., & Passeron, J. C. (1977). *Reproduction in education, society, and culture*. Chicago, IL: University of Chicago Press.
Bourdieu, P., & Wacquant, L. J. (1992). *An invitation to reflexive sociology*. Chicago, IL: University of Chicago Press.

Bowen, W. G., Kurzweil, M. A., & Tobin, E. M. (2005). *Equity and excellence in American higher education.* Charlottesville: University of Virginia Press.

Bowles, S. (2009). When economic incentives backfire. *Harvard Business Review, 87*, 22–23.

Brock, T., & Richburg-Hayes, L. (2006). *Paying for persistence: Early results of a Louisiana scholarship program for low-income parents attending community college.* New York, NY: MDRC.

Cabrera, A. F., Nora, A., & Castaneda, M. B. (1992). The role of finances in the persistence process: A structural model. *Research in Higher Education, 33*, 571–593.

Calarco, J. M. (2011). "I need help!": Social class and children's help-seeking in elementary school. *American Sociological Review, 76*, 862–882.

Cameron, J. (2001). Negative effects of reward on intrinsic motivation—A limited phenomenon: Comment on Deci, Koestner, and Ryan (2001). *Review of Educational Research, 71*, 29–42.

Cameron, J., & Pierce, W. D. (2002). *Rewards and intrinsic motivation: Resolving the controversy.* Westport, CT: Bergin & Garvey.

Carnevale, A. P., & Rose, S. J. (2004). Socioeconomic status, race/ethnicity, and selective college admissions. In R. D. Kahlenberg (Ed.), *America's untapped resources* (pp. 101–156). New York, NY: Century Foundation Press.

Carter, P. L. (2003). "Black" cultural capital, status positioning, and schooling conflicts for low-income African American youth. *Social Problems, 50*, 136–155.

Chen E., & Miller, G. E. (2012). "Shift-and-Persist" strategies: Why being low socioeconomic status isn't always bad for health. *Perspectives on Psychological Science, 7*, 135–158.

Choy, S. P. (2001). *Students whose parents did not go to college: Postsecondary access, persistence, and attainment.* National Center for Education Statistics, U.S. Department of Education, Office of Educational Research and Improvement.

Cohen, G. L., Garcia, J., Apfel, N., & Master, A. (2006). Reducing the racial achievement gap: A social-psychological intervention. *Science, 313*, 1307–1310.

Condly, S. J., Clark R. E., & Stolovitch, H. D. (2003). The effects of incentives on workplace performance: A meta-analytic review of research studies. *Performance Improvement Quarterly, 16*, 46–63.

Credé, M., & Kuncel, N. R. (2008). Study habits, skills, and attitudes: The third pillar supporting collegiate academic performance. *Perspectives on Psychological Science, 3*, 425–453.

Croizet, J. C., & Claire, T. (1998). Extending the concept of stereotype threat to social class: The intellectual underperformance of students from low socioeconomic backgrounds. *Personality and Social Psychology Bulletin, 24*, 588–594.

Deci, E. L. (1975). *Intrinsic motivation.* New York, NY: Plenum.

Dovidio, J. F., Kawakami, K., Johnson, C., Johnson, B., & Howard, A. (1997). On the nature of prejudice: Automatic and controlled processes. *Journal of Experimental Social Psychology, 33*, 510–540.

Dynarski, M. (2008). *Dropout prevention.* National Center for Education Evaluation and Regional Assistance, Institute of Education Sciences, U.S. Department of Education.

Ehrenberg, R. G., & Sherman, D. R. (1987). Employment while in college, academic achievement and post-college outcomes: A summary of results. *Journal of Human Resources, 22*, 1–23.

Federal Register, Vol. 76, No. 13, January 20, 2011, 3637–3638.

Fryberg, S. A., & Markus, H. R. (2007). Cultural models of education in American Indian, Asian American and European American contexts. *Social Psychology of Education, 10*, 213–246.

Fryer Jr., R.G. (2011). Financial incentives and student achievement: Evidence from randomized trials. *Quarterly Journal of Economics, 126,* 1755–1798.

Fryer Jr., R.G., Levitt, S. D., List, J., & Sadoff, S. (2012). *Enhancing the efficacy of teacher incentives through loss aversion: A field experiment* (No. w18237). National Bureau of Economic Research.

George, D., Dixon, S., Stansal, E., Gelb, S. L., & Pheri, T. (2008). Time diary and questionnaire assessment of factors associated with academic and personal success among university undergraduates. *Journal of American College Health, 56,* 706–715.

Gneezy, U., & Rustichini, A. (2000). A fine is a price. *Journal of Legal Studies, 29,* 1–17.

Greene, D., & Lepper, M. R. (1974). Effects of extrinsic rewards on children's subsequent intrinsic interest. *Child Development, 45,* 1141–1145.

Greene, D., Sternberg, B., & Lepper, M. R. (1976). Overjustification in a token economy. *Journal of Personality and Social Psychology, 34,* 1219–1234.

Greenfield, P.M. (1994). Independence and interdependence as developmental scripts: Implications for theory, research, and practice. In P.M. Greenfield & R.R. Cocking (Eds.), *Cross-cultural roots of minority child development* (pp. 1–37). Hillsdale, NJ: Erlbaum.

Greenwald, A. G., & Banaji, M. R. (1995). Implicit social cognition: Attitudes, self-esteem, and stereotypes. *Psychological Review, 102,* 4–27.

Harackiewicz, J. M., Rozek, C. S., Hulleman, C. S., & Hyde, J. S. (2012). Helping parents to motivate adolescents in mathematics and science: An experimental test of a utility-value intervention. *Psychological Science, 23,* 899–906.

Henry, G. T., & Rubenstein, R. (2002). Paying for grades: Impact of merit-based financial aid on educational quality. *Journal of Policy Analysis and Management, 21,* 93–109.

Horvat, E. M., Weininger, E. B., & Lareau, A. (2003). From social ties to social capital: Class differences in the relations between schools and parent networks. *American Educational Research Journal, 40,* 319–351.

Jackson, C. K. (2010). A little now for a lot later: A look at a Texas Advanced Placement Incentive Program. *Journal of Human Resources, 45,* 591–639.

Jenkins, G. D., Mitra, A., Gupta, N., & Shaw, J. D. (1998). Are financial incentives related to performance? A meta-analytic review of empirical research. *Journal of Applied Psychology, 83,* 777–787.

Johns, M., Schmader, T., & Martens, A. (2005). Knowing is half the battle: Teaching stereotype threat as a means of improving women's math performance. *Psychological Science, 16,* 175–179.

Johnson, S. E., Richeson, J. A., & Finkel, E. J. (2011). Middle class and marginal? Socioeconomic status, stigma, and self-regulation at an elite university. *Journal of Personality and Social Psychology, 100,* 838–852.

Kim, H. S. (2002). We talk, therefore we think? A cultural analysis of the effect of talking on thinking. *Journal of Personality and Social Psychology, 83,* 828–842.

Kim, Y. K., & Sax, L. J. (2009). Student–faculty interaction in research universities: Differences by student gender, race, social class, and first-generation status. *Research in Higher Education, 50,* 437–459.

Kuh, G. D., Cruce, T. M., Shoup, R., Kinzie, J., & Gonyea, R. M. (2008). Unmasking the effects of student engagement on first-year college grades and persistence. *Journal of Higher Education, 79,* 540–563.

Lareau, A. (1987). Social class differences in family-school relationships: The importance of cultural capital. *Sociology of Education, 60,* 73–85.

Lepper, M. R., & Greene, D. E. (1978). *The hidden costs of reward: New perspectives on the psychology of human motivation.* Hillside, NJ: Erlbaum.

Lepper, M. R., Greene, D., & Nisbett, R. E. (1973). Undermining children's intrinsic interest with extrinsic reward: A test of the "overjustification" hypothesis. *Journal of Personality and Social Psychology, 28*, 129–137.

Li, J. (2003). U.S. and Chinese cultural beliefs about learning. *Journal of Educational Psychology, 95*, 258–267.

Markus, H. & Conner, A. (2013). *Clash! Eight cultural conflicts that make us who we are.* New York, NY: Hudson Street Press.

Mellström, C., & Johannesson, M. (2008). Crowding out in blood donation: Was Titmuss right? *Journal of the European Economic Association, 6*, 845–863.

Ostrove, J. M., & Long, S. M. (2007). Social class and belonging: Implications for college adjustment. *Review of Higher Education, 30*, 363–389.

Oyserman, D. (2009). Identity-based motivation: Implications for action-readiness, procedural-readiness, and consumer behavior. *Journal of Consumer Psychology, 19*, 250–260.

Oyserman, D., & Destin, M. (2010). Identity-based motivation: Implications for intervention. *Counseling Psychologist, 38*, 1001–1043.

Oyserman, D., Fryberg, S. A., & Yoder, N. (2007). Identity-based motivation and health. *Journal of Personality & Social Psychology, 93*, 1011–1027.

Page-Gould, E., Mendoza-Denton, R., & Tropp, L. R. (2008). With a little help from my cross-group friend: Reducing anxiety in intergroup contexts through cross-group friendship. *Journal of Personality and Social Psychology, 95*, 1080.

Pallais, A. (2009). Taking a chance on college: Is the Tennessee Education Lottery Scholarship a winner? *Journal of Human Resources, 44*, 199–222.

Pascarella, E. T., Pierson, C. T., Wolniak, G. C., & Terenzini, P. T. (2004). First-generation college students: Additional evidence on college experiences and outcomes. *Journal of Higher Education, 75*, 249–284.

Patel, R., & Richburg-Hayes, L. (2012). *Performance-based scholarships: Emerging findings from a national demonstration.* New York, NY: MDRC.

Paulsen, M. B., & St John, E. P. (2002). Social class and college costs: Examining the financial nexus between college choice and persistence. *Journal of Higher Education, 73*, 189–236.

Pettigrew, T. F., & Tropp, L. R. (2006). A meta-analytic test of intergroup contact theory. *Journal of Personality and Social Psychology, 90*, 751–783.

Robbins, S. B., Lauver, K., Le, H., Davis, D., Langley, R., & Carlstrom, A. (2004). Do psychosocial and study skill factors predict college outcomes? A meta-analysis. *Psychological Bulletin, 130*, 261–288.

Scott-Clayton, J. (2011). On money and motivation: A quasi-experimental analysis of financial incentives for college achievement. *Journal of Human Resources, 46*, 614–646.

Sirin, S. R. (2005). Socioeconomic status and academic achievement: A meta-analytic review of research. *Review of Educational Research, 75*, 417–453.

Springer, M. G., Ballou, D., Hamilton, L., Le, V. N., Lockwood, J. R., McCaffrey, D. F., Pepper, M., & Stecher, B. M. (2011). Teacher pay for performance: Experimental evidence from the project on incentives in teaching (POINT). Retrieved from RAND Corporation website: http://www.rand.org/content/dam/rand/pubs/reprints/2010/RAND_RP1416.pdf

Steele, C. M. (2010). *Whistling Vivaldi and other clues to how stereotypes affect us.* New York: W.W. Norton & Company.

Steele, C. M., & Aronson, J. (1995). Stereotype threat and the intellectual test performance of African Americans. *Journal of Personality and Social Psychology, 69*, 797–811.

Stephens, N. M., Fryberg, S. A., & Markus, H. R. (2012). It's your choice: How the middle-class model of independence disadvantages working-class Americans. In S. T. Fiske & H. R. Markus (Eds.), *Facing social class: How societal rank influences interaction* (pp. 87–106). New York, NY: Russell Sage Foundation.

Stephens, N. M., Fryberg, S. A., Markus, H. R., Johnson, C. S., & Covarrubias, R. (2012). Unseen disadvantage: How American universities' focus on independence undermines the academic performance of first-generation college students. *Journal of Personality and Social Psychology, 102,* 1178–1197.

Stephens, N. M., Hamedani, M. H., & Destin, M. (2014). Closing the social-class achievement gap: A difference-education intervention improves first-generation students' academic performance and all students' college transition. *Psychological Science, 25,* 943–953.

Stephens, N. M., Markus, H. R., & Fryberg, S. A. (2012). Social class disparities in health and education: reducing inequality through a sociocultural self-model of behavior. *Psychological Review, 119,* 723–744.

Stephens, N. M., Townsend, S. S., Markus, H. R., & Phillips, L. T. (2012). A cultural mismatch: Independent cultural norms produce greater increases in cortisol and more negative emotions among first-generation college students. *Journal of Experimental Social Psychology, 48,* 1389–1393.

Stinebrickner, R., & Stinebrickner, T. R. (2003). Working during school and academic performance. *Journal of Labor Economics, 21,* 473–491.

Walpole, M. (2003). Socioeconomic status and college: How SES affects college experiences and outcomes. *Review of Higher Education, 27,* 45–73.

Walton, G. M., & Cohen, G. L. (2007). A question of belonging: race, social fit, and achievement. *Journal of Personality and Social Psychology, 92,* 82–96.

Walton, G. M., & Cohen, G. L. (2011). A brief social-belonging intervention improves academic and health outcomes of minority students. *Science, 331,* 1,447–1,451.

Warburton, E. C., Bugarin, R., & Nuñez, A. M. (2001). *Bridging the gap: Academic preparation and postsecondary success of first-generation students* (NCES 2001–153). U.S. Department of Education. National Center for Education Statistics. Washington: Government Printing Office.

Wilson, T. D. (2011). *Redirect: The surprising new science of psychological change.* New York, NY: Little, Brown and Company.

Yeager, D. S., & Walton, G. M. (2011). Social-psychological interventions in education: They're not magic. *Review of Educational Research, 81,* 267–301.

5

PROMPTS, PERSONALIZATION, AND PAY-OFFS

Strategies to Improve the Design and Delivery of College and Financial Aid Information

Benjamin L. Castleman

Introduction

Policy-makers have invested in a range of strategies over the last several decades to reduce disparities in college entry and completion by family income. Historically, many of these interventions have focused on improving students' academic readiness and increasing college affordability for low-income students and their families (Adelman, 2006; Deming & Dynarski, 2009). More recently, however, policy-makers and researchers have devoted increasing attention to how the accessibility and presentation of college information affects whether students apply to college or for financial aid, and the college choices students make (Bettinger, Long, Oreopoulos, & Sanbonmatsu, 2012; Hoxby & Turner, 2013; Carrell & Sacerdote, 2012). A number of studies have documented, for instance, that students and families from disadvantaged backgrounds either do not know or tend to substantially overestimate the actual cost of college tuition (Avery & Kane, 2004; Grodsky & Jones, 2007; Horn, Chapman, & Chen, 2003). Other research has documented how complexities in the Free Application for Federal Student Aid (FAFSA) may deter many students who would qualify for substantial grant and loan assistance from even applying for financial aid (Dynarski & Scott-Clayton, 2006: Bettinger et al., 2012). A separate line of research suggests that a surprisingly large share of students who have sufficient high school achievement to attend academically-rigorous institutions often only apply to and enroll at essentially open-enrollment colleges and universities (Hoxby & Avery, 2013; Bowen, Chingos, & McPherson, 2011; Roderick et al., 2008; Smith et al., 2013).

The recent focus on informational barriers to college entry and success for low-income students has in turn prompted numerous federal initiatives to improve the quality of information that students and their families can access about college and financial aid. For instance, the Higher Education Opportunity Act of 2008 required institutions that participate in Title IV federal student aid programs to post net price calculators on their websites. These calculators allow students and families to obtain personalized estimates of the net cost of attendance at that institution, given their individual financial circumstances. The United States Department of Education (USDOE) also created the FAFSA 4caster to allow students and their families to input a relatively small amount of information about family size, income, and geographic residence, and obtain an estimate of the amount of grant and loan assistance for which they would qualify. More recently, in July 2012 the Obama Administration launched the Financial Aid Shopping Sheet, an attempt to standardize and simplify the presentation of financial aid award information across institutions. In addition, the federal government created both College Navigator and the White House Scorecard, which allow students to obtain information that has typically not been available through most privately-funded college search engines, such as retention and graduation rates.

These initiatives, in addition to a number of additional efforts by states, non-profit organizations, and individual colleges, have substantially increased and simplified the amount of institution- and family-specific college and financial aid information students can access. However, will the *availability* of simpler and more personalized information be sufficient to mitigate the informational obstacles that prevent low-income students from attending colleges and universities that are well matched to their abilities and interests? Recent work in a range of behavioral sciences implies that simplification and personalization are important first steps to address these barriers. Yet research in these disciplines also highlights the importance of going further to improve college and financial aid information. How information is presented and delivered; whether students and their families can access individualized assistance when they need it; and whether students and parents receive timely prompts to complete relevant tasks may be of additional importance.

In the remainder of this chapter I synthesize what recent research in the behavioral sciences suggests about how people process and make decisions based upon information they receive. I focus in particular on adolescent post-secondary decision making, but many of the same insights would apply to adults who are interested in continuing their education. I highlight several recent experimental interventions that apply concepts from these disciplines to further improve the design and delivery of college and financial aid information. Particularly as local, state, and federal governments continue to grapple with limited funding for college access initiatives, these interventions are particularly promising given the magnitude of their impacts relative to their costs. Finally, I propose several additional interventions that could meaningfully affect students' decisions at various stages in the college exploration, application, and choice processes. These suggested interventions are not meant to replace individualized, high-quality counseling, but rather to provide policymakers who face budgetary constraints with cost-effective strategies to supplement existing services available to students.

Behavioral Sciences Perspectives on How People Process and Respond to Information

Perhaps the most important question to address is why College Navigator, the Net Cost Calculators, and tools like them may not be sufficient to address the informational barriers faced by low-income students and their families as they navigate the college and financial aid processes. After all, in the space of a prime-time reality television episode, students could use these sites to identify several institutions in their geographic area from which they have a high probability of graduating and which offer the lowest net costs. The process of identifying potential colleges and universities that are well matched to the student's interests and abilities has arguably never been more straightforward. Yet the current design and structure of these tools make several assumptions about how students and parents access and respond to information that may compromise their effectiveness.

Lack of Access to Information or Assistance

The federal college and financial information tools, along with their state and private counterparts, require that students and parents both know about their existence and will set aside time to make use of them. Both expectations are potentially untenable. Many public high school students have limited access to college counseling, through which they would conceivably learn about these tools. Nationally, the average counselor caseload of 457 students is nearly twice the ratio recommended by the American School Counseling Association (ASCA, 2012; NCES, 2009). Counselors in public schools spend only 22 percent of their time on college admissions, compared with 54 percent among private school counselors (Clinedinst & Hawkins, 2009). Moreover, counselors typically lack a thorough understanding of the financial aid process and may not feel prepared to guide students to apply for aid or evaluate financial aid packages (Civic Enterprises, 2011). Of potentially even greater concern, online college search tools require that students and their families have internet access, yet recent research by the Pew Internet and American Life Project suggests that the majority of students from low-income households may be unable to make use of these online tools from home (Purcell, Heaps, Buchanan, & Friedrich, 2013). While the rapid proliferation of smart phones may somewhat alleviate this obstacle, conducting a college search from a mobile phone may be cumbersome and time-consuming, particularly with search engines like the White House Scorecard that do not currently have a mobile-friendly interface.

The Neurology of Adolescent Decision Making

Even among adolescents who are aware of these tools and who have reliable internet access, however, it may not be realistic to assume that they will be sufficiently disciplined to budget time to make use of them. Recent work in neuroscience confirms what parents of all adolescents (regardless of socioeconomic status) have always known implicitly: the neurological systems that respond to immediate stimulation are at their peak activity during the teen-age years, yet brain systems required for self-regulation are still in development. As a result, adolescents are more impulsive, less likely to consider the long-term consequences of their present actions, and more likely to put off onerous tasks in favor of more pleasurable pursuits (Casey, Jones, & Somerville, 2011; Steinberg, 2008; Steinberg, Cauffman, Woolard, Graham, & Banich, 2009). Neural transformations that take place during adolescence are also shaping individuals' ability to perform higher-order cognitive functions, like organization, attention, and planning (Casey, Tottenham, Liston, & Durston, 2005; Giedd et al., 1999; Strauch, 2003). At the most basic level students may not remember how to access college search tools, even if they were given a handout in school or sent an email by a school counselor (think about the organizational state of a teenager's back pack or email in-box). Strongly college-intending students may still not identify researching institutional graduation rates and net costs as important steps in the college-planning process. The cognitive load required to process college information may be particularly daunting and taxing for students from disadvantaged backgrounds who have to devote their time and energy to addressing immediate stressors, like financially supporting their families or dealing with neighborhood violence (Mullainathan & Shafir, 2013).

Another potential shortcoming in the design of college and financial aid information is that tools designed to educate students about their postsecondary options implicitly assume they will be able to learn independently, without additional professional assistance. This may also be an unrealistic assumption. Because adolescents' higher-order cognitive functioning is still in development, they often need help organizing and analyzing multiple strands of information; understanding the connection between their college choices and future opportunities; and addressing sources of stress that impact their college planning (Schneider, 2009). The process of identity formation is still ongoing, so adolescents may also struggle to define what they want from their adult lives (Schneider & Stevenson, 1999). Without clear goals in mind, students may be particularly reliant on outside guidance to assess which postsecondary paths best align with their interests and abilities.

Lack of Family-Based Support for First-Generation College Students

Among college-educated families, parents implicitly recognize the importance of providing structure and accountability to compensate for their adolescents' cognitive challenges, and accordingly invest considerable time in the college process

(Ramey & Ramey, 2010; White, 2005). The depth and intensity of middle-class parents' involvement in college search and completing college applications is perceived to be so great, in fact, that the term "helicopter parent" has become well-entrenched in the popular lexicon (Gibbs, 2009; Lipka, 2005; Lum, 2006). College-educated families are also considerably more likely to pursue "shadow education" for their children, such as private tutoring and SAT prep courses (Buchmann, Condron, & Roscigno, 2010). Adolescents from disadvantaged backgrounds are considerably less likely to benefit from parental guidance and involvement in the college process. One challenge is that parents from low-income families are more likely to work non-standard hours and to experience unpredictable shifts in their work schedules (Acs & Loprest, 2005; Presser & Cox, 1997). As a result, lower-income families may struggle to establish regular family routines that are conducive to parents helping their child with college applications (Hsueh & Yoshikawa, 2007). Psychological barriers may also inhibit low-income parents from engaging in college planning with their child: they may not believe their involvement would positively influence their child, or they may question whether the colleges allow for their involvement in the process (Perna, 2004; Rowan-Kenyon, Bell, & Perna, 2008). Particularly if parents did not go to college themselves, they may rely on the high school to guide the child through the college process because they do not know how to do so themselves (Lareau, 2000).

In short, faced with strong biological impulses that privilege immediate pleasures over longer-term considerations and lacking sufficient adult guidance and structure, teen-agers from disadvantaged backgrounds may not thoroughly engage in college search, even if they plan to pursue postsecondary education.

Information Complexity and Choice Overload

A related limitation of current college and financial information is that the available tools still involve substantial cognitive processing for students, and require adolescents to choose among a multitude of factors to identify a well-matched set of institutions. For instance, to obtain an estimate of the net price they would pay at a particular college, students need to know, among other information, which federal income tax forms their parents submitted for the previous tax year; how much their parents earned from interest and dividend income; whether their parents claimed educational tax credits; and how much their parents contributed to retirement plans. Students may struggle to persuade their parents of the importance of sharing this information, particularly if their parents do not speak English or have concerns about the privacy of the information they provide (Institute for College Access and Success, 2013).

Similarly, many college search tools expect that students can evaluate a wide range of factors in deciding which colleges and universities best match their interests in abilities. Yet the volume and complexity of this material may be more likely to produce information overload for students than to illustrate a set of well-matched colleges and universities. Using College Navigator as an example, after students indicate the state in which they want to go to college and the level and type of institution they want to attend (public vs. private, two- vs. four-year), they are given a list of all the colleges that meet these basic criteria. Once students click on a specific college, there are twelve category headings of institution-specific information, ranging from "tuition, fees, and estimated student expenses" to "campus security." Within a given heading, there are extensive tables of detailed information. Across all twelve categories, there are literally hundreds of data points for students to consider. Comparing multiple institutions would require students to digest and assess an extraordinary volume of information.

What the designs of sites like the College Navigator fail to sufficiently take into account is that too much complexity can create a "paradox of choice" for students (Schwartz, 2004). People—and adolescents in particular—often struggle to methodically evaluate and compare alternatives that differ on many attributes (Thaler & Sunstein, 2008; Scott-Clayton, 2011). In fact, as the choices become more complex, individuals are more likely to opt for a simplifying strategy to make their selection (Thaler & Sunstein, 2008). From a policy perspective, the challenge is that the simplifying rules teenagers adopt may not lead them to choose postsecondary plans that best position them for future success. Of particular concern is that students may base their postsecondary decisions on factors that have appeal in the short term, like being close to a high school girlfriend, but that may not contribute to their long-term well-being. Even among students who are determined to pursue postsecondary education, rather than select the institution with the highest graduation rate, lowest net cost, and best academic support services, students may instead simplify their choices to focus on attributes that are very tangible but potentially less related to whether they will be successful, like nice dorm rooms or good food. Yet attending institutions with these premium features may require students to incur substantial debt without meaningfully increasing their probability of future success. As a result, search tools that were intended to equip students with the information necessary to make fully-informed college choices may ironically lead them to base their decisions on a small and superficial set of factors.

It is worth noting that this tendency to simplify the college decision to a superficial set of factors is likely true for most adolescents. For students from middle- and upper-income families, however, these simplification strategies are less likely to be constraining, since their parents and counselors likely encourage them to consider a broader range of college characteristics when deciding where to apply, and later matriculate. Adolescents from disadvantaged backgrounds, on the other hand, may not have adults in their lives who can offer broader perspective. As a result, they are more likely to pursue a set of postsecondary choices that are bounded by less-informed considerations.

Bias Toward the Present

Finally, current college and financial aid information makes the costs to students very concrete, yet the potential benefits remain quite hazy. Recent research in behavioral economics suggests that individuals often over-weight immediate costs and forego investments that would be in their long-term interest (Chabris, Laibson, & Schuldt, 2008). Even minor cost barriers may deter students from completing key stages of the college application or choice processes, despite a high probability that the lifetime benefits of higher education would far outweigh short-term investments (Pallais, forthcoming). Students may also face liquidity constraints that prevent them from paying for mandatory fees associated with college applications, deposits, and freshman orientation.[1] These costs are likely to loom particularly large when the potential benefits associated with college seem quite opaque.

While tools like the net cost calculators provide personalized estimates of what students will pay for college, there are currently no corresponding tools that provide students with personalized estimates of the financial return to college that they would likely realize if they matriculated. In fact, much about the college experience may feel very undefined to first-generation college students: whether they will succeed academically; whether they will form new friendships; whether the education and credentials they receive will outweigh the debt they have to incur. Faced with this uncertainty, students may be averse to foregoing the predictability of their current lifestyle (Kahneman & Tversky, 1979). This reluctance to pursue college may be particularly pronounced for students who are deciding whether to attend a residential college, since doing so would require students to opt for an unfamiliar environment and uncertain gains over the stability of their current community and relationships.

Strategies to Improve the Design and Delivery of College and Financial Aid Information

Behavioral sciences research thus highlights a range of limitations in the college and financial aid information currently available to students. Yet these disciplines also offer valuable guidance on how information design and delivery could be improved to increase accessibility for students and their families. It is worth emphasizing that the types of behavioral interventions I propose are not meant to substitute for high-quality college counseling. In the ideal world, all students would have access to the kind of personalized, in-depth college counseling that affluent families can afford for their children. But for many policymakers and school leaders, providing additional counseling may not be a fiscal reality, whereas low-cost behavioral interventions may be feasible.

It is also worth noting that in some cases improvements to the design and delivery of college and financial aid information will necessitate providing students and their families with different information about college than what they currently receive. Yet this creates an inherent tension, since doing so potentially introduces additional complexity about college and financial aid. In the final section of the chapter, I address this tension directly by offering a set of suggestions for how information could be enhanced based on principles from behavioral sciences while minimizing the risk of information overload. In short, I argue for providing information that is likely to be particularly relevant and timely for each student, and providing this information in structured and sequenced increments, so students and their parents progressively learn more about their college options and are able to narrow down a list of viable alternatives without having to digest a large set of information all at once.

Prompts to Complete Important Tasks

One important lesson from the behavioral sciences is that people benefit from prompts to engage in important activities. Procrastination and forgetfulness frequently interfere with whether individuals—and adolescents in particular—follow through on beneficial behaviors (Milkman, Beshears, Choi, Laibson, & Madrian, 2012). Especially if the important event is far into the future, people often struggle to maintain focus on all of the tasks they need to complete in order to achieve the longer-term goal (Karlan, McConnell, Mullainathan, & Zinman, 2010). Providing prompts, however, can trigger people's awareness of the tasks they need to complete and encourage them to deal with the task in the present, rather than putting it off into the future. Prompts have been demonstrated to have positive impacts in a range of settings. Researchers in the public health and development economic sectors, for instance, have found that sending people text message reminders increased flu vaccination rates and individual contributions to financial savings accounts (Karlan et al., 2010; Stockwell et al., 2012). Patients with HIV whose pill bottles lit up and beeped each day if they were not opened were more likely to take their medication (Mullainathan, 2011); individuals were more likely to schedule a colonoscopy if they received a Post-It note prompting them to write down the date of their appointment and the name of the physician who would be conducting the procedure (Milkman et al., 2012). In the context of college and financial aid information, prompts could be used to encourage students and their families to access available information at key stages in the college and financial aid processes. For instance, school districts or state education agencies could send high school students text message prompts to apply for financial aid during the spring of their senior year.

Proactive Delivery of Simplified and Personalized Information

Providers of college and financial aid information could also go beyond providing prompts and bring simplified and/or personalized information right to the student and his/her family. Behavioral economists have frequently pursued this strategy to increase individuals' retirement savings. As with postsecondary information, employees who are eligible to participate in retirement plans face a daunting array of options for how they could invest their money. The complexity of these choices often leads people to put off investing anything, even when they would clearly benefit financially from doing so (Madrian & Shea, 2000). One strategy to increase retirement contributions has been to collapse the broad range of retirement options into one plan with a pre-determined contribution rate and asset allocation in which employees can enroll (Beshears et al., 2012). This approach overcame the complexity employees faced in their retirement decisions, and therefore increased the rate at which they benefited from the financial incentives offered by their employer's retirement plans. Analogously, educational agencies could collapse the broad and complex range of college choices that students face into a simplified set of options tailored to each student's academic profile and geographic residence. For instance, state agencies or school districts could recommend colleges for high school juniors to consider applying to that are close to where the students live, that meet certain benchmarks in net costs and graduation rates, and that the students have a good chance of being admitted to based on their academic profiles.

Utilizing Effective Channels to Deliver Information

Related to the idea of providing students with prompts and personalized information is the question of how information is delivered. As I discuss earlier, most college and financial aid information is passive: tools are available, but students and their families have to seek them out. To the extent that high schools, community-based organizations, or colleges proactively communicate with students, they typically do so through handouts, U.S. Postal Mail, or email. Yet postal mail and email are not the primary means of communication among adolescents. Whereas only 6 percent of teens exchange emails on a daily basis, 63 percent send texts every day (Lenhardt, 2012). The information that institutions are sending to students about college or financial aid may therefore not even be reaching them, let along inducing further college exploration.

Facilitating Connections with Professional College Advisors

For college and financial aid information to be more accessible to students, it is also important to minimize barriers to help-seeking. The psychological literature has documented a range of factors, including adolescents' perception of their academic and social competence, their level of motivation, and their attitudes towards help-seeking, that influence whether students pursue assistance with school-based problems (Boldero & Fallon, 1995; Newman, 1994; Ryan & Pintrich, 1997). In under-resourced schools where counselors have large caseloads and limited time to focus on college planning, high school graduates may have limited personal relationships with counselors. This lack of a personal connection may inhibit students from initiating contact with a counselor to request assistance. On the other hand, students may be quite responsive to proactive and direct outreach from a counselor to discuss college- and financial-aid related issues. Students may be particularly responsive if they can signal their interest in meeting to discuss college and financial aid through media, like text messaging or Facebook messaging, that require less upfront relational investment (Castleman & Page, 2013; Subrahmanyam & Greenfield, 2008).

Shifting Students Perceptions of Social Norms Around College

College and financial aid information could also potentially be more effective by taking into consideration students' perceptions of the social norms around postsecondary choices. A broad literature has documented that the behavior of peers in a social environment influences individuals' responses (Cialdini & Goldstein, 2004). In uncertain situations, individuals may be particularly influenced by peer behavior if they believe that following the actions of others will lead to better outcomes (Cialdini, 2001). Individuals may also be more influenced by the actions of peers whom they perceive to share similar features, such as age and gender (Murray, Luepker, Johnson, & Mittelmark, 1984; White, Hogg, & Terry, 2002). Specific to postsecondary decision making, students from underrepresented groups may not feel that they belong at colleges and universities if they perceive these institutions to be the domain of affluent, white students (Walton & Cohen, 2007). They may also be concerned that they would need to downplay their group identity in order to succeed in college (Cohen & Garcia, 2005). Students' uncertainty about whether they would fit in on campus may result in greater stress, further impeding their ability to complete required tasks over the summer (Lovelace & Rosen, 1996).

Currently, much of the information provided by college search tools is individualistic in its orientation (i.e., "how much will college cost *me*? What major(s) can *I* pursue? How likely am *I* to get in?"). This information could be enhanced to provide students with a more palpable sense of the social attributes of the college experience. Individual colleges have capitalized on this concept by promoting a social identity associated with attending that institution (e.g., "The Morehouse Man").[2] Of several major college search engines (College Navigator, the College Board search tool, and the ACT search tool), however, only the College Board provides information on student activities, and its presentation of the social experience is limited to a static list of some of the student groups on each campus. Low-income students who have never been on a college campus and who did not grow up hearing college anecdotes from family members would likely respond positively to a more tactile presentation of the social dimensions of higher education. At the simplest level this could be achieved by actively highlighting some of the student activities available at each college/university. This information does not need to be restricted to residential colleges: many community colleges and commuter institutions also have a range of student groups and activities on campus. A more sophisticated approach would be to allow students to identify personal characteristics that are central to their identity (race/ethnicity, religion, sexual orientation, etc.), and customize which aspects of collegiate social life are presented to each student. This personalized view of opportunities for social engagement with relevant campus groups could be particularly effective for students who have little familial experience with or conception of college.

Concretizing the Benefits of Going to College

Because individuals tend to prefer certain benefits over potential gains (Kahneman & Tversky, 1979), college and financial aid information could also be improved by concretizing the advantages, both financial and non-pecuniary, of going to college. This may be particularly important for low-income students who would be the first in their family to go to college, for whom college may feel like a particularly risky gamble relative to the certainty of their current relationships and environment. One approach to concretize benefits would be to provide students with a personalized estimate of what their annual earnings could be with a college degree, given the type of institution to which they would have a good chance of being admitted and the field of study they are interested in pursuing. Admittedly, this estimate would be a ballpark approximation at best, and would need to acknowledge both the institution-specific probabilities of earning a degree and the considerable variation in earnings among degree-holders. Particularly given the sizeable earnings gaps between college graduates and high school graduates (Baum, Ma, & Payea, 2013), however, additional personalized information about the returns to college could positively influence students to apply and attend, even with the risks and uncertainties involved. In collaboration with College Measures, a partnership between the American Institutes for Research and the Matrix Knowledge Group, several states have recently moved in this direction by making information available online about the average earnings among graduates from in-state institutions, and/or from specific college majors.[3]

Given the research I document earlier about adolescents' tendency to base their decision making on near-term considerations, however, making the benefits of the college experience more concrete may be more important than emphasizing the long-term financial gains associated with higher education. One strategy for doing so would be to provide the kind of personalized glimpses of the collegiate social experience I describe above. In addition, college search engines could emphasize other aspects of campus life that may be attractive to students, such as better employment opportunities than in their neighborhood or improvements in community safety.

Making Choices in Context

Finally, research in behavioral economics highlights the importance of individuals making choices in context, rather than evaluating each option in isolation (Camerer, Babcock, Loewenstein, & Thaler, 1997). An individual college may seem particularly attractive to a student because of the quality of its dorm rooms and athletic facilities; similarly, another college may be unattractive because its list price appears prohibitively high. Yet to make fully-informed choices, students and their families would ideally consider the gains and drawbacks of each institution relative to other potential options. Accordingly, college information should facilitate students making apples-to-apples comparisons between institutions. While some search engines currently have this functionality in place, they do not necessarily include comparative information that may be particularly important for or impactful on the student, such as graduation rates and opportunities for social engagement.

In the same way that consumer sites like Amazon recommend products based on shoppers' searches, institutional comparisons could also be further enhanced by proactively generating recommendations of additional colleges students should consider based on their initial explorations. These recommendations could be tailored to suggest colleges and universities that meet certain graduation and net cost benchmarks, and that are geographically proximate to the student. Of arguably even greater importance would be to help students and their families consider in concrete terms the potential implications of *not* going to college when they are evaluating postsecondary options. That is, when students decide not to apply to or attend college, they are not necessarily making an affirmative choice to pursue a preferred alternative. Particularly if quality alternatives are scarce, information that effectively communicates the advantages and drawbacks of college relative to the pros and cons of students' best other option could influence whether students decide to pursue higher education. One strategy that may be especially effective is to help students understand what they are losing, so to speak, if they choose not to pursue higher education (e.g., potential for greater earnings, engaging social experiences, etc.).

Applications of Behavioral Sciences to Improve the Design and Delivery of College and Financial Aid Information

As the previous section highlights, there are a variety of mechanisms through which improved information and/or an offer of assistance could increase the probability that students matriculate in college. Information and counseling may increase students' willingness to make short-term investments in expectation of longer-term benefits associated with higher education. With improved information and counseling, students may also overcome the complexities in college and financial aid information. Finally, with regular reminders, students may be better able to devote time to task completion incrementally throughout junior and senior year of high school, and therefore increase their probability of enrollment.

As several recent studies indicate, offering students additional counseling and/or personalized information during the college process does indeed have a substantial impact on whether they enroll in college. The majority of these studies have fallen into one of two broad categories: (1) interventions that provided students with individualized assistance and (2) interventions that provided students with personalized information and prompts, and in some cases the offer of additional assistance. I focus in particular on studies that have employed experimental methodologies. Given their high internal validity, these studies isolate the unique impact of behavioral intervention on students' college outcomes, and demonstrate the magnitude of impact that similar interventions may be able to achieve for a relatively small investment.

Interventions That Provide Students With Individualized Assistance

Researchers have examined a range of strategies for providing students and families with individualized assistance with the college or financial aid processes, beyond what they receive in school. Several studies have employed peer mentors to provide students with individualized help throughout the college process. Across different geographic contexts and stages of the college process, students who were randomly assigned to receive peer mentor support were substantially more likely to enroll in college. For instance, high school seniors in Los Angeles who received regular support with the application process from a college student were several percentage points more likely to attend a four-year institution (Berman, Ortiz, & Bos, 2008). Similarly, researchers matched Dartmouth College students with New Hampshire high school seniors who were behind in the application process. The college mentors met weekly with students during the second half of senior year to help them complete their college applications. The intervention had a pronounced effect for females, but not for males. Females in the treatment group were 12 percentage points more likely to enroll in college; this difference persisted into the second year of college (Carrell & Sacerdote, 2012).

Peer mentor programs that provide outreach to students the summer *after* high school graduation have also positively influenced whether they enroll in college. The post-high school summer is a largely-overlooked time period in students' transition to college. Students have to complete a range of tasks, such as interpreting and acting on their financial aid award letters and tuition bills and registering for orientation and placement tests, yet typically do not have access to professional assistance to help with these tasks. Students are no longer part of their high school, so cannot access help from their school counselors, but have yet to engage with supports available at their intended college (Arnold et al., 2009; Castleman, Arnold, & Wartman, 2012; Castleman & Page, 2013a; Castleman, Page, & Schooley, 2014). High school graduates in three urban Massachusetts districts and from a network of charter schools in Philadelphia were randomly assigned to receive summer outreach and support from peer mentors working under the guidance of professional counselors or financial aid advisors. Throughout the summer, the mentors proactively reached out to students to offer them help addressing potential barriers to college enrollment, and to connect them to professional counselors if they needed additional assistance. Across sites, students randomly assigned to receive peer mentor outreach were 4.5 percentage points more likely to enroll at four-year institutions; male students who received outreach from male mentors appeared to particularly benefit from the intervention (Castleman & Page, 2013b).

Several studies have also examined the impact of offering students additional help directly from school counselors or community-based financial aid advisors during the summer after high school. To investigate the impact of providing students with summer support, researchers randomly assigned students in Providence, Rhode Island, Boston, Massachusetts, and Fulton County, Georgia, several hours of additional college counseling. Counselors helped students interpret and act on their financial aid packages and tuition bills; access, digest, and complete required paperwork; and address potential social/emotional barriers to enrollment. The offer of 2–3 hours of additional support during the summer increased college enrollment by 5–14 percentage points, and in Boston (the only site for which the researchers have been able to examine longer-term persistence trends to date), increased sophomore year persistence by almost nine percentage points (Castleman, Arnold, & Wartman, 2012; Castleman, Page, & Schooley, 2014).

Researchers have also examined the impact of offering students and their families individualized assistance with and information related to the federal financial aid application. Low-income adults who went to H&R Block for their income tax preparation were randomly assigned the offer of help with the FAFSA for themselves or their children. In addition, adults in the treatment group were provided information about their estimated financial aid eligibility compared to the cost of tuition at several nearby colleges. Helping parents complete the FAFSA following their income tax preparation took H&R Block tax professionals less than 10 minutes, but led to an eight percentage point increase in the probability that their children remained enrolled continuously enrolled in college for at least two years following high school (Bettinger et al., 2012).

Each of the studies described above utilized individualized assistance—either from peer mentors, school counselors, or financial aid professionals—to help students and their families overcome complexities in the college and financial aid application processes. The H&R Block intervention ($88 per participant) and the summer college counseling interventions ($100–$200 per participant) were particularly cost-effective strategies to increase college-going among disadvantaged students, while the peer mentor interventions tended to be somewhat more expensive approaches ($100–$1,000).

Two recent studies suggest that providing students with personalized and timely information can yield enrollment impacts of similar magnitude, but with even greater cost efficiency. Capitalizing on records of students' SAT or ACT scores, their geographic residence, and an estimate of their family income, researchers sent high-achieving, low-income seniors in the 2010–2011 and 2011–2012 high school cohorts semi-customized information about the college application process and about the net cost of attending colleges. Students were randomly assigned to one of several intervention groups, in which they received different combinations of information. For instance, students in one intervention group received comprehensive guidance on how to apply to a set of institutions matched to their academic ability. In another intervention group, students received information about the net costs of college, while in a third group, students received fee waivers for their college applications. In a final intervention, students received the application guidance, the net cost information, and the application fee waiver. The latter comprehensive intervention, which cost only $6 per student, had a particularly pronounced impact, increasing the rate at which students applied and were accepted to and matriculated at institutions with higher graduation rates and more resources (Hoxby & Turner, 2013).

In a separate study in summer 2012, researchers sent high school graduates and their parents 8–10 text reminders of important tasks to complete in order to matriculate in college. The text messages were customized to the colleges students planned to attend, and provided timely reminders of important tasks to complete, such as interpreting and acting on financial aid award letters and registering for orientation. Most of the messages also included task- and college-specific web links that enabled students to complete tasks directly from their phones, before their attention was diverted to other activities. Each message also offered students and their parents individualized assistance from a school counselor. The intervention cost approximately $7 per student (counting counselor support when students requested help to complete tasks) and increased enrollment by over four percentage points among students qualifying for free- or reduced-price lunch in a large urban district in the southwestern United States, and by over seven percentage points among students in two urban school districts in Massachusetts (Castleman & Page, 2013b).

Additional Interventions to Increase Student and Family Responsiveness to College and Financial Aid Information

Thus, interventions that increase the simplicity and personalization of college and financial aid information may be able to substantially increase college entry and success among low-income populations. While there have been relatively few field interventions applying behavioral insights to date, these early studies reinforce research in other fields that demonstrate the potential of information simplification and prompts to shape individual decision making. I close by discussing several additional low-cost and easily-scaled interventions that would similarly apply principles and concepts from the behavioral sciences to increase the accessibility of college and financial aid information.[4]

One place to start would be to refine college search tools to share additional salient information with students (e.g., about the social dimensions of college and the returns to postsecondary education), while minimizing the problem of information overload. The solution to doing so likely lies in providing intentional structure and sequence to the way that information is presented (Thaler & Sunstein, 2008). Rather than treat all information as equally valuable, college search engines could both personalize and prioritize particularly important considerations. In the same way that many commercial websites prompt visitors to enter their zip codes to provide more user-specific content, college search engines could prompt students for their zip codes to first feature colleges and universities within a reasonable geographic proximity. Within this set of institutions, college search tools could then highlight key factors about each institution, like their average net cost and graduation rate. The USDOE's College Scorecard, released in February 2013, takes this approach of emphasizing a small set of essential attributes about each college and university.

One criticism of the Scorecard is that it reduces the college decision to an overly narrow set of factors. However, once students have identified a subset of institutions that are within a comfortable geographic radius and that maximize their chance of graduating without incurring an excessive loan burden, search tools provide students with another set of factors to consider about each college. Again, sites could prompt students to anonymously share additional personal details, such as ethnic and cultural groups with which they have affinity, to further customize the search results. College search sites could make strategic decisions about the order in which information is shared. For instance, after first narrowing institutions by cost and graduation rates, sites could provide students with information about the returns to higher education and the social dimensions of college. Once students further narrow their choice set of potential colleges and universities, the sites could then share additional characteristics of each institution, such as academic programs offered and student employment opportunities.

The primary advantage of this approach is that, for students from disadvantaged backgrounds without sufficient access to professional guidance, college counseling would essentially be built into the site. Much as if students were working with an independent college consultant, the site would learn about the student; make specific college recommendations based on this acquired information; and select important attributes about each institution to share with the student. Just as if students were working with a consultant, they would not be restricted from conducting a wider and less-structured search on their own: at each stage in the process, the sites could be designed so that students could still opt to view a broader set of institutions, or additional details about each college and university in their choice set.

The personalization and prioritization of information could be further enhanced in two important ways. First, college search sites could partner with social network platforms like Facebook to provide an even more personalized viewing experience. If students were logged into their Facebook accounts, for instance, the personalized college recommendations could be based on a rich set of information about the student: where they live; the kind of groups with whom they have identified an affinity; where students from their high school or community have successfully enrolled. Another enhancement to the basic refinement would be to provide students with access to real-time support via a chat or instant message function built into the college search site. In this sense, personalized college counseling could be incorporated into the platform by enabling students to get individualized guidance about their college options. Particularly if implemented at a state or federal level, this approach could also be a more cost-effective approach to increasing students' access to college counseling than adding counseling capacity to many individual schools or districts. Another advantage is that, as with corporate sites that offer live chat, the real-time support could be available to students during nights and weekends, when they may be more likely to be exploring their college options.

A different approach would be to apply the strategy of sending students personalized and timely text messages at earlier stages in the college exploration process. One potential barrier that personalized messaging could address, for instance, is that high school students from disadvantaged backgrounds do not have a full sense of the range of colleges to which they would likely be admitted based on their academic achievement. Researchers or policy makers could draw on student- and college-level data to send high school juniors personalized recommendations of colleges to consider applying to, based on their academic profiles and geographic residence. The recommendations could be delivered via text message, and could highlight institutions that meet certain benchmarks in graduation rates and net costs, and to which the student has a good chance of being admitted. As with the summer text message campaign, each message could also offer high school juniors individualized assistance with the college application process.

Text messaging (or digital messaging more broadly) could likewise be leveraged to provide students and their families with personalized information at other important stages in the college planning process. For instance, low-income students who perform well on state assessments or national exams like the PSAT may nonetheless not recognize the benefits of taking rigorous courses like Advanced Placement exams; not have access to these courses; or not have access to sufficient academic support to succeed in these courses. Researchers or policy makers could send personalized messages that encourage students to take AP courses; offer to connect them to online AP courses if their high school does not offer a sufficient range of AP options; and offer to connect them to online tutoring if they need assistance in more rigorous courses. Digital messaging could also be used to prompt high school seniors who have not applied to college but based on their academic records appear college-ready to complete applications before high school graduation.

Another strategy would be to harness the reach and influence of social networks to nudge students to complete important college and financial aid tasks. Researchers applied this concept to influence voting behaviors in the 2010 U.S. mid-term elections (Bond et al., 2012). On November 2, 2010, domestic Facebook users over 18 years old were randomly assigned to receive a message at the top of their news feed reminding them to vote. Users could share that they had voted with their friends, and were able to see a counter of how many of their friends had already voted. Users assigned to receive these messages were more likely to actually vote on election day. Voting impacts were even greater for the users' friends, particularly for close friends that the user likely interacted with in person on a regular basis. A parallel approach could be used to encourage students to register for the SAT or ACT exam, or to complete the FAFSA. As with the voting study, these tasks may be particularly appropriate for a social network nudge because there are common and discrete deadlines faced by all high school students within a given state.[5] Social network sites like Facebook also have the functionality, like instant messaging and live chat capability, to provide students with in-the-moment, professional assistance if they need help with any aspect of their college or financial aid applications.

An even lower-touch but potentially effective intervention would be to capitalize on the rich information available from individuals' web searches to identify people whose profiles suggest they are from disadvantaged backgrounds and of an age where they could be applying for college. In the same way that for-profit companies use this information to target people with customized product-oriented advertisements, policy makers or researchers could target adolescents with advertisements that encourage them to register for college entrance exams, complete the FAFSA, or search for college. Ad-clicks could bring users to web pages that provide simplified information about college and financial aid. The web page to which students were directed could also prompt students to share basic information about their geographic residence and academic performance in high school, and offer more personalized guidance, as well as access to individualized assistance.

Conclusion

Policy makers have invested in a range of strategies over the last several decades to reduce disparities in college entry and success by family income. Initiatives have focused on increasing students' and families' access to better information about their college and financial aid options, and have substantially increased and simplified the postsecondary information to which students have access. Yet recent work in the behavioral sciences suggests that simply making better information available may not be sufficient to meaningfully influence students' and families' decision making about higher education. These disciplines highlight the importance of bringing high-quality and personalized information directly to students and their parents; of providing students with prompts and reminders to complete important tasks in both the college and financial aid processes; and of minimizing barriers to students and families accessing professional and individualized guidance when they need assistance. A growing body of research has applied these principles to the design of college access interventions, and has consistently found pronounced and positive impacts on whether students enroll and succeed in college. Equally importantly, these interventions are typically low-cost and easily-scalable. Particularly as governments continue to grapple with constrained budgetary resources, policies and programs that deliver personalized information and that facilitate access to professional assistance will likely play an increasingly essential role in policy efforts to improve the postsecondary and career prospects of students from disadvantaged backgrounds.

Notes

1. There is a related informational barrier, since students may be able to qualify for fee waivers for any of these charges, but they may not know these fee waivers are available.
2. I am indebted to Michael McPherson for this helpful observation.
3. For more information, visit: www.collegemeasures.org
4. Many of these intervention ideas emerged from ongoing collaborations with several researchers, including Chris Avery, Josh Goodman, Doug Harris, Bridget Terry Long, Mike Luca, Lindsay Page, Bruce Sacerdote, and Barbara Schneider.
5. States have different priority dates for FAFSA submission. Both the ACT and SAT exam are administered at several points during the year, with registration deadlines in advance of each test administration.

References

Acs, G., & Loprest, P. (2005). *Who are low-income working families?* Washington, D.C.: The Urban Institute.

Adelman, C. (2006). *The toolbox revisited: Paths to degree completion from high school through college.* Washington, D.C.: U.S. Department of Education.

American School Counselor Association (ASCA). (2012). Student-to-school-counselor ratios. Retrieved from www.schoolcounselor.org/content.asp?contentid=658

Arnold, K. C, Fleming, S., DeAnda, M., Castleman, B.L., & Wartman, K. L. (2009). The summer flood: The invisible gap among low-income students. *Thought and Action, Fall,* 23–34.

Avery, C., & Kane, T. J. (2004). Student perceptions of college opportunities. The Boston COACH program. In C. Hoxby (ed.). *College choices: The economics of where to go, when to go, and how to pay for it* (pp. 355–394). Chicago, IL: University of Chicago Press.

Baum, S., Ma, J., & Payea, K. (2013). *Education pays.* New York, NY: The College Board.

Berman, J., Ortiz, L., & Bos, J. (2008). *Evaluation of the SOURCE program: An intervention to promote college application and enrollment among urban youth.* Oakland, CA: Berkeley Policy Associates.

Beshears, J., Choi, J. J., Laibson, D., & Madrian, B. C. (2012). *Simplification and saving.* (No. 12659). NBER Working Paper. Retrieved from www.nber.org/papers/w 12659

Bettinger, E., Long, B. T., Oreopoulos, P., & Sanbonmatsu, L. (2012). The role of application assistance and information in college decisions: Results from the H&R Block FAFSA experiment. *Quarterly Journal of Economics, 127*(3), 1205–1242.

Boldero, J., & Fallon, B. (1995). Adolescent help-seeking: What do they get help for and from whom? *Journal of Adolescence, 18,* 193–209.

Bond, R. M., Fariss, C. J., Jones, J. J., Kramer, A. D. I., Marlow, C., Settle, J. E., & Fowler, J. H. (2012). A 61-million person experiment in social influence and political mobilization. *Nature, 498,* 295–298.

Bowen, W. G., Chingos, M. M., & McPherson, M. S. (2011). *Crossing the finish line: Completing college at America's public universities.* Princeton, NJ: Princeton University Press.

Buchmann, C., Condron, D., & Roscigno, V. (2010). Shadow education, American style: Test preparation, the SAT and college enrollment. *Social Forces, 89,* 435–642.

Camerer, C., Babcock, L., Loewenstein, G., & Thaler, R. (1997). Labor supply of New York City cabdrivers: One day at a time. *Quarterly Journal of Economics, 112*(2), 407–441.

Carrell, S., & Sacerdote, B. (2012) *Late interventions matter too: The case of college coaching in New Hampshire.* National Bureau of Economic Research Working Paper No. 19031. Cambridge, MA: National Bureau of Economic Research.

Casey, B. J., Tottenham, N., Liston, C., & Durston, S. (2005). Imaging the developing brain: What have we learned about cognitive development. *Trends in Cognitive Sciences, 9*(23), 104–110.

Casey, B., Jones, R. M., & Somerville., L. H. (2011). Braking and accelerating of the adolescent brain. *Journal of Research on Adolescence, 21*(1), 21–33.

Castleman, B. L., Arnold, K. C., & Wartman, K. L. (2012). Stemming the tide of summer melt: An experimental study of the effects of post-high school summer intervention on low-income students' college enrollment. *Journal of Research on Educational Effectiveness, 5*(1), 1–18.

Castleman, B. L., & Page, L. C. (2013a). A trickle or a torrent? Understanding the extent of summer "melt" among college-intending high school graduates. *Social Sciences Quarterly 95*(1), 202–220.

Castleman, B. L., & Page, L. C. (2013b). *Summer nudging: Can text messages and peer mentor outreach increase college going among low-income high school graduates?* Paper presented at the Society for Research on Educational Effectiveness Spring Conference. Washington, D.C.

Castleman, B. L., Page, L. C., & Schooley, K. (2014). The forgotten summer: The impact of college counseling the summer after high school on whether students enroll in college. *Journal of Policy Analysis and Management, 32*(2), 320–344.

Chabris, C., Laibson, D., & Schuldt, J. (2008). Intertemporal choice. In Steven N. Durlauf & Lawrence E. Blume (Eds), *The new Palgrave dictionary of economics* (2nd ed.). New York, NY: Palgrave Macmillan.

Cialdini, R. B. (2001). *Influence: Science and practice.* Boston, MA: Allyn & Bacon.

Cialdini, R. B., & Goldstein, N. J. (2004). Social influence: Compliance and conformity. *Annual Review of Psychology, 55,* 591–621.

Civic Enterprises. (2011). *School counselors literature and landscape review.* New York, NY: College Board.

Clinedinst, M. E., & Hawkins, D. A. (2009). State of College Admission. Washington, D.C.: National Association for College Admission Counseling.

Cohen, G. L., & Garcia, J. (2005). I am us: Negative stereotypes as collective threats. *Journal of Personality and Social Psychology, 89,* 566–582.

Deming, D., & Dynarski, S. M. (2009). *Into college, out of poverty? Policies to increase the postsecondary attainment of the poor* (No. 15387). NBER Working Paper. Retrieved from www.nber.org/papers/w15387

Dynarski, S. M., & Scott-Clayton, J. E. (2006). The cost of complexity in federal student aid: Lessons from optimal tax theory and behavioral economics. *National Tax Journal, 59*(2), 319–356.

Giedd, J. N., Blumenthal, J., Jeffries, N. O., Castellanos, F. X., Liu, H., Zijdenbos, A., Paus, T., Evans, C., & Rappaport, J. (1999). Brain development during childhood and adolescence: A longitudinal MRI study. *Nature Neuroscience, 2*(10), 861–863.

Gibbs, N. (2009, November 30). The growing backlash against overparenting. *Time Magazine.* http://content.time.com/time/magazine/article/0,9171,1940697,00.html

Grodsky, E., & Jones, M. T. (2007). Real and imagined barriers to college entry: Perceptions of cost. *Social Science Research, 36*(2), 745–766.

Horn, L., Chapman, C., & Chen, X. (2003). *Getting ready to pay for college: What students and their parents know about the cost of college tuition and what they are doing to find out.* U.S. Department of Education, National Center for Education Statistics: Washington, D.C.

Hoxby, C. & Avery, C (2013). The missing "one-offs": The hidden supply of high-achieving, low-income students. *Brookings Papers on Economic Activity.* Spring, 1–61.

Hoxby, C. M., & Turner, S. (2013). *Expanding college opportunities for high-achieving, low-income students.* Stanford University: Stanford Institute for Economic Policy Research.

Hsueh, J., & Yoshikawa, H. (2007). Working nonstandard schedules and variable shifts in low-income families: Associations with parental psychological well-being, family functioning, and child well-being. *Developmental Psychology, 43*, 620–632.

Institute for College Access & Success. (2013). *Aligning the means with the ends: How to improve federal student aid and improve college access and success.* Washington, D.C.: Institute for College Access and Success.

Kahneman, D., & Tversky, A. (1979). Prospect theory: An analysis of decision under risk. *Econometrica, 47*(2), 263–291.

Karlan, D., McConnell, M., Mullainathan, S., & Zinman, J. (2010). *Getting to the top of mind: How reminders increase saving* (No. 16205). NBER Working Paper. Retrieved from www.nber.org/papers/w16205

Lareau, A. (2000). *Home advantage: Social class and parental intervention in elementary education* (2nd ed.). Lanham, MA: Rowman & Littlefield Publishers.

Lenhardt, A. (2012). *Teens, smart phones, and texting.* Washington, D.C.: Pew Research Center.

Lipka, S. (2005, December 16). Some helicopter parents play politics to protect their children's interests. *Chronicle of Higher Education, 52*(17), A22.

Lovelace, K., & Rosen, B. (1996). Difference in achieving person-organization fit among diverse groups of managers. *Journal of Management, 22*(5), 703–722.

Lum, L. (2006). Handling helicopter parents. *Diverse Issues in Higher Education, 23*(20), 40–42.

Madrian, B. C., & Shea, D. F. (2000). *The power of suggestion: Inertia in 401(K) participation and savings behavior.* (No. 7682). NBER Working Paper. Retrieved from www.nber.org/papers/w7682

Milkman, K. L., Beshears, J., Choi, J. J., Laibson, D., & Madrian, B. C. (2012). *Following through on good intentions: The power of planning prompts.* (No. 17995). NBER Working Paper. Retrieved from www.nber.org/papers/w17995

Mullainathan, S. (2011). The psychology of poverty. *Focus: Institute for Research on Poverty. 28*(1), 19–22.

Mullainathan, S., & Shafir, E. (2013). *Scarcity: Why having so little means so much.* New York, NY: Times Books.

Murray, D. M., Luepker, R. V., Johnson, A. C., & Mittelmark, M. B. (1984). The prevention of cigarette smoking in children: A comparison of four strategies. *Journal of Applied Social Psychology 14*(3), 274–88.

National Center for Education Statistics (NCES). (2009). Common Core of Data. Washington, D.C.: U.S. Department of Education, Institute of Education Sciences.

Newman, R. S. (1994). Adaptive help seeking: A strategy of self-regulated learning. In D. Schunk & B. Zimmerman (Eds.), *Self-regulation of learning and performance: Issues and educational applications.* Hillsdale, NJ: Lawrence Erlbaum Associates.

Pallais, A. (forthcoming). Small differences that matter: Mistakes in applying to college. *Journal of Labor Economics.*

Perna, L. W. (2004). Understanding the decision to enroll in graduate school: Sex and racial/ethnic group differences. *Journal of Higher Education, 75,* 487–527.

Presser, H. B., & Cox, A. G. (1997). The work schedules of low-educated American women and welfare reform. *Monthly Labor Review, (120)*4, 25–34.

Purcell, K., Heaps, A., Buchanan, J., & Friedrich, L. (2013). *How teachers are using technology at home and in their classrooms.* Pew Center: Pew Internet and American Life Project.

Ramey, G., & Ramey, V. A. (2010). The rug rat race. *Brookings Paper on Economic Activity, Economic Studies Program, The Brookings Institution 41*(1), 129–1999.

Roderick, M., Nagaoka, J., Coca, V., Moeller, E., Roddie, K., Gilliam, J., & Patton, D. (2008). *From high school to the future: Potholes on the road to college.* Chicago, IL: Consortium on Chicago School Research.

Rowan-Kenyon, H. T., Bell, A., & Perna, L. W. (2008). Contextual influences on parental involvement in college going: Variations by socioeconomic class. *Journal of Higher Education, 79,* 564–586.

Ryan, A. M., & Pintrich, P. R. (1997). Should I ask for help? The role of motivation and attitudes in adolescents' help seeking in math class. *Journal of Educational Psychology, 89,* 329–341.

Schneider, B. (2009). *College choice and adolescent development: Psychological and social implications of early admission.* Arlington, VA: National Association for College Admissions Counseling.

Schneider, B., & Stevenson, D. (1999). *The ambitious generation: America's teenagers, motivated but directionless.* New Haven, CT: Yale University Press.

Schwartz, B. (2004). *The paradox of choice: Why less is more.* New York: Harper Perennial.

Scott-Clayton, J. (2011). *The shapeless river: Does a lack of structure inhibit students' progress at community colleges?* (No. 25). Community College Research Center, Teachers College, Columbia University, Working Paper. Retrieved from http://ccrc.tc.columbia.edu/publications/lack-of-structure-students-progress.html

Smith, J., Pender, M., & Howell, J. (2013, February). The full extent of academic undermatch. *Economics of Education Review, 32,* 247–261.

Steinberg, L. (2008). A social neuroscience perspective on adolescent risk-taking. *Development Review, 28,* 78–106.

Steinberg, L., Cauffman, E., Woolard, J., Graham, S., & Banich, M. (2009). Are adolescents less mature than adults? Minors' access to abortion, the juvenile death penalty, and the alleged APA "Flip-Flop." *American Psychologist, 64,* 583–594.

Stockwell, M. S., Kharbanda, E. O., Martinez, R. A., Vargas, C. Y., Vawdrey, D. K., & Camargo, S. (2012). Effects of a text messaging intervention on influenza vaccination in an urban, low-income pediatric and adolescent population. *Journal of the American Medical Association, 307*(16), 1702–1708.

Strauch, B. (2003). *The primal teen.* New York, NY: Anchor Books.

Subrahmanyam, K., & Greenfield, P. (2008). Online communications and adolescent relationships. *Future Child, 18*(1), 119–146.

Thaler, R., & Sunstein, C. (2008). *Nudge: Improving decisions about health, wealth, and happiness.* New Have, CT: Yale University Press.

Walton, G. M., & Cohen, G. L. (2007). A question of belonging: Race, social fit, and achievement. *Journal of Personality and Social Psychology, 92*(1), 82–96.

White, W. S. (2005, December 16). Students, parents, colleges: Drawing the lines. *Chronicle of Higher Education, 52*(17), B16.

White, K. M., Hogg, M. A., & Terry, D. J. (2002). Improving attitude-behavior correspondence through exposure to normative support from a salient in-group. *Basic and Applied Social Psychology, (24)*, 91–103.

6

THE SHAPELESS RIVER

Does a Lack of Structure Inhibit Students' Progress at Community Colleges?

Judith Scott-Clayton

> You've got to know the shape of the river perfectly. It is all there is left to steer by on a very dark night. . . [I]t was a villainous night for blackness, we were in a particularly wide and blind part of the river, where there was no shape or substance to anything, and it seemed incredible that Mr. Bixby should have left that poor fellow to kill the boat trying to figure out where he was.
>
> Mark Twain, *Life on the Mississippi* (1883)

Introduction

Community colleges are the most common starting point for college entrants, with 43 percent of students beginning at such institutions. But out of 100 students entering a community college for the first time, only 16 will complete a degree or certificate within three years. Even after six years, only 34 will have a credential, while 46 will have left school without completing a degree or certificate.[1] There are many reasons for low rates of degree completion at community colleges, and in search of potential solutions, researchers and policymakers have appropriately focused on obvious targets such as improving students' academic preparation (through remediation, high school outreach, and dual enrollment programs) and strengthening their financial supports (through subsidized tuition, Pell Grants, and other forms of financial aid).

A less obvious but potentially important determinant of student success is the structure, or lack thereof, of student pathways from initial entry through completion. For many students at community colleges, finding a path to degree completion is the equivalent of navigating a shapeless river on a dark night. And as the above quotation illustrates, navigation is particularly difficult when there is "no shape or substance to anything." Compared to high school, entering a large community college can be overwhelming in terms of the choices to be made about which program to pursue, which courses to take within it, when to take them, how to pay for them, and whom to approach if a problem or question arises. Without clear signposts, an experienced guide, or a visible shoreline to follow, many students make false starts, take wrong turns, and hit unexpected obstacles, while others, like the inexperienced pilot in Twain's story, simply "kill the boat" trying to figure out where they are.

This chapter sets forth an argument for what has been called, in the community college context, the "structure" hypothesis: that students will be more likely to succeed in programs that are tightly structured, with relatively little room for individuals to deviate on a whim—or even unintentionally—from paths toward completion, and with limited bureaucratic obstacles to circumnavigate. The lineage of this hypothesis can be traced back in part to Tinto's seminal work on student persistence (1993), which recognized that the dropout phenomenon is not solely an individual failure but also an institutional one. In the community college context, this hypothesis was prominently raised by Rosenbaum, Deil-Amen, and Person (hereafter referred to as RDP, 2006) who examine differences in "organizational procedures" between public and private two-year institutions in their book *After Admission*.

This chapter focuses on community colleges because this is where non-completion is particularly concentrated; however, many of the issues raised and policy tools examined are relevant for thinking about student progress at for-profit institutions and large comprehensive four-year institutions as well.[2] While perhaps narrower than Tinto's idea that schools should support "integrative interactions," the definition of structure used in this chapter is broadened from RDP's (2006) construct to include not only explicit institutional policies and procedures, but also norms and nudges that may more subtly influence individuals' decisions at a point of action. This broad definition is influenced by the concept of choice architecture, or the way in which choices are structured and presented that can influence the decisions people ultimately make. Just as physical architecture influences our physical movements, choice architecture influences how we navigate complex decisions (Thaler & Sunstein, 2008).

Providing students with more structured paths to graduation is not without tradeoffs, particularly if "more structure" is taken to imply "less choice and flexibility." A broad range of services and program options, combined with flexible course scheduling options, is what makes college attractive and feasible for many students. There is a risk that while streamlined programs, policies, and procedures may improve the college experience for some students, they may unintentionally push others out. Because the consequences of increased structure are not always obvious, empirical research is essential to moving the debate forward. Strategies for increasing structure without restricting choice will be among those considered in this chapter.

Very few studies have explicitly examined the role of institutional or program structure in student persistence, though any intervention may have structural features worth examining. Thus, rather than attempting to comprehensively review the structural features of all potential reforms, this chapter aims to integrate previously disconnected evidence and especially to inject into the conversation ideas from behavioral economics and psychology that have been under-applied in higher education. It will evaluate substantive findings from both inside and outside higher education, as well as review the state of the research evidence in general. It is intended to provoke discussion rather than serve as a final word.

The next section provides a brief description of the decision context facing college students—what do they have to do in order to successfully progress towards completion?—and illustrates how community college students often depart from the idealized linear path. Section III introduces several concepts from the behavioral economics and psychology literature to examine how the structure of a decision-making process may influence students' choices within the community college setting, with special attention paid to the role of structure in ameliorating or exacerbating educational inequality. Section IV reviews the evidence regarding promising potential structure-based solutions in the community college context, and Section V concludes with suggestions for future research and practice.

The Decision Context: What Must a Student Do to Navigate College?

In order to successfully navigate college, students at some point must determine what they want to do, plan how to do it, and then follow through on these plans. We know that students do not always go through these stages in an organized, sequential fashion, and students often may change their minds and have to start again from the beginning. Thus, this section describes not what actually happens but rather what needs to happen at some point if students are to ultimately navigate college successfully—and it is illustrated with qualitative evidence regarding how students often depart from this idealized process. Of course, this is not to imply that community colleges are uniform, or to ignore the reforms that some institutions are moving towards to address the challenges highlighted below (these reform efforts will be the focus of a subsequent section).

Deciding What to Do

An important first step in the pursuit of a postsecondary credential is to decide what credential to pursue. Yet incoming students often lack well-defined, pre-established preferences, as illustrated by the following excerpt from a qualitative study by MDRC (Gardenhire-Crooks, Collado, & Ray, 2006):

> Once they decided to go to college, some students were starting from scratch in determining their academic goals and what they wanted from college, as this somewhat older blue-collar father revealed:

I'm illiterate as far as college; I just always wanted to come back to school." This same student highlighted how basic the guidance he needed might be: "I didn't know what (I was in college) for. Even now I don't know what I want to take up. (p. 16)

The abundance of program options offered by the typical community college may be particularly appealing to these undecided students; at the same time, it also may serve to perpetuate their indecision.

As noted by Goldin and Katz (2008), a variety of choices and a high degree of flexibility are two of the defining features of the U.S. educational system, particularly in higher education: "No nation in the world offers as much choice to potential undergraduates . . . as does the United States" (p. 254). And the comprehensive community college is perhaps the most diverse type of institution in this diverse postsecondary system. The typical community college serves multiple functions— preparing students to transfer to baccalaureate programs, offering associate degrees in both academic and occupational subjects, providing adult basic education and remedial instruction, providing occupational training and certification, and providing continuing education and recreational courses. Students may have literally hundreds of programs to choose from. Macomb Community College in Michigan, for example, offers thousands of courses in nearly 200 degree and certificate programs ranging from History to Nursing to Mechatronics.[3]

Whatever their deficiencies may be, community colleges cannot be criticized for offering a dearth of options—or can they? As RDP (2006) conclude, "Although community colleges offer many choices, we find that they rarely offer one: highly structured programs that curtail choice but promise timely graduation and an appropriate job" (p. 21). Cohen and Brawer (2008) note that the variety of programming offered by the typical comprehensive community college is virtually unique to the United States, perhaps because compared to the citizens of other countries, "Americans seem more determined to allow individual options to remain open for as long as each person's motivations and the community's budget allow" (p. 27).

Planning How to Do it

Previous studies have noted the complexity of choosing the right school (e.g., Avery & Hoxby, 2004), and several websites attempt to help students navigate that decision.[4] But even after choosing a school and program, consider the complexity of the additional decisions students must make. They must choose how many courses to take and when to take them, based on course descriptions that may provide only partial information about course content and difficulty, and program descriptions that provide little guidance about which courses should be taken when. On top of this, students may have to make tradeoffs depending upon the vagaries of class schedules and work schedules. Logistically, just obtaining all of the information needed to make wise course choices can be difficult. Information about course content and prerequisites is often located in one place, while course schedules are in another place, and the requirements for specific degree programs are spelled out in yet another location.

Moreover, unlike the typical elite four-year institution, where courses all usually cost the same and count the same, at the typical community college (and many public four-year institutions), not all credits are treated equally. Students may be surprised to find that enrolling at a college does not necessarily imply that they can take college-level courses. More than half of entering community college students are assigned to "developmental" coursework in at least one subject (Bailey, Jeong, & Cho, 2010; Bailey, 2009). Developmental credits may qualify a student for financial aid, but may not count as "degree credits" toward graduation; or, a college-credit bearing course may count toward general graduation requirements but not program-specific requirements. A common problem in community colleges is that even courses that count toward specific program requirements for a two-year degree may not be transferable if the student decides to continue at a four-year institution. Finally, community colleges may offer credit and noncredit programs in related fields (e.g., Nursing and Nursing Assistant programs), in which the noncredit program may cost as much or even more per term, but may result in only a certificate of completion that is not applicable toward an academic credential should the student decide to switch programs within the same institution or transfer to another institution.

Ideally, students should consider how their course choices in the current term will alter the set of choices for the following term, but at many institutions it is difficult to confirm in advance what courses will be offered in a future semester. Thus, term after term, this complex decision process must be repeated. Successfully navigating a single semester is no guarantee of smooth sailing in subsequent semesters.

Following Through

Even if they make a conscientious plan, students may encounter bureaucratic hurdles and unexpected obstacles that throw them off course. As Tinto (1993) has written, "[E]arly withdrawal from college need not always imply a lack of commitment or the absence of intention . . . Lest we forget, most new students are teenagers who have had precious little chance to live on their own and attend to the many challenging issues of adult life. For them, college is as much a social testing ground as an academic one" (p. 47).

One of the first tests students encounter is the financial aid application process. The Free Application for Federal Student Aid (FAFSA) is, for many students, longer and more complicated than their income tax return (Dynarski & Scott-Clayton, 2006).[5] Federal student aid information, packaging, verification, and disbursement is administered primarily by the institutions themselves, which may not have the staff to provide each student with patient, individualized attention. As RDP (2006) find in their qualitative study, "Students who apply for financial aid complain about the difficulty of the forms, and the lack of assistance at these colleges. Unfortunately, many students faced unpleasant and even hostile encounters with financial aid staff in their attempts to complete the financial aid process" (p. 117).

This intimidating form and the subsequent aid application verification process—which need to be repeated annually—appear to be a significant impediment to aid access, enrollment, and persistence. A recent study found that aid access and college enrollments both increased among prospective students who were randomly assigned to receive assistance with completing and submitting a FAFSA (Bettinger, Long, Oreopoulos, & Sanbonmatsu, 2012). Another study found that sending text messages with FAFSA reminders and assistance to community college freshmen increased sophomore year re-enrollment rates by nearly 12 percentage points, compared to a randomized control group that did not receive the texts (Castleman & Page, 2014).

The course registration process may be equally or more frustrating. While students at some schools may be able to register online, other institutions still hold "grueling registration ordeal[s]" involving long lines, crowds, and confusion (RDP, 2006, p. 117). Students who arrive at (or log into) course registration with a specific plan in hand may find that their preferred courses are already full. One student interviewed by RDP reported: "I wanted a math class, but they said the math classes were too full. . . . I didn't really need the reading though because they said I scored high and I didn't need the reading. I just took it anyway because they didn't have math" (p. 78). Even a single unavailable course can disturb the student's entire carefully balanced schedule, not only for the current term but for future terms as well.

Finally, even after successfully registering and beginning coursework, a student may encounter unexpected obstacles along the way. Financial aid may be delayed. A course may be more difficult than expected, or not difficult enough, but it may be too late to gain access to an appropriate course. A student may fail a placement exam (which are often, but not always, administered prior to registration). At each of these points, the student needs to make some active adjustments to get back on track, and with every active adjustment that is required, the risk increases that on their own some students simply won't react quickly enough. A problem encountered in one semester may reverberate or even amplify into future semesters, or the student may simply drop out.

Resources for Students Along the Way

While the specific resources available to help students through these three stages will vary from school to school, the level of assistance that can be provided by advisors and counselors is limited by extraordinarily high caseloads, which average one advisor/counselor for up to 1,500 students (Bettinger, Boatman, & Long, 2013). A national survey of entering community college students found that less than a quarter of students were assigned a specific person that they could contact for information or assistance, and less than half reported that any college staff (besides instructors) knew their names (Center for Community College Student Engagement, 2009).

The advising that does take place is often by necessity focused on mechanics of course registration, rather than bigger questions about goals. As O'Banion (1972, reprinted 1994) states: "It is assumed that students have already made choices regarding life goals and vocational goals when they enter the college—a questionable assumption for college students in general and a harmful assumption for community college students in particular" (p. 83). Even schools that recognize their role in guiding students to career decisions may have virtually no career counseling (Grubb, 2006).

In some decision contexts, family and peer networks may compensate for a lack of formal guidance. But because the students at community colleges are disproportionately first-generation college-goers, many from minority and/or low-income families, they may be less able to glean information from the experiences of their families and friends (Bailey, Jenkins, & Leinbach, 2005). Moreover, information may not circulate very well among classmates, because no two students are likely to be following the same exact path, campuses are generally non-residential, and many students attend part time and often intermittently (skipping terms).

Finally, community college advising systems often rely on students proactively seeking assistance. Poor institutional data systems may limit advisors' ability to detect and track struggling students; schools may not know a student has encountered a problem until a semester or more after that student is gone.

Research on Choice and Complexity: Is This Decision Context a Problem?

Usually, we think of choice as a good thing; in fact, classical economic theory implies that more choice can never be a bad thing. An abundance of choice usually develops for a reason: to serve a diversity of preferences. A plethora of postsecondary program options may improve individual welfare by providing individually-tailored alternatives, enabling students with diverse backgrounds, preparation, interests, and constraints to match with similarly diverse programs and attendance schedules. Indeed, this wide variety of alternatives has been central to the rise of open-access community colleges, which Cohen and Brawer (2008) attribute to the characteristically American belief "that all individuals should have the opportunity to rise to their greatest potential. Accordingly, all barriers to individual development should be broken down" (p. 11). Psychological evidence also suggests that choice can strengthen individuals' intrinsic motivation and sense of self-determination, as well as improve subjective evaluations of decision outcomes (see review by Botti & Iyengar, 2006). Postsecondary education without choice might begin to feel much like high school, and for many students this resemblance may be de-motivating.

As discussed in the introductory chapter of this book, however, recent work in psychology, marketing, and behavioral economics presents compelling evidence that more choice is not always better. This section reviews some of the key findings from this literature and relates them to students' decision-making process in the community college context. It concludes with a discussion of the critical implications of these findings for inequality in educational experiences and outcomes.

Limitations on Human Rationality and Self-Control

Human beings are not choice-making machines but rather function with "bounded rationality," a phrase first coined by Herbert Simon (1976). Behavioral research has repeatedly demonstrated that irrelevant contextual factors often influence choices, even when the choices seem fairly simple. For example, students given a choice between a fancy pen and $6 cash chose the fancy pen only 36 percent of the time, but a second group of students who were offered a cheap pen, a fancy pen, or $6 chose the fancy pen 46 percent of the time (Tversky & Simonson, 1993). In another experiment, men were much more likely to take up an identical loan when the loan offer letter included a woman's picture instead of a man's (Bertrand, Karlan, Mullainathan, Shafir, & Zinman, 2005).

The key conclusion from these and similar studies is that "preferences are actually constructed—not merely revealed—during their elicitation" (Bertrand et al., 2005, p. 30). The implication for higher education is that for students, "deciding what to do" may not be as straightforward as simply reflecting upon their preferences and selecting a program that fits those preferences. Indeed, research indicates that preferences may be least well-defined when choices involve complexity, limited personal experience, third-party marketing, and costs/benefits that occur across different time frames (Beshears, Choi, Laibson, & Madrian, 2008). All of these factors apply to college planning. Thus, students' choices between programs of study or courses within programs may not reflect well-defined preferences but rather may be highly dependent upon how these choices are structured and marketed.

Even if students' preferences were clear, another aspect of bounded rationality that can lead to poor decision making is pure cognitive overload. Choosing between two pens or $6 is one thing, but choosing between multiple institutions—offering dozens of programs and hundreds of individual courses each—is another thing altogether. Additionally, unlike the choice of pens, students' college, program, and course options rarely differ along a single dimension of "quality;" rather, they typically vary along multiple dimensions including cost, location, relevance to personal interests, expected future labor market payoffs, timing of course offerings, and difficulty of coursework. Choices like this that differ along many dimensions that are difficult to directly compare (known as "non-alignable" assortments in the behavioral sciences) can exacerbate cognitive overload because they require individuals to evaluate trade-offs between dimensions that are not easily compared (Gourville & Soman, 2005). Consumers seem to prefer having more choices when the assortment of choices is alignable, and tend to avoid brands and decisions when assortments are non-alignable (Gourville & Soman, 2005; Dhar & Nowlis, 1999).

While research has shown that cognitive overload may lead to significant mistakes in financial planning (Lusardi & Mitchell, 2007), college planning is arguably even more complex because it involves making financial and academic choices simultaneously. Simply *reading* all of the relevant academic and financial information can be prohibitively time-consuming, let alone figuring out how to weigh all of the present and future costs and benefits appropriately. Moreover, young adults may be particularly susceptible to cognitive overload because of their relative inexperience and low levels of financial literacy (Agarwal, Driscoll, Gabaix, & Laibson, 2008; Lusardi, Mitchell, & Curto, 2010).

Finally, even after deciding on the best course of action, individuals may suffer from what economists refer to as "present bias" or "time-inconsistent preferences" (Laibson, 1997). In other words, individuals may have no problem mentally committing themselves to do something costly or unpleasant in the future, but have trouble following through on those plans when the future becomes the present. Just as many people mentally commit every day to go to the gym *tomorrow*, students may delay taking important classes or may take a lighter than optimal load because they think they will be able to focus more on their studies *next term*.

Importantly, several features of the college decision context may aggravate this self-control problem. First, college—like going to the gym—involves trading certain, current pain for uncertain future gain. Second, the plethora of choices available to students may aggravate a phenomenon known as regret aversion (Bell, 1982). Even after an individual has decided which among several majors is preferred, she may hesitate to declare because of the potential regret associated with closing off other options. Finally, "hassle factors"—having to travel to inconvenient locations, wait in lines, fill out paperwork, or explain things repeatedly to different staff as a problem gets referred from person to person—can also cause individuals to delay taking an action they know to be beneficial (Bertrand, Mullainathan, & Shafir, 2004). Similarly, individuals may avoid or put off interactions that highlight negative aspects of one's identity—having to discuss one's poverty with financial aid staff, for example, or discuss prior failing grades with an advisor—simply because of unpleasant associations. Hassle factors and unpleasant associations may help explain why some students fail to claim financial aid; and why many students fail to complete remedial course sequences (Bailey, Jeong, & Cho, 2010).

Adverse Consequences

These human limitations can lead to three potential problems: mistakes, delay, and dissatisfaction. First, individuals who are uninformed or overwhelmed with too much complicated information may make systematically biased decisions that are not in their best interest. Psychological and behavioral economic researchers have identified a number of decision-making rules-of-thumb that individuals often resort to in the face of complexity. For example, Madrian and Shea (2001) find strong evidence of default bias (also called status quo bias) in a study of 401(k) enrollment procedures at a large U.S. corporation. When the corporation instituted a policy of automatically enrolling new hires in the 401(k) plan unless they actively opted out, participation immediately increased by about 50 percentage points. This indicates the large potential role for seemingly small differences in bureaucratic procedures.

In the community college context, the pathway from initial application to course enrollment requires numerous active decisions, where the default is simply not to enroll. In the face of confusion, students also may be unduly influenced by idiosyncratic factors such as whether a friend is enrolling in a particular program or course. This tendency to base decisions on easily accessible information is often referred to as "availability bias" (see, e.g., Tversky & Kahneman, 1974; Kahneman, 2011). In RDP's (2006) qualitative study, 42 percent of community college students indicated that they did not have enough information about requirements and prerequisites; 26 percent were unsure which of their courses counted toward a degree (p. 104). Students also undertake surprisingly minimal search efforts regarding educational options, given their importance. Instead, they often resort to trial and error: Beggs, Bantham, and Taylor (2006) find in a qualitative study that "that very few participants mentioned having performed any type of information search in the process of choosing their major. Only one participant talked about using career planning tools" (p. 385). RDP describe students as pinballs "bouncing from one thing to another" (quoting a community college administrator, p. 126), and Grubb (2006) similarly finds that students often "develop information by taking courses almost at random" (p. 197).

But program/course enrollment mistakes are neither the only nor even necessarily the most important adverse consequence when imperfect humans are confronted with unstructured, complex decision problems. A second potential problem is decision deferral. Greenleaf and Lehmann (1995) find that among other reasons, consumers delay decision making when they are uncertain about the consequences of their actions, uncertain about how to identify and weigh the key attributes of alternative choices, and when they must wait on the advice of others. Moreover, consumers are more likely to defer decisions when the choices under consideration involve multi-dimensional tradeoffs (see, e.g., Tversky & Shafir, 1992; see also a brief review of the literature in Dhar & Nowlis, 1999, p. 370). Finally, individuals may be *more* likely to procrastinate on consequential goals than inconsequential ones, because of unrealistic planning: "A person might forgo completing an attractive option because she plans to complete a more attractive but never-to-be-completed option" (O'Donoghue & Rabin, 2001, p. 121). In higher education, we thus might be worried that some students, unsure about which courses to take, may simply never complete the registration process or, once they register, may delay decisions about degree concentration.

Finally, a third potential adverse consequence is dissatisfaction with the ultimate decision once it is made. Evidence from psychology and marketing suggests that consumers are less satisfied when they are uncertain about their final choice and when the decision involves highly consequential tradeoffs (Heitmann, Lehmann, & Herrmann, 2007; Botti & Iyengar, 2006). Moreover, satisfaction is positively related to customer loyalty and the likelihood of repeat purchases (Heitmann et al., 2007). Drawing a parallel between "customer loyalty" and students' institutional attachment, this marketing perspective complements Tinto's (1993) model of student dropout, which he suggests is a consequence of student frustration and disengagement. Students who experienced an unpleasant decision process or who have lingering doubts about their choices may dread having to go through the process all over again the next semester.

Relationship of Structure and Complexity to Inequality

The lack of structure at many community colleges may reinforce inequality, both because the choices they offer are more complicated and because the students they serve may be least equipped to navigate this complexity. First, given the "vast variety of students" that community colleges serve (Grubb, 2006), students at such institutions are likely to face more choices and more complex choices than students enrolled at an elite four-year institution. For example, Harvard offers only full-time, residential bachelor's degree programs in 43 academic fields and requires all students to complete a core curriculum, while nearby Bunker Hill Community College offers 72 full-time or part-time associate degree or certificate programs in 63 academic and applied fields with no required core and with some courses available online. Thus, at a community college, any given student is relatively unlikely to be following exactly the same path as another—and even students who do follow the same path may be unlikely to know it. Moreover, schools serving low-income students are often disadvantaged themselves in terms of resources, thus explaining the high student-to-counselor ratio at community colleges.

Second, this unstructured complexity may be the most daunting for disadvantaged students—particularly first-generation college students—who may have limited access to college networks. Deil-Amen and Rosenbaum (2003) are among those who argue that lack of structure increases the importance of "social know-how" or "college knowledge," which in turn tends to place already disadvantaged groups (low-income, minority, and first-generation college enrollees) at an even further disadvantage. Unable to ask a parent or older sibling who has already been through the process, these students are especially in need of effective guidance from the institution. Yet they may also have a smaller margin for error. As argued by Bertrand, Mullainathan, and Shafir (2006), "The poor may exhibit basic weaknesses and biases that are similar to those of people from other walks of life, except that in poverty, there are narrow margins for error, and the same behaviors often manifest themselves in more pronounced ways and can lead to worse outcomes" (p. 419). A student who experiences a delay in financial aid or who cannot get a course enrollment question answered prior to the registration deadline may simply drop out.

Finally, it is worth noting that the lack of structure at some institutions is not always an accident. Some institutions have philosophical objections to "intrusive advising" and restrictions on students' choices, believing that it is the student's job to be engaged and proactive in their education. For example, Fonte (1997) describes how some community colleges consciously eschew restrictive curricula and services in favor of a laissez-faire approach. One argument of the laissez-faire proponents is that external interference may crowd out students' intrinsic motivation, although there is evidence that even students who are "cajoled" into increasing their educational investment (e.g., via financial incentives for passing AP exams in high school) may, by accident, learn something and perform better even after incentives are removed (Jackson, 2010).[6]

Interestingly, Fonte's description of restrictive versus laissez-faire institutional philosophies parallels the "concerted cultivation" versus "natural development" approaches that Lareau (2003) identifies in her qualitative study of class differences in child rearing. Lareau finds that low-income families are more likely to take a "hands off" approach to parenting. While Lareau does not pronounce one parenting style as better than another, she describes how the children of "natural development" parents were often more passive and less effective in their interactions with institutions such as schools and doctors. This description accords with the assessment of one community college dean of students, who reported that it is not "the natural tendency of these students to be aggressive, to be astute, self-directed, and all of those kinds of strategies that the successful student is able to do" (quoted in Grubb, 2006, p. 199).

Evidence on Potential Solutions

The lack of structure in the community college experience encompasses several types of problems that could be addressed by a range of solutions, from very "light-touch" informational interventions, to moderately intensive interventions restructuring aspects of the curricula and student services, to drastically overhauling the entire institution. In general, the evidence presented thus far regarding the extent of the *problems* is much stronger and deeper than the evidence regarding potential *solutions*. Nevertheless, all of the potential structure-based solutions discussed below have at least suggestive evidence of positive effects.

Improving Information Access and Navigation

Perhaps the most straightforward approach to addressing the complexity of the community college experience is simply to enhance student advising. There is evidence that doing so can at least modestly improve student outcomes (for recent reviews of the advising literature, see Karp, 2011, and Bettinger et al., 2013). For example, a randomized evaluation by MDRC found that lowering student-to-advisor ratios to 160:1 or less in the first year, and providing modest financial incentives for students to meet with their advisors twice per term for the first year, improved re-enrollment rates by about 10 percent (65 percent in the treatment group versus 58 percent in the control group returned in the second term, and 44 versus 40 percent returned in the third term after entry), though the effects did not remain significant in subsequent semesters (Scrivener & Weiss, 2009). Positive, and potentially longer-lasting effects have been found for more intensive student coaching services, such as those provided by InsideTrack, a for-profit company that contracts with individual institutions to coach students via phone, email, text message, and social media interactions. A randomized study of InsideTrack's services found significant impacts on persistence and graduation, for a cost of approximately $500 per student per semester (Bettinger & Baker, 2014).

One implication of the choice-architecture approach is that big problems do not always require big solutions (Thaler & Sunstein, 2008). While intensively advising students one-on-one continuously throughout the school year may be prohibitively expensive for some institutions, smaller solutions could generate impacts by taking advantage of technology and reaching out to individuals at critical moments. One example comes from a randomized experiment conducted by Bettinger et al. (2012) in conjunction with the tax preparer H&R Block. In the experiment, some low-income families who visited a tax-preparation center were randomly assigned to receive personal assistance with completing and submitting the FAFSA. This intervention, which took less than ten minutes and cost less than $100 per participant, increased immediate college entry rates by eight percentage points (24 percent) for high school seniors and 1.5 percentage points (16 percent) among independent participants with no previous college experience. After three years, participants in the full-treatment group had accumulated significantly more time in college than the control group. They also were much more likely to have received a Pell Grant.

Other evidence comes from interventions aimed at reducing "summer melt," the phenomenon that many college-intending students—high school seniors who graduate on time, are accepted to college, and apply for financial aid—nonetheless fail to matriculate in the fall (Castleman & Page, 2014). In a series of randomized experiments, Castleman and Page found that text messaging, peer mentoring, and proactive outreach were all successful at reducing summer melt, with costs as little as $7 and no more than $200 per student served (Castleman & Page, 2013; Castleman, Page, & Schooley, 2014). Targeting another type of choice problem— that high achieving students often don't apply to the most selective institutions they could attend—the Expanding College Opportunities (ECO) project sent information packets and application fee waivers to a random sample of high-achieving, low-income students (Hoxby & Turner, 2013). Despite an average cost of just $6 per participant, the intervention had substantial impacts on the number of applications submitted and on the quality of institutions actually attended (in terms of instructional spending and peer achievement).

The success of these interventions, primarily targeted at students on the cusp of college entry, raise the prospect that technological simplifications in other domains (such as course registration) might produce similarly dramatic results. Community colleges present a particularly target-rich environment for technological innovations that could improve students' access to and navigation of information about programs, courses, requirements, and prerequisites. For example, many college websites simply provide an alphabetical listing of program offerings, requiring students to click into each one to see what it involves, and making it difficult to compare substantively related programs. This may quickly frustrate students accustomed to the sophisticated search tools of online retailers like Amazon and Netflix.

Recent innovations attempt to address this void by offering interactive tools to help students plan and track their own progress toward a degree. For example, MyEdu.com offers an online subscription service that integrates information about degree requirements at specific schools with details about individual courses from course catalogs, schedules, and student course evaluations. Individual institutions are also developing their own tools: Austin Peay State University in Tennessee developed Degree Compass, which "combines hundreds of thousands of past students' grades with each particular student's transcript to make individualized recommendations for each student" (Austin Peay State University, 2014).

Learning Communities

Learning communities (LCs) are "a variety of approaches that link or cluster classes, during a given term, often around an interdisciplinary theme, and enroll a common cohort of students" (Arnett & Van Horn, 2009, p. 31).[7] For example, at Kingsborough Community College in New York City (a City University of New York [CUNY] institution), students enrolled in LCs take three courses together, usually a developmental English course, an orientation or student success course, and an academic course (such as health or psychology). Learning communities may address problems described in previous sections in at least two ways: first, they simplify students' course choices (and schedules) by offering them bundles of two or more courses together; second, they may improve peer networks since students are clustered together in the same set of courses.

The learning community model at Kingsborough was evaluated in a randomized experiment conducted by MDRC (as part of the "Opening Doors" study; see Scrivener et al. 2008). The study found statistically significant positive impacts on a range of outcomes during the treatment period, including credits attempted, credits completed, GPA, and self-reported student experience; however, these impacts tended to fade in post-program semesters. At the end of four semesters, treated students had enrolled for slightly more semesters, had earned slightly more credits, and had slightly higher GPAs (effect sizes around 0.10). One limitation of this study is that because the LCs involved a cluster of intertwined interventions (including smaller classes, a textbook voucher, enhanced counseling, and tutoring), it is not possible to attribute positive impacts to the more "structured" curriculum versus other aspects of the intervention.

Results from subsequent replication efforts around the country, however, have tempered enthusiasm for the learning communities model somewhat. A synthesis of findings from six randomized evaluations of learning communities found no impact on student persistence and only a small (one half-credit) impact on credit attainment overall (Visher, Weiss, Weissman, Rudd, & Wathington, 2012).

Overall, then, learning communities do not appear to have persistent, transformative effects on student success (at least as currently implemented). But it may be unrealistic to expect large and lasting impacts from programs that generally ran for just a single semester. The original Kingsborough model also included additional student supports that were not part of the subsequent interventions. Thus, expanding such communities beyond the first semester is one potential solution (though block scheduling is more difficult to implement once students begin branching out in their coursework); the results also may suggest interventions need to be bundled rather than implemented piece by piece (a point that will be explored further below).

Whole-Institution Reform

Producing meaningful and lasting improvements in college students' persistence and degree completion may require more than tweaking around the edges; it may require overhauling the organization so that all aspects of the institution are aligned to promote student success. High-performing for-profit institutions, despite the negative perceptions of the sector overall, provided some early models of the type of streamlined student programs and services that some public institutions now seek to implement. For example, in a study comparing seven typical community colleges to seven well-regarded private two-year institutions in the same area, Rosenbaum, Deil-Amen, and Person (2006) find that the private colleges had more structured programs, making it easier for students to understand and follow important information, and providing students with fewer opportunities to "mess up." Advising at the private two-year schools was also more structured and intrusive, requiring mandatory meetings each term. Finally, students at the private schools advanced through programs in cohorts, providing a level of peer support and streamlining the guidance process from initial registration through job placement. As a result, the private two-year students were significantly more likely than the community college students in the sample to know which courses were needed for degree plans and which offered college credit. Private two-year students were also less likely to take a course they later discovered would not count toward a degree. Although the students who choose to enter public and for-profit institutions may be different to begin with, these differences in survey outcomes remained significant even after controlling for observable student characteristics. On the basis of these findings, RDP's key recommendations include that community colleges simplify their curricula, improve counseling and more proactively monitor student progress, and improve information systems.

These were some of the motivations behind the newly-established Guttman Community College (GCC), a CUNY system that enrolled its first students in 2012. The school takes a comprehensive approach to student success. First, the school offers a highly structured curriculum, including a mandatory "summer bridge" program just prior to the first semester, mandatory full-time enrollment requirement, a highly standardized first year curriculum (with embedded remediation for those that need it). In the second year, students can choose from a limited set of 10–12 majors in high-need fields. In addition to the structured curriculum, GCC also provides structured student supports, including small learning communities, designated "student success advocates," and one-stop student services, and peer mentors. While it is too early for external evaluation, staff are optimistic about student outcomes based upon preliminary data showing that 75 percent of Fall 2012 enrollees returned in Fall 2013, and 20 percent were expected to graduate by August 2014 (Zweifler, 2014).

One prominent advocacy organization, Complete College America (CCA) has developed and promoted a model called "Guided Pathways to Success" (GPS) which includes structured programs of study, informed choice, block schedules, and more "intrusive" advising as key elements (Complete College America, 2012). Tennessee's technical colleges, called Technology Centers or "Tennessee Techs" incorporate these elements and have received accolades and attention for their unusually high (75 percent) graduation rate. This rate is several times higher than at most community and technical colleges, although not all of the difference may be causal (those who choose to enroll at the Tennessee Techs may already be more focused than average). Elements of the GPS model have been adopted by four-year institutions as well, including Arizona State University and Florida State University.

Another major community college reform along these lines that has received national attention is the Accelerated Study in Associate Programs (ASAP) intervention, currently operating in six CUNY community colleges. Though not a whole-institution reform, ASAP is an unusually comprehensive program—in some ways like a school-within-a-school—designed to help students stay in school and graduate with an associate's degree quickly. Similar to GCC, ASAP students are required to enroll full-time and groups of ASAP students by major are block-scheduled for three or more courses during the first year. ASAP students receive enhanced advisement (with advisers responsible for only 60–80 students each), tutoring and career services. The program also offers significant financial supports including tuition waivers, free textbooks, and free public transportation provided when students meet with their advisers.

Early findings from a rigorous random assignment evaluation by MDRC shows that ASAP is having a dramatic impact (Scrivener & Weiss, 2013): after two years, ASAP students had earned 25 percent more credits than their counterparts in the control group (38 versus 30 credits), and were 66 percent more likely to have earned a degree (15 percent versus 9 percent). Degree completion impacts are expected to get even bigger over time, based on early evidence from the first cohort to participate in the study.

If GCC and ASAP prove to be as effective as early findings suggest, it will add significant weight to the hypothesis that students are more likely to succeed when programs are tightly structured, with limited bureaucratic obstacles and little room for students to unintentionally stray from paths toward completion. But comprehensive models may cost significantly more per student than the typical services provided to community college students. While GCC's costs will not be clear for a few years until it reaches its full capacity (the first cohort entered in Fall 2012, and was limited to 300 students), ASAP appears to cost roughly twice as much per enrollee as the status quo (Levin & Garcia, 2013). These higher costs may be justified by the better outcomes they support: Levin & Garcia (2013) find that CUNY's cost-per-graduate is 10 percent less for ASAP than for the typical community college program.

Conclusions and Future Directions

The observational evidence clearly indicates that community college students are often confused and sometimes overwhelmed by the complexity of navigating their community college experience. And the evidence from other fields (such as consumer choice and financial planning) demonstrates that individuals' ability to make good decisions—or to make any decision at all—can be adversely affected by several of the factors that are present in the community college context. The evidence relating to specific solutions in the community college context is more limited, but growing. Enhanced advising, assistance in navigating bureaucracy (e.g., financial aid forms), and the provision of linked cohorts/curricula through learning communities are among the interventions that have been evaluated and found to have positive (if not always transformational) impacts. Comprehensive reforms like GCC and ASAP indicate both the potential for and the cost of making dramatic improvements.

In terms of future directions for policy and research, it is worth emphasizing that the concept of "structure" as discussed above encompasses several different types of problems, each of which might require different types of solutions. For example, "hassle factors" such as long lines at registration, burdensome and/or redundant paperwork, or negative interactions with financial aid staff may require behind-the-scenes streamlining of bureaucratic processes, additional support staff, and/or new staff training. While the cost and effort required for such reforms may not be trivial, the argument for reducing hassle factors is uncontroversial.

Similarly, there is little substantive argument against providing students with better information—and better ways to search and navigate this information—to help them manage the sheer complexity of gathering and correctly utilizing all of the relevant information on the costs, benefits, and requirements of alternative educational paths (and then updating this information every semester). One potential light-touch intervention to test in this area would be a sophisticated online college advising tool, which would integrate career exploration and goal setting, prerequisite navigation, course planning and recommendations, tracking of student progress in meeting requirements, and early warnings when students fall off track. Such a tool would not replace trained counselors, but would assist currently overburdened counselors by automating the nuts-and-bolts aspects of college guidance, thus freeing up staff to focus on more complicated individual issues.

A related, but distinct challenge is the number of complex program options students must choose from, which psychological evidence suggests can cause decision paralysis, arbitrary decision outcomes, and dissatisfaction. Simply providing students with more information may not solve this problem, but reducing options is certainly more controversial. CUNY's new Guttman Community College, which explicitly limits students' choice of major upfront, is one potential solution, but it may be possible in part because students' choices remain unconstrained at other local community colleges in the CUNY system. There are dangers in reducing choice complexity too much; while it may be easier for students to choose among fewer options, there is no guarantee that this will always make all students better off. Some students may make better decisions in a world where they must wrestle with the tradeoffs among many options, even if it is more unpleasant in the short term.

However, helping students navigate an abundance of options need not imply restricting student choice. A middle path would be for schools to provide the equivalent of a "prix-fixe" menu, offering a limited selection of pre-packaged college pathways that students could choose from instead of planning their schedules a la carte. Similarly, colleges might experiment with setting "smart defaults," as companies have begun to do with their employees' retirement plan choices. These defaults do not limit students' ability to customize their own path through college, but provide them with a starting point. For example, incoming students could be "pre-registered" for a set of common foundational courses, which they would then be free to change; returning students could be pre-registered for a set of logical follow-up courses based on their major and previous coursework.

Overall, the evidence that a problem exists is very strong, though the evidence on what policies best address it—particularly in terms of cost-effectiveness and scalability, as well as in terms of figuring out which types of interventions work best for whom and under which circumstances—is more limited. But the reality that there is no silver bullet need not be cause for discouragement. Instead, the issue of structure in higher education decision making appears ripe for continued innovation and research.

Notes

1. Author's calculations using NCES QuickStats with BPS:2009 Beginning Postsecondary Students database.
2. For example, completion rates at open-access four-year institutions are not much better (39 percent after six years), but such institutions enroll a much smaller proportion of first-time entrants (3 percent). Completion rates at moderately selective public four-years (which represent the vast majority of public four-year entrants) are much higher— 66 percent after 6 years—though such institutions may still be concerned about students taking longer than necessary to graduate.
3. For a complete list, see www.macomb.edu/Current+Students/Educational+Offerings/ Areas+of+Study.htm
4. For example, The College Board's College MatchMaker (http://collegesearch. collegeboard.com/search/adv_typeofschool.jsp) and the U.S. Department of Education's College Navigator (http://nces.ed.gov/COLLEGENAVIGATOR/).
5. Since 2006 several efforts have been made to simplify the FAFSA, including eliminating unnecessary questions entirely and improving the online application so that students can skip questions which are not relevant for them. However, even those applying online are encouraged to fill out a worksheet that is longer and more complicated than an IRS 1040EZ, the tax form many students are eligible to use.
6. Interestingly, in the domain of financial planning, similar objections were raised early on regarding the perceived intrusiveness of automatic 401(k) enrollment policies, but these objections tended to fade as evidence accumulated on program effectiveness.
7. This is the definition adopted by LaGuardia Community College (CUNY); see www. lagcc.cuny.edu/lc/overview/ppt/keyslidescore.ppt

References

Agarwal, S., Driscoll, J. C., Gabaix, X., & Laibson, D. (2008). *The age of reason: Financial decisions over the lifecycle* (No. 13191). NBER Working Paper. Retrieved from www. nber.org/papers/w13191

Arnett, A., & Van Horn, D. (2009). Connecting mathematics and science: A learning community that helps math-phobic students. *Journal of College Science Teaching, 38*(6), 30–34.

Avery, C., & Hoxby, C. (2004). Do and should financial aid packages affect students' college choices? In C. M. Hoxby (Ed.), *College choices: The economics of where to go, when to go, and how to pay for it* (pp. 239–302). Chicago, IL: University of Chicago Press.

Austin Peay State University. (2014). *Degree compass: What is it?* Clarksville, TN: Office of Information Technology, Austin Peay State University. Retrieved from www.apsu. edu/information-technology/degree-compass-what

Bailey, T. (2009). Challenge and opportunity: Rethinking the role and function of developmental education in community college. *New Directions for Community Colleges, 145,* 11–30.

Bailey, T., Jenkins, D. W. & Leinbach, T. (2005). *What we know about community college low-income and minority student outcomes: Descriptive statistics from national surveys.* New York, NY: Columbia University, Teachers College, Community College Research Center.

Bailey, T., Jeong, D. W., & Cho, S.-W. (2010). Referral, enrollment, and completion in developmental education sequences in community colleges. *Economics of Education Review, 29*(2), 255–270.

Beggs, J. M., Bantham, J. H., & Taylor, S. T. (2006). Distinguishing the factors influencing college students' choice of major. *College Student Journal, 42,* 381–394.

Bell, D. E. (1982). Regret in decision making under uncertainty. *Operations Research, 30*(5), 961–981. doi:10.1287/opre.30.5.961

Bertrand, M., Karlan, D., Mullainathan, S., Shafir, E., & Zinman, J. (2005). *What's psychology worth? A field experiment in the consumer credit market* (No. 11892). NBER Working Paper. Retrieved from www.nber.org/papers/w11892

Bertrand, M., Mullainathan, S., & Shafir, E. (2004). A behavioral-economics view of poverty. *American Economic Review, 94*(2), 419–423.

Bertrand, M., Mullainathan, S., & Shafir, E. (2006). Behavioral economics and marketing in aid of decision making among the poor. *Journal of Public Policy & Marketing, 25*(1), 8–23.

Beshears, J., Choi, J. J., Laibson, D., & Madrian, B. (2008). How are preferences revealed? *Journal of Public Economics, 92*(8–9), 1787–1794.

Bettinger, E. P., & Baker, R. (2014). The effects of student coaching: An evaluation of a randomized experiment in student advising. *Educational Evaluation and Policy Analysis, 36*(1): 3–19.

Bettinger, E. P., Boatman, A. & Long, B. T. (2013). Student supports: Developmental education and other academic programs. *Future of Children, 23*(1), 93–115

Bettinger, E. P., Long, B. T., Oreopoulos, P., & Sanbonmatsu, L. (2012). The role of application assistance and information in college decisions: Results from the H&R Block FAFSA Experiment. *Quarterly Journal of Economics, 127*(3): 1205–42.

Botti, S., & Iyengar, S. S. (2006). The dark side of choice: When choice impairs social welfare. *Journal of Public Policy & Marketing, 25*(1), 24–38.

Castleman, B., & Page, L. (2013). *A trickle or a torrent? Understanding the extent of summer "melt" among college-intending high school graduates.* Harvard University manuscript, presented at the Annual meeting of the Association for the Study of Higher Education. Retrieved from http://scholar.harvard.edu/files/bencastleman/files/castleman_and_page_-_trickle_or_torrent_ssq_final_manuscript_-_02–06–13.pdf and http://scholar. harvard.edu/files/bencastleman/files/castleman_page_schooley_-_the_forgotten_summer_-_july_2013.pdf

Castleman, B., & Page, L. (2014). *Freshman year financial aid nudges: An experiment to increase FAFSA renewal and college persistence.* (No. 29). University of Virginia EdPolicyWorks Working Paper. Retrieved from http://curry.virginia.edu/uploads/resourceLibrary/29_Freshman_Year_Financial_Aid_Nudges.pdf

Center for Community College Student Engagement. (2009). *Benchmarking & benchmarks: Effective practice with entering students.* Austin: University of Texas at Austin, Community College Leadership Program.

Cohen, A. M., & Brawer, F. (2008). *The American community college* (5th ed.). San Francisco, CA: Jossey-Bass.

Complete College America. (2012). *Guided Pathways to Success (GPS): Boosting college completion.* Indianapolis, IN: Complete College America.

Deil-Amen, R., & Rosenbaum, J. E. (2003). The social prerequisites of success: Can college structure reduce the need for social know-how? *Annals of the American Academy of Political and Social Science, 586*(1), 120–143.

Dhar, R., & Nowlis, S. M. (1999). The effect of time pressure on consumer choice deferral. *Journal of Consumer Research, 25*(4), 369–384.

Dynarski, S. M., & Scott-Clayton, J. (2006). The cost of complexity in federal student aid: Lessons from optimal tax theory and behavioral economics. *National Tax Journal, 59*(2), 319–356.

Fonte, R. (1997). Structured versus laissez-faire open access: Implementation of a proactive strategy. *New Directions for Community Colleges, 100*, 43–52.

Gardenhire-Crooks, A., Collado, H., & Ray, B. (2006). *A whole 'nother world: Students navigating community college.* New York, NY: MDRC.

Goldin, C., & Katz, L. F. (2008). *The race between education and technology.* Cambridge, MA: Belknap Press of Harvard University Press.

Gourville, J. T., & Soman, D. (2005). Overchoice and assortment type: When and why variety backfires. *Marketing Science, 24*(3), 382–395.

Greenleaf, E. A., & Lehmann, D. R. (1995). Reasons for substantial delay in consumer decision making. *Journal of Consumer Research, 22*(2), 186–199.

Grubb, N. (2006). "Like, what do I do now?": The dilemmas of guidance counseling. In T. Bailey & V. Morest (Eds.), *Defending the community college equity agenda* (pp. 195–222). Baltimore, MD: Johns Hopkins University Press.

Heitmann, M., Lehmann, D. R., & Herrmann, A. (2007). Choice goal attainment and decision and consumption satisfaction. *Journal of Marketing Research, 44*(2), 234–250.

Hoxby, C. M., & Turner, S. (2013). *Expanding college opportunities for high-achieving, low income students.* SIEPR Discussion Paper No. 12–014. Stanford University, Stanford, CA.

Jackson, C. K. (2010). *A stitch in time: The effects of a novel incentive-based high school intervention on college outcomes* (No. 15722). NBER Working Paper. Retrieved from www.nber.org/papers/w15722

Kahneman, D. (2011). *Thinking, fast and slow.* New York: Farrar, Straus and Giroux.

Karp, M. M. (2011). *Toward a new understanding of non-academic student support: Four mechanisms encouraging positive student outcomes in the community college* (No. 28). Community College Research Center, Teachers College, Columbia University, Working Paper. Retrieved from http://ccrc.tc.columbia.edu/publications/non-academic-student-support-mechanisms.html

Laibson, D. (1997). Golden eggs and hyperbolic discounting. *Quarterly Journal of Economics, 112*(2), 443–477.

Lareau, A. (2003). *Unequal childhoods: Class, race, and family life* (1st ed.). Berkeley and Los Angeles, CA: University of California Press.

Levin, H. M., & Garcia, E. (2013). *Benefit-cost analysis of Accelerated Study In Associate Programs (ASAP) of the City University Of New York (CUNY).* New York: Center for Benefit-Cost Studies in Education, Teachers College, Columbia University.

Lusardi, A., & Mitchell, O. S. (2007). Financial literacy and retirement preparedness: Evidence and implications for financial education. *Business Economics, 42*(1), 35–44.

Lusardi, A., Mitchell, O.S., & Curto, V. (2010). *Financial literacy among the young: Evidence and implications for consumer policy* (No. 15352). NBER Working Paper. Retrieved from www.nber.org/papers/w15352

Madrian, B. C., & Shea, D. F. (2001). The power of suggestion: Inertia in 401(k) participation and savings behavior. *Quarterly Journal of Economics, 116*(4), 1149–1187.

O'Banion, T. (1994). An academic advising model. *NACADA Journal, 14*(2), 10–16.

O'Donoghue, T., & Rabin, M. (2001). Choice and procrastination. *Quarterly Journal of Economics, 116*(1), 121–160.

Rosenbaum, J.E., Deil-Amen, R., & Person, A.E. (2006). *After admission: From college access to college success.* New York, NY: Russell Sage Foundation.

Scrivener, S., Bloom, D., LeBlanc, A., Paxson, C., Rouse, C.E., & Sommo, C. (with Au, J., Teres, J. J., & Yeh, S.) (2008). *A good start: Two-year effects of a freshman learning community program at Kingsborough Community College.* New York, NY: MDRC.

Scrivener, S., & Weiss, M. J. (2009). *More guidance, better results? Three-year effects of an enhanced student services program at two community colleges.* New York, NY: MDRC.

Scrivener, S., & Weiss, M. J. (2013). *More Graduates: Two Year Results from an Evaluation of Accelerated Study in Associate Programs (ASAP) for Developmental Education Students.* New York, NY: MDRC.

Simon, H. (1976). *Administrative behavior.* New York, NY: The Free Press.

Thaler, R.H., & Sunstein, C.R. (2008). *Nudge: Improving decisions about health, wealth, and happiness.* New Haven, CT: Yale University Press.

Tinto, V. (1993). *Leaving college: Rethinking the causes and cures of student attrition* (2nd ed.). Chicago, IL: University of Chicago Press.

Tversky, A., & Kahneman, D. (1974). Judgment under uncertainty: Heuristics and biases. *Science, 185*, 1124–1131.

Tversky, A., & Shafir, E. (1992). Choice under conflict: The dynamics of deferred decision. *Psychological Science, 3*(6), 358–361.

Tversky, A., & Simonson, I. (1993). Context-dependent preferences. *Management Science, 39*(10), 1179–1189.

Visher, M. G, Weiss, M. J., Weissman, E., Rudd, T., & Wathington, H. (2012). *The effects of learning communities for students in developmental education: A synthesis of findings from six community colleges.* New York, NY: MDRC.

Zweifler, S. (2014). A new community college keeps students on track with structure. *Chronicle of Higher Education,* 2014, May 27. Retrieved from http://chronicle.com/article/A-New-Community-College-Keeps/146731/

7

PREPARE FOR CLASS, ATTEND, AND PARTICIPATE!

Incentives and Student Success in College

Robert M. Shireman and Joshua A. Price

The dream of every caring teacher is that students will seek knowledge because they are curious and love learning for its own sake. But few people are so self-motivated and self-directed that, on their own, they will take the steps to achieve basic mastery of an academic discipline. Most of us need significant guidance and encouragement to identify and engage in all of the necessary tasks to achieve academic success, even if we are intrinsically motivated. Indeed, that direction and inspirational prodding is what a college, ideally, is supposed to provide.

In this chapter we use the tools and terminology of behavioral economics to examine strategies that can promote learning for students in college and increase the probability they earn a degree. By applying a behavioral lens to the task of improving college completion we are not attempting anything novel. It would be more accurate to say that we are returning to the very roots of the higher education enterprise and how it should ideally operate to support students in their pursuit of a degree.

Motivations vs. Methods vs. Behaviors

A college degree has become strongly associated with having a successful life, due largely to higher earnings and the ability of a college degree to open doors to a variety of occupations and careers. Many people who begin college say they want a college degree, yet a substantial share fail to engage in the behaviors necessary to achieve that goal. Why does this discrepancy exist? To examine that question, it is helpful to distinguish the ultimate goals people are trying to achieve from the route they are taking to achieve those goals, and to differentiate both of those from the behaviors that people actually display. Physical fitness offers a useful analogy, because like a college education it requires sustained work over a long time to achieve the reward. There are many reasons someone might want to be physically fit, like being more attractive, but here we assume that good health is the motivating factor.

Ultimate goal: Live a healthy lifestyle.
Route to the goal: Lose weight.
Behavior: Substitute fresh vegetables for potato chips.

Applying the same construct to higher education might produce something like the following:

Ultimate goal: A career with financial security.
Route to the goal: Earn a college degree.
Behavior: Read, write, go to class.

In both examples, the motivating goals are compelling while the behaviors themselves often face countervailing impulses. Even with the goals in mind, conflicting motivations can lead individuals to adopt behaviors that will lead them away from their goal: the weight loss goal being undermined by ice cream consumption and the goal of a college degree being undermined by social activities. Two of the major reasons that goals are undermined are lack of salience and present-biasedness.

Lack of Salience

Sometimes people do not engage in the behaviors that lead to their goals because they do not fully appreciate the association between their actions and their consequences (positive or negative). Posting calorie counts on menus can change people's food choices because it increases the *salience* of food choice: the connection between what they eat and their weight-loss goal. A college degree is salient because of its association with success later in life. Courses are salient because they are the building blocks to the degree. Within each course, instructors create even smaller salience units, the specific expectations of what students need to do to earn a specific grade or credit, such as points for completing assignments satisfactorily, passing exams, or participating in class. Students can calculate the effect that their performance on each component will have on course credit and, in the end, on graduating with the degree. The chain of salience, at least theoretically, reaches all the way from writing the term paper to earning a good salary (if that is the student's ultimate goal).

In behavioral economics terms, breaking down a salient goal into smaller units (courses, assignments, exams) is known as *narrow bracketing*. When the action steps are narrowed and individually rewarded, even small incentives can be powerful motivators (Read et al., 1999). Telling a child that eating his spinach will make him strong is rarely the effective motivator we hope for, even if the child has a Superman obsession. But a mere nickel can be enough to incentivize children to eat their vegetables at lunch (Just & Price, 2013). Adults in the workplace setting are constantly subjected to employers' efforts to incentivize behavior using money and other types of rewards (see Chapter 2 in this volume). Popular video games like Farmville use points to promote game-based behaviors in the same way that grades and credits in college are intended to incentivize learning-related behaviors.

The idea of attaching monetary rewards to behavior can spark worries that extrinsic rewards might crowd out intrinsic motivation. The concern may be misplaced, however: course credits and grades themselves are extrinsic rewards, designed to manipulate behavior that is, presumably, inadequately incentivized through intrinsic motivation alone. Furthermore, extrinsic rewards can help to introduce people to behaviors without undermining their potential willingness to later continue the activities without the incentive, as shown in studies involving exercise (Royer, Stehr, & Sydnor, 2012), eating fruits and vegetables (Just & Price, 2013), and performance on reading and math tests (Levitt et al., 2012). Indeed, a good college education ideally transforms someone who starts out wanting a piece of paper (the degree) or a salary into someone who is a self-motivated lifelong learner, creating, leading, and learning out of curiosity and personal commitment.

The salience of tasks can be influenced by the way they are presented, or *framed*, such as calling an assignment a "requirement" versus "extra credit." Reframing a task as allowing a student to avoid a loss rather than leading to a potential gain can increase its power to affect behavior.[1] For example, the best golfers in the world, even Tiger Woods in his prime, were more likely to make a putt if they were putting for par than if they were putting for birdie (Pope & Schweitzer, 2011). If they missed their birdie putt they could settle for a par—the salient reference point for the hole. But if they missed their par putt they got a dreaded bogey. In higher education, an analogy could be multi-year scholarships which some students are eligible to earn. However, these scholarships can be lost by failing to meet set requirements. Loss aversion implies that students would be more likely to meet the set requirements to retain their current scholarship than to meet the same requirements to earn a new scholarship. As individuals are averse to losing what they already have or perceive that they have, actions can be taken to encourage students to adopt the behaviors that lead to college success.

Present-Biasedness

Many of the actions necessary to earn a college degree require sacrifices now in exchange for expected benefits in the future. Bracketing choices, framing them creatively, and attaching rewards all help to counteract the human tendency to be biased in favor of the present: wanting to do what is best for the long term but in the moment focusing on the short term (Downs & Loewenstein, 2011).

Many of us have had this feeling: *I want to lose weight soon, but I want the cookie now.* Both are true and legitimate desires, but the reward from losing weight is in the future, while the scrumptiousness of the cookie is immediate. So the cookie is eaten, and the weight-loss goal is pushed (again, and again) into the future. Taking advantage of people's present-biasedness can be a profitable business strategy. Before consumer protection laws curbed the practice, gyms would charge a large fee for a long-term membership that seemed reasonable on a per-use basis to consumers who were eager to commit to frequent exercise. But of course the buyers were vastly over-estimating their likelihood of actually going to the gym. Using this strategy, the gym could sell far more memberships than would fit in the facility because they knew that most of the people were fooling themselves when they bought the membership. The gyms had no financial incentive to implement strategies to get people to actually *use* the gym. Much the opposite: it was best if members stayed away, because more memberships could be sold. And the buyers couldn't really complain, since after all their own laziness could be blamed for failing to make use of the membership they had purchased (DellaVigna & Malmendier, 2006).

Of course, even *with* the specific commitment to a course, present-bias can undermine success. For example, as a student selects and enrolls in classes she might say to herself, *I am going to dedicate myself to being an exemplary student this term. I will sign up for that class that meets at 8:00 in the morning.* Her determination is strong and she is pleased that the schedule fits her other commitments and will provide her with more flexible time each afternoon. However, during the second week in school when her alarm sounds to wake her with just enough time to get ready for that 8 o'clock class, she is faced with a new decision: Should I stay or should I go? She knows she should attend class—she is the same person who enrolled in the class—but she now faces a conflict between the long-term desire to succeed academically and the short-term impulse to sleep. Present-biasedness gets in the way of her goal of a college degree.

In the college context, one strategy for addressing bias towards the present is to ask students to make a *specific commitment* towards achieving a longer-term goal. A scheduled "course" is essentially that: a construct to get students to engage in tasks that lead to the credit towards graduation. By signing up for a course, a student is telling the college: *For the next 15 weeks, I will show up, prepared for class, every Tuesday and Thursday at 10 a.m.* Much of the excitement about online education fails to appreciate the importance of time-and-place commitments to battling the human tendency toward procrastination. It may seem like a good idea to let students sign up for online courses in which they can watch lectures and do assignments "at their own pace." However, without the specific up-front commitment, it becomes extremely difficult for people to battle the short-term desires to do something else. Life gets filled up with other tasks, to the point that it is never "convenient" to actually perform the learning tasks necessary to complete the wonderfully convenient online course.

Our discussion of incentives and student behavior should not be interpreted as placing all of the blame on students and their cognitive biases for failing to complete college. At most, the ideas we lay out should be seen as adjustments worth trying in the context of broader efforts to improve students' experiences and achievement in higher education through advising, creative scheduling, improved teaching, engaging extracurricular activities, and supportive peer groups.

Student Behaviors That Matter

When faced with the college dropout problem, policy makers and college leaders frequently undertake efforts to increase the salience of graduation as a goal. They launch information campaigns designed to remind students of the career and salary benefits of having the degree, for example. However, trying to make an already-salient motive more salient is not likely to make much difference. Students have chosen to enroll because of the expected career and salary benefits of having a degree, so the general incentive to enroll in courses and do assignments is already there. Trying to make graduation more salient is like telling someone who already has a gym membership that they need to work on getting physically fit. They already know that.

Instead of trying to increase students' desire for the degree, interventions need to focus on changing the near-term behaviors that will help the student make progress toward the degree. Just as the person who wants to lose weight needs help eating right and exercising, college students can benefit from interventions that prompt them to engage in the specific actions that contribute to learning. Rather than focus on the motivation that caused them to set their goal, strategies should target the *behaviors* that lead to achieving the goal that they have already set.

The oft-cited examples of successful interventions in behavioral economics involve relatively simple, measurable actions and outcomes: increasing savings by making enrollment in a 401K the default; reducing the spread of germs by washing hands; improving health by eating fruit or by exercising regularly. To make use the insights of behavioral economics requires first identifying the behaviors that contribute to earning a degree, something that is far more complicated than preventing infection or boosting assets. Analyzing 57 different measured student activities, Astin (1993) identified those that were associated with retention or degree attainment, after adjusting for student characteristics. They include:

Factors that Are Positively Related to Student Success

Hours spent studying or doing homework
Working on an independent research project
Giving class presentations
Taking essay exams
Interacting with faculty

Hours spent attending classes or labs
Participation in internship programs
Participation in intramural sports
Working part-time on campus
Participating in volunteer work
Alcohol consumption (see Note 4)

Factors that Are Negatively Related to Student Success

Working at a full-time job
Working part-time off campus
Hours spent watching television
Hours spent commuting to campus

Strategies from behavioral economics could be applied to any of the identified behaviors. We focus below on three behaviors that are particularly closely associated with learning in the traditional, classroom-based college: studying (doing assignments and otherwise coming to class well-prepared), attending class, and participating in class.

Studying

Hours spent studying was identified by Astin (1993) as having a particularly strong positive association with student success: "the most basic form of academic involvement—studying and doing homework—has stronger and more widespread positive effects than almost any other involvement measure or environmental measure." Studying not only contributes to retention and completion, students learn more when they dedicate more time to a given task (Frederick & Walberg, 1980). Students who spend more time doing homework get higher scores on exams and are more likely to get A's and B's (Grodner & Rupp, 2011). One study found that completing extra homework is more strongly related with students' performance than other measures, such as class size (Eren & Henderson, 2008).

Despite the importance of studying, many students fail to put sufficient time into preparing for class and completing assignments. Some evidence indicates that the time students spend studying has dropped dramatically over the past few decades (Babcock & Marks, 2010). Today, the average college student spends less time *in class and studying* than a high school student spends *in class* without including homework. Experiments can be designed to encourage students to spend more time learning outside of the classroom, but there is a bit of chicken or egg problem that must be considered. For students to spend time on assignments that take serious time and effort, they need assignments that take serious time and effort. For faculty to make those assignments, they need to believe that the students will be ready and willing to do the work.

Attending

In addition to studying and completing assignments, going to class is a strong predictor of student success. As obvious as it may seem that students should go to class, skipping out is surprisingly common in many colleges. A survey conducted at three different types of institutions to measure absenteeism rates during a "typical" week of school found that 34 percent of students were absent at a medium-sized private university, 40 percent at a large public university, and 23 percent at a small liberal arts college (Romer, 1993). A survey at another university found that absenteeism averaged 20.7 percent and increased as the semester progressed (Marburger, 2001).

The evidence suggests that showing up to class does correlate with higher grades. A meta-analysis indicates that class attendance is also a very strong predictor of college grades even more so than scores on standardized admissions tests such as the SAT (Credé et al., 2010). One study attempted to quantify the effects of student absenteeism on performance by investigating the relationship between absenteeism and performance in an introductory economics class. The course was structured with three non-cumulative exams; each exam question was connected to the class period when the topic was covered. Students who were absent during the relevant class session were 14 percent more likely to get the corresponding questions wrong on the first two midterms and 7 percent more likely on the final (Marbuger, 2001). Overall, if students never had missed a class, their grade would have been slightly more than a quarter of a letter grade higher. While this study does not control for student characteristics, studies that do include student characteristics (i.e., prior GPA, gender, major, homework completion) find similar results (Romer, 1993; Dobkin, Gil, & Marion, 2010).

Absenteeism doesn't only affect the student who misses class. There is also suggestive evidence indicating that absenteeism of classmates can negatively affect the performance of other students within a course. Collaborative learning—involving students in team or group activities and discussions—is a common and effective teaching strategy. Koppenhaver (2006) finds that students who had team members absent from class performed worse on homework assignments and on exams. Therefore, increasing attendance can benefit not only the students who weren't coming to class but also other students in the course.

The decision by a student to attend class is often hampered by the lack of salience and of immediate rewards to attending class. Consider for example a student who attends class wherein an instructor lectures from presentation slides drawn directly from the textbook. The benefit of actually attending class might not be apparent as the student could get the same information from reading the book and looking at lecture slides posted on a course website. Additionally, if there is no assignment due, no quiz, no exam in class, the student receives no immediate benefit, or at least no immediate reward, for attending. Even if there are salient and immediate benefits from attending class, a present-biased student may face more compelling alternatives in the present moment that preclude class attendance. Consider a student who, the night before class, is invited to a social activity. The student knows that this activity may extend into the late hours of the night, thus making it more challenging to wake up for the 8 a.m. class. What should the student do? He knows the importance of going to class as that will lead to better grades, but the benefits of a night out are so immediate that any benefit in the future, even the next morning, are soon dismissed. Thus the student stays out late and doesn't wake up in time to attend class.

Participating

Getting students to class is not sufficient if they are not engaged once they are there. Student participation is such a core element of effective college pedagogy that the U.S. Department of Education commissioned a study in 1984 entitled "Involvement in Learning: Realizing the Potential of American Higher Education" (National Institute of Education, 1984). Subsequent studies have confirmed that "active learning" in the classroom improves student performance (Tinto, 1987; Nunn, 1996; Tinto, 1997; Billings & Hallstead, 2009). Efforts to improve teaching in college continue to promote the central importance of active participation by students in class. For example, the 2013 standards of the Association to Advance Collegiate Schools of Business state that course curricula will "facilitate and encourage active student engagement in learning" and "facilitate and encourage frequent student-student and student-faculty interaction designed to achieve learning goals" (AACSB, 2013). Yet often students find themselves in class with no apparent reason to do anything more than just sit there. There seems to be a disconnect from their participation in class to subsequent performance in class and progress toward a college degree.

What are the obstacles that impede students from active learning?[2] First, even in an environment conducive to active learning, students may resist active engagement, preferring a passive approach more akin to the traditional college class with a professor speaking and students taking notes: the "sage on the stage." These students feel they are learning, even though they are passive and would learn more if they were engaged in active learning (Benware & Deci, 1984). If they are interested and are learning, students may not recognize the need to learn *better*, especially if the current learning method meets their expectations for a college class. Instructors, meanwhile, may lack the skills to effectively draw these students out.

Second, in large classes it is simply not feasible for every student to participate regularly by asking a question or making a comment. Students recognize this and decide to let others raise their hands to respond to or ask questions. Third, research suggests that the dominant reason students do not proactively participate in class is that they lack the confidence to do so (Fassinger, 1995), and are particularly worried about peer approval (Weaver & Qi, 2005). Saying something they worry may be unintelligible in front of their peers, not communicating their ideas clearly, or even simply having to speak in front of others makes many students nervous. These studies find that higher levels of student preparation can improve confidence. However, even with proper preparation students may still choose not to participate because they perceive the risks of embarrassment outweigh the expected benefits.

Strategies and Incentives to Increase Studying, Attendance, and Participation

Systematic efforts to improve instruction are too rare in our colleges and universities (Bok, 2006). Our intent in suggesting specific interventions is to provide some initial ideas for consideration in the context of more comprehensive efforts to analyze student progress and identify strategies for improvement both inside and outside of the classroom. We discuss this important context more in the final section.

Strategies Directly Connected to Credit and Grades

Grades and course credit are behavioral devices invented as tools to send signals to students about what is important. If students are failing to engage in an important behavior, the first question should be whether the behavior should be linked directly, or more effectively, with a grade.

Assign homework and give credit: Assigning homework makes studying salient: effort spent out of class directly relates to overall performance in the course. Assigning the homework on a regular basis is a way to take the material that students are expected to learn and to narrowly bracket each task. Further, providing credit for the assignment provides immediate rewards (or penalties) if assignments are done correctly (or not). These immediate rewards can be used as short-term benchmarks towards a long-term goal (i.e., an exam), addressing the present-biasedness that students face.

A wrinkle that can be applied to assigning homework and providing credit is how the assessment of homework assignments is framed. Consider the following examples. First, "For each assignment completed, you will earn 5 percent towards your final grade." Second example, "For each assignment not turned in completed, you will lose 5 percent from your total grade. Thus missing just two assignments will lower your overall score by one letter grade." Both examples provide the same credit for completing assignments, but the second scenario frames it in such a way that the consequences of missing assignments are more salient. Further, it frames the assignments in such a way that not completing the assignment will cause the student to lose rather than gain credit. Individuals have a greater response to losing something they already have than gaining something new, so this simple twist in how the assignments are framed can have positive impacts on getting students to complete assignments.

While providing students with regular, graded assignments may lead to more time studying and engaging with class materials, one survey showed that almost one-third of courses do not provide credit for the completion of homework assignments (Grodner & Rupp, 2011). Why don't more courses require regular homework assignments? One of the primary limitations may be the time instructors have to invest in grading these assignments. Two potential strategies are: (1) assign homework but grade only completion (5 points for completing it, 0 if not). Then provide solutions for students to grade themselves. (2) Assign and collect regular homework assignments but only grade a random subset or assign and collect each homework assignment and grade only a subset of the questions. In both of these ways, students see the salient benefit from studying outside of class and are given immediate rewards for doing so, but the time required for grading is reduced.

Lost credit for non-attendance.[3] To promote more regular attendance in class, instructors can deduct credit from students for each class they miss or for missing a predetermined number of sessions. Many students dislike policies requiring attendance, but variations of this can be implemented. For example, Baylor University mandates that "a student must attend at least 75 percent of all scheduled class meetings. Any student who does not meet this minimal standard will automatically receive a grade of 'F' in the course" (Baylor, 2011). Eastern Florida State College (EFSC) requires students to attend 85 percent of classes to receive credit (EFSC, 2014). Lafayette College allows instructors to refer students who miss an excessive number of classes (as determined by the course syllabus) to the dean for a review assessment of the "student's commitment to the class" (Lafayette, n.d.).

Dobkin et al. (2010) demonstrated the effectiveness of a mandatory attendance rule implemented in the middle of the term for a subset of students: those who scored below the median on the midterm exam. Using a regression discontinuity approach (which compares students just below the median to students just above the median) the study shows that attendance increased by a whopping 28 percentage points as a result of making attendance mandatory for students who scored just below the median, and scores on the final exam increased significantly.

Credit for participation: Making class participation a part of the course grade has been shown to increase participation in class. In fact, multiple studies suggest that the level of participation is proportional to the amount it counts toward the final grade in the course (Berdine, 1986; Smith, 1992). If when students look at the syllabus they can see exactly how participation affects their grade, participation becomes more salient.

Credit for written comment or question: Students could be provided credit for turning in a question or comment written on a provided index card, or in an online forum. Foster et al. (2009) used this method to record participation in their study. This may be especially effective in large classes where there may not be time for every student to participate in class. It may also benefit small classes by encouraging students to prepare their comments or questions before vocalizing them. During class the instructor might ask for questions and students who have already written something may feel more confident about speaking up.

Online discussion groups have been shown to be effective in improving student performance in college courses (Cheng et al., 2011). Students could be rewarded for posing questions or discussion topics on the forum, and provided with extra rewards for the types of interactions that help to connect discussion threads and deepen learning for the group. Rewards can be structured to provide a large reward to encourage first-time participants and then provide smaller rewards for continued participation.

Strategies Indirectly Linked to Credit and Grades

It is not always necessary to micromanage student behavior by formally offering class credit. There are strategies that may be able to achieve similar results.

Social priming: The stereotype of the student who answers questions in class is the overachieving student in the front two rows who raises her hand at every opportunity possible. Or there is the student who asks a stupid question that causes everybody to laugh. These stereotypes are examples of descriptive norms—perceptions of behaviors that individuals perform. An instructor can provide a prime to modify this perception (Cialdini, 2003). An example of this kind of prime is a statement like, "students who ask questions are the ones who do the best on the exam." The statement gives insight that those who ask questions do better and students are asking questions during class and not those that fit the stereotypes. Another example is, "the best students in past semesters are those who participate in our small group discussions." Seeing others participate in group discussions can then help a student who wants to be one of the best students to participate in the class activity.

Along with priming with descriptive norms, a prime can be given to inform on injunctive norms. Injunctive norms "involve perceptions of which behaviors are typically approved or disapproved" (Cialdini, 2003). For example, "students who fail this course are those who come to class and use their cell phones instead of engaging in the lecture." While this kind of statement is directed towards disapproved behavior, it also introduces a caution on the hazards of priming. Students may hear the phrase "use their cell phones" and might perceive this as a descriptive norm—other students use cell phones in class—and adopt the undesired behavior. Caution is warranted when using primes to describe norms.

Just as priming can be used to affect attendance, it can also be used as a strategy aimed at increasing time that students spend studying. For example, the prime given can be directed at students who desire to do well in the course. The instructor can make a statement like, "Students with a schedule similar to yours set aside significant amounts of time to study outside of class." Or, "Those who get A's and B's set aside 2–3 hours for every hour they are in class." These statements describes a norm that students spend time outside of class studying, but also establishes an injunctive norm that 2–3 hours is required to earn an A or B.

Exam prep in class: Research indicates that attendance in class spikes the days before a midterm or final exam (Romer, 1993). One way to make the benefits of attending class more salient for students is to be more explicit about exam preparation being a part of every class throughout the semester rather than on a specific day before the exam. Students may be more motivated to attend class when they know material on an exam will be discussed. Using phrases like, "this would be a good test question" or "this might be something you will see on the midterm" may help make the benefits of attending class more salient for students. Doing this on a daily basis makes each class period provide a well-defined benefit for the students, preparation for an exam.

Quizzes: Many instructors already provide rewards for students who show up to class. One of the more common rewards used for attendance is the use of pop quizzes. Unannounced quizzes can increase attendance in classes (Wilder, Flood, & Stromsnes, 2001). Frequent unannounced quizzes for extra credit may be particularly effective (Thorne, 2000). Similar quizzes worth minimal class credit have also been shown to increase student motivation to attend class (Kouyoumdjian, 2004). These studies indicate that for quizzes to be effective in encouraging attendance they should be frequent and unannounced, but need not be worth a significant number of points.

Aiding and Prompting Strategies

Another type of strategy to influence behavior is to create the educational equivalent of tying a string around your finger or leaving a note on the refrigerator.

Peer nudges: The University of Tennessee at Chattanooga has implemented a Freshmen Academic Success Tracking program (FAST) to make the benefits of attending class more salient. The FAST program identifies students who miss two or more classes in a term and reaches out to "gently nudge them back on course." The program has peers talk with students face-to-face, explaining the "connection between attending class and academic success." Introduction of the program was associated with the highest ever recorded average freshmen GPA and a fall-to-spring retention increase of seven percent (McClane, 2009).

Distraction limit: Even when students sit down to study or work on assignments, they can often be easily distracted by the electronic addiction: updating your social media page, checking the score of the game, finding out if Kevin Bacon really was in that movie, or even reading the news. These can all distract students from effectively studying. In an intervention to keep students on task, Patterson (2014) utilizes software where students pre-commit to the amount of "distraction" time when studying for an online course. Prior to beginning an assignment, the student determines the amount of distraction time available, e.g., 30 minutes. As students leave the course website for distraction time, once the time limit is reached, they receive a reminder of their commitment and then all other websites are blocked until the assignment is finished. Students can provide a reason and unblock websites, but must do so on a site-by-site basis. Using a pre-commitment device like this can help overcome time-inconsistent preferences and help students stay actively engaged in studying.

Note cards: In large classes, expecting each student to participate may simply be infeasible and impractical. So rather than have students participate vocally, note cards can be used instead (or electronic equivalents). Students can participate in class by putting a comment or question on a note card and handing the note card in. Note cards can be turned in for credit or they can be used as entries into a lottery drawing, with each note card serving as an entry. At the end of class, the instructor pulls one note card at random and the winner receives a reward. The use of a daily note card then further highlights how participation affects grades by narrowly bracketing and rewarding the note card as a form of class participation.

This method provides a way for students to participate without having to bear the costs of how they are perceived by their peers. It allows them time to formulate their thoughts and communicate them in a non-threatening way instead of being called upon in front of the entire class. It also is a method that can be used in large classrooms, where time does not make it feasible for every student to participate.

Other variants can be added to reward active engagement in learning. When a card is drawn there can be a quality control measure to validate the note card as a winner (e.g., it must answer the question or provide a contribution to the discussion). Furthermore, note cards can be collected more than once per class period to ensure that students stay actively engaged the whole class period.

Using Monetary Rewards

There can sometimes be a negative reaction to the idea of using money to influence school behaviors. While the concerns should not be completely dismissed, it is important to recognize that monetary rewards already play a major role in higher education: for example, students are offered scholarships or discounts based on grades and test scores (sometimes linked to studying particular topics), or they receive greater subsidies for enrolling full-time, enrolling immediately after high school graduation, or for enrolling in their home state. The money is already linked to choices and behaviors. The strategies we describe are simply more specific to key behaviors.

Study-time wage: Providing a set location for students to study allows them to work on assignments individually or in groups as needed. One of the reasons students may fail to finish homework is that they have job responsibilities in addition to the courses in which they enroll. In order for financial incentives to induce the desired behavior, it may be necessary for them to be substantial enough (to account for opportunity cost) and more certain (salient) than, say, the higher future earnings that may come after graduating. This could be achieved by paying for the time spent in a study area or academic support center as if it were an hourly wage. (The rate need not necessarily be as a high as a wage since there are benefits to studying beyond the payment).

Reward for keeping a study log: Sometimes just by keeping track of something, people are more attentive to it. Students can be rewarded for keeping a study log by, for example, making it a requirement of scholarship programs. It could be based on time and subject, or could ask for a brief reflection on the value of the activity. The information could be used by administrators or scholarship programs to identify the student's needs and ways the institution and instructors could better support students.

Pay for attendance: Financial aid and other subsidies (such as in-state tuition) are provided based on the assumption that a student actually goes to college. One way to make the benefits of attending class more salient as well as immediate would be to condition a payment or financial aid on attendance. By having students "earn" their subsidy for each class attended, or by reaching attendance milestones, the importance of showing up is made more salient.

Conditioning aid on attendance may well be too high stakes, with potential unintended consequences. A different approach would be to offer small rewards, either directly or through a lottery for attending class. A lottery can be more cost-effective than directly paying students because individuals are not very good at assessing low probabilities, imagining that very low probabilities are more likely than they actually are (Kahneman & Tversky, 1979). Routinely, individuals overestimate the value of the reward. Students are no different. Consider the two scenarios in a class with 100 students. Scenario 1: each day you come to class you earn 25 cents. Scenario 2: each day you come to class there will be a lottery where the winner will earn $10 in cash. Which would you choose? The value of the prize in the first scenario is known with certainty, 25 cents. The second scenario is based on the probability of winning. Assuming that all 100 students are in class, there is a 1/100 chance of winning $10, or if you multiply those numbers together, your expected winning each day is 10 cents. Clearly not as good as 25 cents, but many choose the latter because they overestimate the probability that they will be that winner. As a result, each student could get a lottery entry for every class attended (or some variant of class attendance) as an immediate salient reward for attending class.

Multiple Motivations and Complex Causation

While students may *enter* college because they know it's good to have a degree, they may *stay* in part because they like the people they are spending time with and they feel good about themselves. If they feel disconnected socially, they are more likely to leave.[4] The motivations that can influence what students do and don't do in college are complicated, certainly at least as challenging and nuanced as this summary of the complex and highly individualistic psychology of motivation in the workplace:

> [P]eople will be better motivated if . . . incentive schemes are designed by making use of their understood needs and wants; the rewards are linked to efforts; the performance goal is challenging and individuals accept and are committed to it; the rewards are perceived to be equitable; people feel confident they can perform better; the incentive schemes are in line with both expectations and the individual's goals and values; the incentive scheme design takes into consideration outcome uncertainty that may be unrelated to the effort contribution; and a model of positive leadership can be provided in the process of performance.
>
> *(Liu and Mills, 2007)*

While present-biasedness and the inadequate salience of particular tasks are worthy of attention, one hazard of an overly myopic approach would be to blame students for what are actually failures of a college. For example, once students start college, they learn more about the amount of time and effort they need to commit in order to pass, or to earn high grades. They may begin to doubt their own abilities, or to recalculate their initial thoughts about the costs and benefits of college, which may lead them to drop out. Is the decision to drop out, after recalculating based on better information, a "rational" decision that should be accepted? The question itself ignores the responsibility of the college and its faculty to pay attention to the more nuanced student motivations, including confidence and self-esteem. Effective instructors help students feel like they are making real progress, from wherever they are starting. Interpersonal strategies tied to specific assignments can be more effective than mass implementation of external incentives. For example, an instructor may tell a student that his ideas matter and he would really like him to speak up more in class discussions. If that doesn't work because the student is nervous, the instructor might help the student prepare before class by telling him what he will call on him to discuss, or having him write down some thoughts. The way an instructor manages student participation can serve as a promotion or deterrent to future participation.[5]

Effective instructors—those who simultaneously inspire, challenge, and support students—contribute to higher rates of attendance.[6] While strategies like smaller class sizes do not guarantee better, more interactive and personalized learning, they do make them more likely and more possible, and have been shown to decrease absenteeism (Devadoss & Foltz, 1996; Romer, 1993). Further, it should be no surprise that colleges with higher graduation rates tend to have built a lot of social and academic supports that surround students.

The behavioral strategies we have laid out are best employed in the context of efforts to consider the broad array of factors that motivate students to engage and learn in college. Encouraging students to study more, attend class, and participate more actively have been and will continue to be part and parcel of efforts to improve instruction and the overall design of the college experience. The concrete and psychologically-informed approaches we highlight can be important elements of faculty and administrators' ongoing efforts to provide an enriching education for all students.

Notes

1. Loss aversion is sometimes referred to as the "endowment effect"—the tendency to fight harder to keep what you feel you have rather than to gain the same item. For example, most people will demand more to give up their concert tickets than they would be willing to pay in the first place.
2. For ease of measurement, all of the studies cited below define "active" engagement as whether a student vocally participates in class—that is, asks a question or makes a comment. Some give credit for participating once, while others measure intensity by considering the number of times a student participated. Since there is evidence that grading based on participation can lead to discussions dominated by a small number of students (Michael, 2006), it may be useful to base incentives on participating at least once. Over longer periods, however, encouraging more intensive involvement may be the better approach.
3. Keeping track of attendance might seem tedious, especially if the instructor is responsible for marking and tracking the attendance of each student. Technology provides mediums which allows attendance to be recorded in the largest of classes with little to no instructor involvement. One example are clicker devices—specific devices that a student purchases that link a given student to the clicker and the class. Other examples can rely on students using their own phones or mobile devices. There are many websites and other software which allows students to link their cell phone number to their roster id in a given class. So attendance can be monitored by simply writing a number of the board and asking students to text or enter that number using their phone.
4. Careful readers may have noticed a curious item on the list of statistically-significant correlates of student success on pages [128–129]: alcohol consumption is positively associated with completing a college degree. While the correlation does not prove causation (perhaps those who are already inclined to drink are also more academically committed), there is some logic to the idea that drinking does play a role. A logical explanation for the positive association of alcohol use with college completion is that it plays a role in social bonding. One downside among many is that alcohol consumption is negatively correlated with students' grades.
5. Loftin, Davis, and Hartin (2010) discuss specific actions of faculty during class which impede students from participating. These include both verbal and nonverbal actions: ridiculing or disregarding student comments, not providing adequate time for responses or interjections, answering questions with questions, negative body language, and facially expressing displeasure. Students participate more if the instructor moves around the classroom to be in closer physical proximity.

6. Weaver and Qi (2005) find that "faculty-student interaction seems to have the largest direct, indirect, and total effects on participation as reported by students." Fassinger (1995) added that the faculty's greatest impact on class participation comes from course designs. Therefore, changing the design of the class, from a talk-and-chalk lecture to one involving students more in the learning process through class exercises, activities, or discussion, can be an effective way to actively engage students in the learning process.

References

AACSB. (2013). The Association to Advance Collegiate Schools of Business. www.aacsb.edu/accreditation/business/standards/2013/ viewed on May 6, 2013.

Astin, A. (1993). *What matters in college: Four critical years revisited.* San Francisco, CA: Jossey-Bass.

Babcock, P., & Marks, M. (2010). Leisure college, USA: The decline in student study time. *American Enterprise Institute for Public Policy Research, 7*, 1–7.

Baylor University. (2011). Attendance policy. Retrieved from www.baylor.edu/artsandsciences/index.php?id=86320

Benware, C. A., & Deci, E. L. (1984). Quality of learning with an active versus passive motivational set. *American Educational Research Journal, 21*(4), 755–765.

Berdine, R. (1986). Why some students fail to participate in class. *Marketing News, 20*(15), 23–24.

Bok, D. (2006) *Our underachieving colleges: A candid look at how much students learn, and why they should be learning more.* Princeton, NJ: Princeton University Press.

Cheng, C. K., Paré, D. E., Collimore, L. M., & Joordens, S. (2011). Assessing the effectiveness of a voluntary online discussion forum on improving students' course performance. *Computers & Education, 56*(1), 253–261.

Cialdini, R. B. (2003). Crafting normative messages to protect the environment. *Current Directions in Psychological Science, 12*(4), 105–109.

Credé, M., Roch, S. G., & Kieszczynka, U. M. (2010). Class attendance in college a meta-analytic review of the relationship of class attendance with grades and student characteristics. *Review of Educational Research, 80*(2), 272–295.

DellaVigna, S., & Malmendier, U. (2006). Paying not to go to the gym. *American Economic Review*, 694–719.

Devadoss, S., & Foltz, J. (1996). Evaluation of factors influencing student class attendance and performance. *American Journal of Agricultural Economics, 78*(3), 499–507.

Dobkin, C., Gil, R., & Marion, J. (2010). Skipping class in college and exam performance: Evidence from a regression discontinuity classroom experiment. *Economics of Education Review, 29*(4), 566–575.

Downs, J. S., & Lewenstein, G. (2011). Behavioral economics and obesity. In J. Cawley (Ed.), *The Oxford Handbook of the Social Science of Obesity.* New York, NY: Oxford University Press.

EFSC. (2014). Eastern Florida State College Attendance Policy. Retrieved December 30, 2014. Retrieved from www.easternflorida.edu/admissions/registrars-office/attendance-policy.cfm

Eren, O., & Henderson, D. J. (2008). The impact of homework on student achievement. *Econometrics Journal, 11*(2), 326–348.

Fassinger, P. A. (1995). Understanding classroom interaction: Students' and professors' contributions to students' silence. *Journal of Higher Education, 66*(1), 82.

Foster, L. N., Krohn, K. R., McCleary, D. F., Aspiranti, K. B., Nalls, M. L., Quillivan, C. C., & Williams, R. L. (2009). Increasing low-responding students' participation in class discussion. *Journal of Behavioral Education, 18*(2), 173–188.

Fredrick, W. C., & Walberg, H. J. (1980). Learning as a function of time. *Journal of Educational Research*, 183–194.

Grodner, A., & Rupp, N. (2011). The role of homework on student learning outcomes: Evidence from a field experiment. http://papers.ssrn.com/sol3/papers.cfm?abstract_id=1592889

Halstead, J. A., & Billings, D. M. (2009). Teaching and learning in online learning communities. In D. M. Billings & J. A. Halstead (Eds.), *Teaching in nursing: A guide for faculty*, 369–387. St. Louis, MO: Elsevier.

Just, D. & Price, J. P. (2013). Using *Incentives to Encourage Healthy Eating in Children. Journal of Human Resources, 48*(4), 855–872.

Kahneman, D., & Tversky, A. (1979). Prospect theory: An analysis of decision under risk. *Econometrica, 47*(2), 263–292.

Koppenhaver, G. D. (2006). Absent and accounted for: Absenteeism and cooperative learning. *Decision Sciences Journal of Innovative Education, 4*(1), 29–49.

Kouyoumdjian, H. (2004). Influence of unannounced quizzes and cumulative exam on attendance and study behavior. *Behavior Analyst, 14*, 229–239.

Lafayette College. (n.d.). Class attendance policies. Retrieved from http://deanofthecollege.lafayette.edu/advising-network/deans-excuse

Levitt, S. D., List, J. A., Neckermann, S., & Sadoff, S. (2012). *The behavioralist goes to school: Leveraging behavioral economics to improve educational performance* (No. w18165). National Bureau of Economic Research.

Liu, X., & Mills, A. (2007). Motivation and performance related pay. In Preker, A. S. (Ed), *Public ends, private means: strategic purchasing of health services* (pp. 237–258). New York, NY: World Bank Publications.

Loftin, C., Davis, L. A., & Hartin, V. (2010). Classroom participation: A student perspective. *Teaching and Learning in Nursing, 5*(3), 119–124.

Marburger, D. R. (2001). Absenteeism and undergraduate exam performance. *Journal of Economic Education, 32*(2), 99–109.

McClane, J. G. (2009). Novel idea: Go to class. Retrieved from www.timesfreepress.com/news/news/story/2009/oct/06/novel-idea-go-to-class/237590/

Michael, J. (2006). Where's the evidence that active learning works? *Advances in Physiology Education, 30*, 159–167.

National Center for Education Statistics. (2012). Digest of Education Statistics, Table 345. nces.ed.gov/programs/digest/d11/tables/dt11_345.asp

National Institute of Education (U.S.). Study Group on the Conditions of Excellence in American Higher Education. (1984). *Involvement in learning: realizing the potential of American higher education: final report of the Study Group on the Conditions of Excellence in American Higher Education.* National Institute of Education, U.S. Department of Education.

Nunn, C. E. (1996). Discussion in the college classroom: Triangulating observational and survey results. *Journal of Higher Education*, 243–266.

Patterson, R. W. (2014). Identifying and Addressing self-control problems for online students: evidence from a field experiment. Paper Presented at Western Economic Association International Annual Meetings, Denver, CO. Retrieved from https://88bbbbb8-a-62cb3a1a-s-sites.googlegroups.com/site/richpattersoncornell/PattersonJMP11_23.pdf

Pope, D. G., & Schweitzer, M. E. (2011). Is Tiger Woods loss averse? Persistent bias in the face of experience, competition, and high stakes. *American Economic Review*, *101*(1), 129–157.

Read, D., Loewenstein, G., Rabin, M., Keren, G., & Laibson, D. (1999). Choice bracketing. In *Elicitation of Preferences* (pp. 171–202). Springer Netherlands.

Romer, D. (1993). Do students go to class? Should they? *Journal of Economic Perspectives*, 7(3), 167–174.

Royer, H., Stehr, M. F., & Sydnor, J. R. (2012). *Incentives, commitments and habit formation in exercise: Evidence from a field experiment with workers at a Fortune-500 company* (No. w18580). National Bureau of Economic Research.

Smith, D. H. (1992). Encouraging students' participation in large classes: A modest proposal. *Teaching Sociology*, *20*(4), 337–339.

Tarrant County College. (2013). Tarrant County College Mandatory Attendance Policy. www.tccd.edu/Courses_and_Programs/Mandatory_Attendance.html

Thorne, B. M. (2000). Extra credit exercise: A painless pop quiz. *Teaching of Psychology*, 27 (3), 204–205.

Tinto, V. (1987). *Leaving college: Rethinking the causes and cures of student attrition*. Chicago, IL: University of Chicago Press.

Tinto, V. (1997). Classrooms as communities: Exploring the educational character of student persistence. *Journal of Higher Education*, 599–623.

Weaver, R. R., & Qi, J. (2005). Classroom organization and participation: College students' perceptions. *Journal of Higher Education*, *76*(5), 570–601.

Wilder, D. A., Flood, W. A., & Stromsnes, W. (2001). The use of random extra credit quizzes to increase student attendance. *Journal of Instructional Psychology*, *28*(2), 117–120.

8

BEHAVIORAL NUDGES FOR COLLEGE SUCCESS

Research, Impact, and Possibilities

Jill Frankfort, Ross E. O'Hara, and Kenneth Salim

Introduction

A college degree remains a crucial stepping-stone for upward economic mobility. As college graduates continue to outperform less-educated peers on multiple measures of economic well-being, including employment rates and personal earnings, increasing college completion rates is an issue of utmost importance for our country's students and our economic future (Pew Research Center, 2014). To achieve this goal, higher education institutions must determine how to effectively support students from orientation to graduation at the same time that students are entering and returning to college in greater numbers than ever before (Hussar & Bailey, 2014). Moreover, as the non-traditional college student—the adult learner returning to college, the first-generation college-goer, the online learner—becomes the norm, colleges and universities must determine how best to help an increasingly wide-ranging population of students who need differentiated support to reach graduation.

In this context, a critical question for higher education administrators is: Why do some students withdraw, and what can we do about it? Among first-time full-time students, only 59 percent of those who enroll in a four-year degree program graduate from the institution in which they first enrolled within six years, and only 31 percent of those who enroll at two-year institutions earn an associate's degree within three years (U.S. Department of Education, 2013). Graduation rates are, on average, even lower for black, Hispanic, and low-income students (Knapp, Kelly-Reid, & Ginder, 2012). While some students withdraw from college for financial reasons or because of academic struggles, there is a population of students who fail to persist because they lack the academic behaviors and mindsets necessary to succeed—characteristics referred to as non-cognitive factors

(Farrington, 2012). There is growing evidence that non-cognitive factors such as students' level of commitment to earning a college degree, ability to manage time effectively, study habits, and confidence in being successful in an academic environment have a substantial influence on persistence and degree completion (Lotkowski, Robbins, & Noeth, 2004).

Supporting students in these non-cognitive domains and helping them to develop new academic behaviors and mindsets are not simple objectives. However, concepts from the field of behavioral science have facilitated behavior change in a range of contexts and lend themselves to thinking about how to cultivate these non-cognitive factors. For example, the placement of less healthy foods in the interior of a salad bar where they are more difficult to reach lowers consumption of those items by up to 16 percent compared to when they are placed in the front (Rozin et al., 2011). Also, informing a student that they shared the same birthday as a recent graduate from the math department significantly increased their motivation and persistence on a subsequent math task (Walton, Cohen, Cwir, & Spencer, 2012). From public health to environmental conservancy to education, researchers have shown that small changes based on behavioral principles—"nudges"—can benefit individuals and society without restricting personal choice (Thaler & Sunstein, 2008). This idea is so powerful that in 2010 United Kingdom Prime Minister David Cameron established the Behavioral Insights Team—nicknamed "the Nudge unit"—to develop low-touch and low-cost interventions for improving problems facing their nation (Bennhold, 2013).

In this chapter, we first describe the challenges facing colleges today in finding effective ways to support and retain a heterogeneous population of students, as recounted from our discussions with higher education administrators at two-year and four-year institutions across the country.[1] We then address how insights from behavioral science can reshape how institutions approach student support. Next we discuss models of student support that utilize lessons learned from behavioral science, including the approach piloted by our organization, Persistence Plus. We conclude by addressing future considerations for institutions and behavioral researchers in applying behavioral science to the challenge of college completion.

The Challenge for College Administrators

Attrition runs contrary to the mission of colleges and universities, which is to improve the life prospects of their students. Moreover, student withdrawals harm institutions by damaging their reputations and costing them valuable tuition revenue. Freshman attrition alone costs higher education institutions $8.4 billion in net tuition revenue over five years (Schneider, 2010) and in 2010–11, four-year colleges lost $16.5 billion due to overall attrition (Raisman, 2013). As a result, colleges are actively looking for ways to boost tuition dollars and lower recruitment costs through even small retention gains. As one provost at a large four-year public university shared, "We are delighted if we increase our yearly retention rate by 1 percent," while another senior administrator talked about the importance of "moving the needle just a little" on retention.

Yet, in our discussions with more than a hundred higher education administrators at two-year and four-year institutions, we have heard countless challenges that confront colleges and universities as they try to reduce attrition. While many administrators voiced concerns about the financial impact of student attrition, they also noted the difficulty of reaching and engaging with students in a cost-effective manner and the challenge of scaling innovative support models. One college dean expressed dismay with the system of reaching out to students who receive poor midterm grades saying, "At that point, it is far [too] late." College administrators also have shared their frustrations with outdated models of engaging with and supporting students: "Students just don't check their personal emails, let alone the college email addresses we provide them," shared one academic dean at a two-year institution. Student support staff as well are looking for new ways of interacting with students: "We need to move away from a model of information saturation as a way of communicating with our students. We need to diagnose student weaknesses and tailor our supports better," noted a senior academic administrator at a large public university.

Schools also struggle with the underutilization of traditional on-campus supports, including tutoring centers and academic advisors. "Students either don't know about these resources or don't know how to take advantage. We are looking for ways to eliminate the barriers that prevent students from seeking out these resources," explained another college dean. Another administrator at a community college noted that all too often, students feel uncomfortable using these services because they erroneously believe that using these resources would mean they are not worthy of college.

One way in which institutions are now addressing these challenges is through new models of student support that utilize insights from behavioral science to influence students' behaviors and beliefs in such a way as to promote college success. In the following section, we outline some of the academic research from inside and outside the education sector that highlights how behavioral nudges may be applicable to many of the challenges facing higher education today.

Nudging Goes a Long Way

Conventional wisdom suggests that significant lifestyle changes are often necessary to realize goals we have set for ourselves. Yet, in recent years, research has shown that low-touch interventions that leverage behavioral mechanisms can dramatically influence behavior and mindsets, often with lasting effects. These findings are not limited by sector or to the laboratory: from energy reduction to voter engagement to education, field experiments have shown that nudges—easy and low-cost interventions that influence people's behavior or perspectives but preserve personal choice—can lead to improved outcomes for individuals and society. In the following, we highlight four levers that show significant promise for shaping student outcomes in higher education: social norms, social belonging, implementation intentions, and growth mindsets.

Social Norming of Behaviors

No matter a student's background, success in college requires learning "the rules of the game" (Bourdieu & Wacquant, 1992). Unfortunately, these rules are largely taken for granted by institutions, leaving many students confused as to what constitutes appropriate behavior and adequate performance in college. When lacking objective criteria, individuals often observe the behavior of others for information, a process known as social norming (Cialdini et al., 2006). Social norms are a powerful way to influence behavior. We want to act the way others act—whether consciously or unconsciously—and when we know what others are doing, particularly those like us, we are likely to follow.

For example, knowing the energy usage habits of our neighbors encourages us to reduce our own energy expenditure (Alcott & Mullainathan, 2010). OPower is a company that offers a suite of services to utilities providers. Of particular relevance is their use of social norming, among other behavioral mechanisms, to reduce people's energy use. When households receive their bill, it not only displays their own energy use, but also compares their use to that of their most energy-efficient neighbors. Randomized experiments have shown OPower reduces household energy use by up to 3 percent (Alcott 2009; Ayres, Raseman, & Shih, 2009). Although the effect on each individual is small (an annual savings of about $25 per household), compounding those minor changes in behavior across the hundreds of thousands of customers served by a single utility provider, the environmental benefits are impressive: a reduction in carbon emissions equivalent to over 14 million gallons of gasoline burned.

Even the behavior of complete strangers can change the way we act. If you have stayed in a hotel in recent years, you no doubt have seen signs hanging in the bathroom asking guests to reuse their towels. These requests often appeal to environmental concerns: For instance, the JW Marriott hotel towel reuse sign (shown on Hotelchatter, 2013) proclaims "Save Our Planet. Every day million of gallons of water are used to wash that towels that have only been used once. You make the difference: A towel hanging up means 'I will use again.' Thank you for helping us conserve the Earth's Vital Resources." Goldstein, Cialdini, and Griskevicius (2008), however, suspected that these social mission appeals were not the most effective way to encourage towel reuse in hotels. In their experiment, they randomly placed different towel reuse signs in different rooms in a hotel. Although all signs mentioned the environmental benefits of reusing towels, only some signs provided social norms information, such as "Almost 75 percent of guests who are asked to participate in our new resource savings program do help by using their towels more than once." They found that guests were more likely to reuse their towels when staying in a room that included the social norms information. In fact, towel reuse increased 33 percent when the sign indicated that the majority of prior guests in that specific room reused their towels (Goldstein et al., 2008).

Together, these studies speak to the potential utility of using social norms to teach college students "the rules of the game." These approaches are familiar on many college campuses, as they have been a primary method by which schools have combated excessive alcohol use (Borsari & Carey, 2003; Wechsler et al., 2003). When applying this lever, however, it is important to select appropriate norms. First, a social norms message may change performance of a behavior by implying that a behavior is common or uncommon. For example, signs in the Petrified Forest National Park in Arizona which read "Your heritage is being vandalized every day by theft losses of petrified wood of 14 tons a year, mostly a small piece at a time" appeared to do little to stop theft (and may have even increased it) by telling people that "everybody does it" (Cialdini, 2003). Social norms messages that imply that a productive behavior is uncommon among students, such as visiting the tutoring center, could therefore reinforce students' unwillingness to utilize this resource. Moreover, norms must be carefully selected for their target audience as they can influence behavior for better or for worse. For example, a norm that signifies to individuals that they use less energy than the average homeowner can lead to an increase in consumption (Ayres, Raseman, & Shih, 2009). Inadvertently telling some students that they study more than the average student, therefore, could lead to a reduction in study time. Despite these caveats, social norms strategies may be an effective means by which to promote behaviors associated with college student success such as going to professors' office hours, using the college's tutoring center, or renewing financial aid. For first-generation and low-income students who may not be familiar with or know the benefit of such steps, leveraging social norms should have powerful effects.

Social Belonging

The power of social norms is predicated on the core human motivation to belong to social groups (Baumeister & Leary, 1995). Whether a student feels that their need to belong can be satisfied at their institution—or, for that matter, any higher education institution—can have important consequences for their persistence. A meta-analysis of over 100 studies examining over 26,000 college students showed social belonging to be a primary predictor of retention (Robbins et al., 2004). Unfortunately, underrepresented students may have a more difficult time developing a sense of belonging in college due to the implicit biases they face based on their race/ethnicity, gender, or socioeconomic background. Research on stereotype threat demonstrates that when individuals are aware of negative stereotypes about their own group, they become cognitively occupied with avoiding behaviors that may confirm that stereotype, either to themselves or to others (Steele & Aronson, 1995). Ironically, this vigilance against confirming the stereotype often leads the individual to act in a stereotype-consistent manner. On college campuses, this threat is sometimes felt by racial and ethnic minorities, low-income students, and first-generation students, who can be stereotyped as academically inferior (Croizet & Claire, 1998; Sherman et al. 2013); the same threat exists for women specifically in STEM fields (Spencer, Steele, & Quinn, 1999).

Small interventions that target students' thoughts and feelings surrounding social belonging have had striking effects on achievement even over months and years (Yeager & Walton, 2011). For example, an intervention designed to buttress African American college students' sense of belonging in college increased the GPA of these students over the next year (Walton & Cohen, 2007). In this study, first-year African American students read survey results provided by African American and white juniors and seniors, including specific quotations sharing how when these students first came to college, they felt like they were not connecting with peers or faculty members, but that over time these issues got much better. The first-year students then wrote their own essays and gave video-recorded speeches about how the transition to college can produce temporary challenges. This short intervention increased target students' sense of academic fit while also buffering their sense of fit against daily adversity—presumably by helping students see challenges during the start of college as universal rather than interpreting these challenges as signs that they themselves did not belong in college.

A similar intervention showed similar benefits for first-generation college students (Stephens, Hamedani, & Destin, 2014). In this study, incoming students were randomly assigned to one of two discussion panels comprised of junior and senior students discussing their transitions to college. The only difference between panels was that in one setting panelists emphasized how their particular backgrounds (e.g., first-generation, low-income) shaped their transition experiences. Students who attended this version of the panel showed higher usage of campus resources (e.g., meeting with professors), which, in turn, led to higher grade point averages compared to the control condition. These studies demonstrate not only the importance of encouraging social belonging among college students, but also the myriad of non-cognitive factors that can be influenced by small interventions.

Planning Behavior: Implementation Intention

Successfully navigating college requires impressive planning and time management skills. If balancing the demands of multiple classes was not enough, more college students than ever are working in paid employment and taking care of family. Studies have shown that implementation intention prompts, which nudge individuals to commit to a specific time and place to complete a task, significantly increase the likelihood that a task will be completed or goal achieved. In one such study, individuals who received mailings about the schedule of free flu shot clinics that prompted them to write down the date and time they planned to attend had a 4.2 percentage point higher vaccination rate than individuals who received mailings that just listed the schedule of the clinics (Milkman et al., 2011). By associating a novel behavior with an already routine one (e.g., "I will get my flu shot after I eat lunch"), performance of the desired behavior no longer requires volitional control; rather, the behavior is automatically triggered by the relevant environment cues (Gollwitzer, 1999).

In another study, a random sample of unlikely voters (i.e., individuals who had participated in one or fewer primary elections since 2000) received robo-calls shortly before the 2008 Pennsylvania Democratic presidential primary (Nickerson & Rogers, 2010). These calls asked "Around what time do you expect to head to the polls on Tuesday? Where do you expect you will be coming from when you come to the polls on Tuesday? What do you think you will be doing before you head out to the polls?" Voters who lived alone and received a robo-call had voting turnout rates nearly 10 percentage points higher than voters who lived alone and did not receive such a call. What was particularly interesting is that these calls had no impact on voters living in multi-person households, suggesting that voters in these households were already discussing these questions as they planned their Election Day schedules with their spouses, partners, or roommates (e.g., "We can go together after dinner"). This study highlights the power that automated prompts focused on helping individuals plan their schedules can have on promoting a desired behavior. Applied to higher education, the utility of implementation intentions is evident for students who must schedule and execute plans to study, complete assignments, and visit professors or tutors for extra help, all while juggling demands outside of the academic realm.

Growth Mindsets

Poor planning is not the only non-cognitive factor that may inhibit students from seeking help with their academic difficulties. Academic help-seeking is a multistage process that can be undermined at many points, such as students not realizing they need help or not knowing where to turn for help (Karabenick & Dembo, 2011). Equally derailing are students' beliefs surrounding help-seeking—specifically, that to ask for help would indicate one's own inadequacy (Ryan, Pintrich, & Midgley, 2001). As previously noted by college administrators, too many students believe visiting a professor or tutor for help indicates that they are not worthy of college, instead of viewing help-seeking as an integral part of the college experience.

This association between help-seeking and inadequacy relates to Carol Dweck's (2007) seminal work on theories of intelligence. Individuals who believe intelligence is an inborn trait—a "fixed mindset"—are unlikely to seek help because doing so would indicate their own natural deficiencies. Moreover, these individuals tend to believe that effort is unrelated to performance. When faced with academic challenges, individuals with a fixed mindset tend to give up because they assume that they "just don't get it." Individuals who instead believe that intelligence is malleable and can be improved with practice—a "growth mindset"—are more likely to persevere through academic struggles. These individuals believe that effort is correlated with success and that seeking help is a normal (and, therefore, non-threatening) part of the learning process.

Dweck and several others have shown that small behavioral interventions can effectively teach students of all different ages and backgrounds to internalize a growth mindset and subsequently improve their academic performance. For example, college students in one study were led to believe that they were partici-pating in a pen pal program to mentor at-risk middle school students (Aronson, Fried, & Good, 2002). In one condition, undergraduates were instructed to tell their pen pals that intelligence is malleable, whereas in a second condition students wrote to their pen pals about the theory of multiple intelligences. Students who wrote about a growth mindset were more likely to believe that intelligence is malleable one year later, and this change led to higher GPAs than students in the comparison group. These effects were particularly pronounced for African American students, a difference which may be indirectly related to stereotype threat. Stereotypes, by their very nature, assume fixed traits among a group of people. African American students may be more likely to have internalized a fixed mindset due to repeated experiences with negative stereotypes (i.e., African Americans are unintelligent). These types of interventions, therefore, have shown particular promise for helping members of stereotyped groups improve their academic performance (Yeager & Walton, 2011)

Although not an exhaustive list, these principles of behavioral science present a wealth of possibilities for how colleges and universities could adapt their sup-port services to better foster students' non-cognitive abilities. In the following section, we discuss a range of innovative support models employed by various universities to increase student persistence and performance. The next section concludes with a description of two case studies in which we have piloted our approach, Persistence Plus, a mobile-based service that leverages these behavioral mechanisms to encourage student motivation, perseverance, and success.

Innovative Approaches to Improving Retention

Success Coaches

Success coaches counsel students on academic decisions and school and life chal-lenges. While many colleges have staff charged with these roles, some colleges contract with outside vendors that use a call center model to connect with students during their first years of college. For example, one company, InsideTrack, offers access to professional success coaches who proactively reach out to students to provide one-on-one counseling. A one-year, randomized control trial showed this call-center coaching model to be quite successful: across eight diverse institutions that included a wide range of student samples, many of whom were considered 'at-risk,' college retention was 12 percentage points higher among the treatment group at the end of treatment, and 15 percentage points higher one year after the treatment had ceased (Bettinger & Baker, 2011).

While this approach can relieve the burden on institutional staff, the high-touch nature of this support can be expensive for higher education budgets. As one provost at a two-year public school employing such practices explained to us, "We are only piloting with small numbers because of the cost. How do we scale this up to all of our students?" This sentiment was echoed by a senior vice provost at a large four-year public research university who explained that he needs to provide support to the thousands of students attending his institution and so can only implement options for which the per-student costs are feasible for the university's budget. Moreover, further research is necessary to determine the non-cognitive factors affected by success coaching. Despite the financial restrictions, success coaches appear to be an effective means of increasing student persistence.

Early Alert Systems and Predictive Analytics

Early alert and predictive analytics vendors help colleges identify at-risk students and manage outreach to these students. One system that was developed initially by a public university uses data analytics to flag struggling students and facilitate communication between these students and their advisors (Arnold & Pistilli, 2012). The system classifies students' likelihood of success in a class using an algorithm that weighs students' current course performance, prior academic performance, interaction with online resources, and demographics. Professors can utilize this information to intervene with students electronically or in-person (e.g., scheduling an advising appointment or referral to other campus resources). The system also provides ongoing feedback to students at the instructor's discretion so that students remain aware of their likelihood for success in a course.

This system offers promising results: across three cohorts of incoming students who were tracked for up to four years, year-to-year persistence was consistently higher among students who took at least one course that used the program. Although randomized trials are necessary to determine the causal effect of this system, there appears to be merit in using data analytics to help identify and reach out as early as possible (i.e., before it's "too late") to students who may be struggling. While more affordable than success coaches, these approaches depend on teaching faculty or support staff to make regular use of the early alert system to identify struggling students and reach out to them, as well as an institution's capacity to then provide support to the identified students. In under-resourced colleges, advising staff may be stretched too thin to make productive outreach feasible once students have been flagged.

Another data analytics system, originally designed by another public university and acquired by a learning management system company, aims to increase persistence by matching students to the courses in which they will be most successful. This system recommends courses to students based on their (planned) major, past academic performance, and the past performance of similar students in each course (Young, 2011). Institutions using this system hope that students who follow these recommendations will be more likely to accrue credit, achieve higher grades, and take more direct routes to completing their programs. Early tests of this system show promise although more data are needed to determine the effect of such a system on student retention and performance. Moreover, this kind of system addresses an important yet specific issue facing college students, making it appear to work best in conjunction with other student support services.

Incorporating Non-Cognitive Factors into Developmental Courses

Many entering college students are required to take developmental or remedial math courses to prepare themselves for college-level math; this is particularly true at community colleges where 60 percent of students require developmental math to continue toward a degree. These courses present a significant obstacle to increasing college completion. However, new curriculum programs that utilize behavioral science in the classroom are helping students excel in developmental math. Students using this curriculum are explicitly taught that they are capable of learning math, that math has practical value, and that faculty and staff support them in their learning. These lessons tackle a host of non-cognitive factors that might hinder success, such as reducing stereotype threat among those who believe that they are deficient in math, encouraging a growth mindset, and enhancing students' sense of social belonging. Ultimately, the goal is for students to develop "productive persistence"—strategies that allow them to persevere in the face of adversity. Early results are very exciting, with completion rates in developmental math courses at participating institutions rising from 6 percent to 51 percent in the first year (Silva & White, 2013). This type of approach shows great promise for helping at-risk students by promoting the skills and mindsets that encourage persistence, but further work is necessary to expand such a program beyond developmental math courses.

Persistence Plus

Finally, Persistence Plus provides an additional example of how behavioral nudges can be used to foster the mindsets and behaviors associated with college persistence and success. Students using Persistence Plus receive personalized and interactive daily nudges through text messages or mobile apps to support them on the path to college success. As we and others have highlighted (e.g., Castleman & Page, 2014), programs accessible via mobile and smart phone technology have the potential to put support in the hands of all students—98 percent of young adults own a mobile phone, 83 percent own a smart phone, and black and Hispanic adults have higher rates of smart phone ownership than white adults (Brenner, 2013). Text messaging and mobile devices are effective media for fostering positive behaviors because they are cost-effective, easily automated and personalized, and embraced by populations that would otherwise be difficult to reach and support. Mobile interventions have been shown to be effective in reminding patients to take medication correctly (Wei, Hollin, & Kachnowski, 2011), increasing physical activity among postnatal women (Fjeldsoe, Miller, & Marshall, 2010), and preventing "summer melt" among high school seniors (Castleman & Page, 2014; see Chapter 5). In an era when college advisors are responsible for hundreds if not thousands of students, mobile technology can reach a much wider population at risk for not completing college, including students who do not typically seek help.

Persistence Plus mobile nudges consist of questions and messages that are customized based on college context, student demographics, and student responses. This level of personalization, which has been shown to bolster effects of mobile interventions in a variety of health-related domains (Head, Noar, Iannarino, & Harrington, 2013), allows the provision of tailored support and interventions in a scalable fashion. The nudges help students deal with academic setbacks and external obstacles, organize their time and responsibilities, and make progress toward short- and long-term goals. The content of nudges is grounded in the behavioral science principles discussed previously, such as leveraging social norms to encourage help-seeking, fostering good academic habits through the use of implementation intentions, and encouraging social connections on campus to reduce the specter of stereotype threat. Moreover, the Persistence Plus platform enables students to easily share information on their well-being, goals, and challenges, thereby enabling the referral of students whose responses indicate they need additional support to college staff well before they might otherwise be identified as at risk (e.g., at midterms). Figure 1 in the appendix shows examples of typical nudges we have delivered through Persistence Plus.

Two case studies provide encouraging evidence that this approach can have a positive impact on college student success. Although these initial studies lack a randomized design, early results support the utility of Persistence Plus in bolstering student success and support the need for further research. The first case study took place at Middlesex Community College (MxCC) in Connecticut, an institution serving more than 3,000 students across 50 degree and certificate programs. Beginning in the fall of 2013, approximately 325 students registered to receive Persistence Plus nudges. Nearly a third of these students (31 percent) were first-generation college goers, 41 percent were students of color, and approximately one in five (18 percent) were 25-years or older. These students received nudges six days a week that were designed to promote positive academic behaviors, mindsets, and connection to MxCC.

Initial outcomes are promising. The participating cohort at MxCC had a seven-percentage point higher fall-to-spring retention rate (73 percent) in 2013–2014 than the general population (66 percent). Even more striking was the 78 percent retention rate of first-generation college-goers in the participating cohort—a population that has, on average, twice the rate of attrition of students who are not first in their family to attend college (Chen, 2005). Rigorous experimental testing is now underway to determine the extent to which this increase in retention can be attributed directly to the mobile-based nudges students received.

Our second case study involves a four-year public university and a population of students in online, introductory math courses. University of Washington Tacoma (UWT) is an urban-serving campus of 4,300 students where more than 60 percent of those enrolled are first-generation college-goers. As it launched its first online courses in 2012, UWT was interested in providing additional support to students given the challenges they faced in these introductory courses and in online courses in general. Again, students who opted to receive Persistence Plus support—more than 200 students in introductory STEM courses—have outperformed their peers who did not use this support each term. In online pre-calculus courses, for instance, pass rates among participating students over the six terms have been an average of 12 percentage points higher, and final grades an average of 0.54 points higher, than among non-participating students. Results for online statistics courses that have incorporated the behavioral support system since winter 2014 were similar: over two terms, participating students had passing rates an average of 17.5 percentage points higher and GPAs an average of 0.39 points higher than students not receiving support. One explanation for these positive results may be that students who opted in to Persistence Plus engaged in more effective academic behaviors than non-participating students. For instance, participating students had a missed assignment rate a third of that of non-participating students, and 20 percent of students using Persistence Plus sought tutoring compared to only 4 percent of non-Persistence Plus students.

Although these case studies suggest a positive impact of Persistence Plus on student retention and performance, challenges remain in the development of this system. First, we must ask whether students who choose to participate in these programs have higher levels of motivation or academic achievement than those in the general student population. We have found no evidence of self-selection effects, although by no means has our examination been comprehensive. For example, students who signed up for Persistence Plus at UWT scored lower on a required math pretest at the start of a term than non-participating students, and yet their final course GPAs were higher on average, indicating that students who opted-in were not stronger students at onset. It is possible though, that online students who enrolled in Persistence Plus were aware of their lower math abilities and were more motivated to succeed. However, surveys revealed no differences between students who signed up for the program and those who did not on measures of planfulness, general self-efficacy, or "grit," a construct that taps an individual's "perseverance and passion for long-term goals" (Duckworth, Peterson, Matthews, & Kelly, 2007, p. 1087). Randomized trials are underway to determine the extent to which Persistence Plus has a causal impact on student outcomes, as well as the behaviors and mindsets that may mediate any such effects.

Another important challenge with this model of support is that for some colleges, it upends the traditional relationship that they have and embrace with students. For such campuses, the use of automated personalized nudges is at odds with the close face-to-face connection they want faculty and staff to cultivate with students. While automation might relieve burden on institutional staff and budgets and allow for the custom experience necessary to address the unique issues experienced by a diverse range of students, this model requires a comfort with technology-enabled interventions serving as a first layer of support. This is not a fit for all institutions.

Conclusion

Using interventions rooted in behavioral science to make significant changes in behavior has been successful in a number of sectors, but this approach is relatively new in higher education. However, early results are promising. Multiple studies have shown that the students who traditionally struggle the most are the very students who garner the most benefit from these types of interventions (e.g., Cohen et al., 2006; Sherman et al., 2013; Stephens et al., 2014). Such findings set the stage for what we predict will be rapid growth in the development of low-touch behavioral interventions for higher education. This approach is apparent in the recent announcement of the $5 Million College Success Prize, sponsored by the Robin Hood Foundation and ideas42. The Robin Hood Foundation's mission is to alleviate poverty, and their efforts emphasize education as a primary means of doing so; ideas42 is dedicated to the notion that behavioral science is key to alleviating many social problems. Their co-sponsored competition calls for scalable innovations that combine behavioral science and technology to keep students on track to a timely graduation. As is apparent from the collaboration of these two organizations, behavioral science is coming into focus as an effective solution for addressing many of the challenges facing higher education and, indirectly, the country as a whole.

Yet, there are many questions still to be answered. Moving forward, research that employs randomized experimental models will provide greater opportunity to show the causal relations between behavioral nudges and student outcomes. Moreover, further empirical research will be needed to explore how student behaviors, cognitions, and emotions are directly impacted by interventions and illustrate the mechanisms that lead to positive results.

Equally important will be determining how to weigh student input in the design of behavioral interventions to facilitate student success. In fact, research suggests that many students remain unaware of interventions in which they actively participated, and interventions may even be more effective under these conditions (Walton & Cohen, 2011). Similarly, some interventions might be most effective under conditions that run counter to student input. For example, it is possible to imagine that asking students their personal preferences for how often they want to receive nudges on a daily or weekly basis may not actually result in the optimal dosage. This scenario underscores the need for both field tests with students and more rigorous research.

Finally, as the potential for broader implementation of technology- and behavioral-based interventions grows in higher education, college administrators and support staff might also need to consider how traditional models of academic support can most effectively incorporate and complement these new intervention models. The prospect of identifying struggling students earlier could have implications for how academic advisors and support staff members reach out to students or how students are assigned to services. It is possible that the use of services or technologies with behavioral focus on college campuses may enable support staff to redefine their roles and direct their attention to the students most likely to benefit.

These are challenging questions lacking simple answers. However, as colleges and universities seek more efficient ways to support their increasingly diverse student bodies, these are some of the many interesting issues with which administrators, researchers, and innovators will need to wrestle. Ultimately, small behavioral interventions present a multitude of exciting opportunities in higher education to improve support for college students and move students toward graduation. These interventions are low-cost and relatively low-touch, making them scalable to large and ever more diverse populations who are at-risk of falling through the cracks of current advising systems. Through use of these approaches, colleges and universities can take positive steps toward keeping students enrolled, thereby ensuring students' future success as well as that of the institutions themselves.

Note

1. The authors (Frankfort and Salim) are co-founders of Persistence Plus, a mission-driven social venture that works with colleges to improve student success. Founded as part of the Kauffman Foundation's Education Ventures Program, Persistence Plus has engaged hundreds of higher education administrators and experts in discussions as part of the development of their model.

References

Allcott, H. (2009, October). *Social norms and energy conservation.* Center for Energy and Environmental Policy Research.

Allcott, H., & Mullainathan, S. (2010). Behavior and energy policy. *Science*, M327, 1204–1205.

Arnold, K. E., & Pistilli, M. D. (2012). Course signals at Purdue: Using learning analytics to increase student success. In *Proceedings of the 2nd International Conference on Learning Analytics and Knowledge* (pp. 267–270). New York, NY. doi:10.1145/2330601.2330666

Aronson, J., Fried, C. B., & Good, C. (2002). Reducing the effects of stereotype threat on African American college students by shaping theories of intelligence. *Journal of Experimental Social Psychology, 38*(2), 113–125.

Ayres, I., Raseman, S., & Shih, A. 2009. *Evidence from two large field experiments that peer comparison feedback can reduce residential energy usage.* NBER Working paper series.

Baumeister, R. F., & Leary, M. L. (1995). The need to belong: Desire for interpersonal attachments as a fundamental human motivation. *Psychological Bulletin, 117*, 497–529.

Bennhold, K. (2013, December 7). Britain's Ministry of Nudges. *New York Times.*

Bettinger, E., & Baker, R. (2011, March 7). *The effects of student coaching in college: An evaluation of a randomized experiment in student mentoring.* National Partnership for Educational Access Research Brief.

Borsari, B. B., & Carey, K. B. (2003). Descriptive and injunctive norms in college drinking: A meta-analytic integration. *Journal of Studies on Alcohol, 64*, 331–341.

Bourdieu, P., & Wacquant, L. J. D. (1992). *An invitation to reflexive sociology.* Chicago, IL: University of Chicago Press.

Brenner, J. (2013). *Pew Internet: Mobile.* The Pew Research Center's Internet and American Life Project. Retrieved from www.pewinternet.org/fact-sheets/mobile-technology-fact-sheet/

Castleman, B. L., & Page, L. C. (2014) *Summer nudging: Can personalized text messages and peer mentor outreach increase college going among low-income high school graduates?* University of Virginia Center for Education Policy and Workforce Competitiveness Working Paper No. 9. http://curry.virginia.edu/uploads/resourceLibrary/9_Castleman_Summer TextMessages.pdf

Chen, X. (2005). *First-generation students in postsecondary education: A look at their college transcripts.* Washington, DC: National Center for Education Statistics.

Cialdini, R. B. (2003). Crafting normative messages to protect the environment. *Current Directions in Psychological Science, 12*, 105–109.

Cialdini, R. B., Demaine, L. J., Sagarin, B. J., Barrett, D. W., Rhoads, K., & Winter, P. L. (2006). Managing social norms for persuasive impact. *Social Influence, 1*(1), 3–15.

Cohen, G. L., Garcia, J., Apfel, N., & Master, A. (2006). Reducing the racial achievement gap: A social-psychological intervention. *Science, 313*(5791), 1307–1310.

Croizet, J.-C., & Claire, T. (1998). Extending the concept of stereotype threat to social class: The intellectual underperformance of students from low socioeconomic backgrounds. *Personality and Social Psychology Bulletin, 24*, 588–594.

Duckworth, A. L., Peterson, C., Matthews, M. D., & Kelly, D. R. (2007). Grit: Perseverance and passion for long-term goals. *Journal of Personality and Social Psychology, 92*(6), 1087–1101.

Dweck, C. (2007). *Mindset: The new psychology of success.* New York, NY: Ballantine Books.

Farrington, C. A., Roderick, M., Allensworth, E., Nagaoka, J., Keyes, T. S., Johnson, D. W., & Beechum, N. (2012). *Teaching adolescents to become learners: The role of noncognitive factors in shaping school performance.* University of Chicago Consortium on Chicago School Research.

Fjeldsoe, B. S., Miller, Y. D., & Marshall, A. L. (2010). MobileMums: A randomized controlled trial of an SMS-based physical activity intervention. *Annals of Behavioral Medicine, 39*, 101–111.

Goldstein, N. J., Cialdini, R. B., & Griskevicius, V. (2008). Using social norms to motivate environmental conservation in hotels. *Journal of Consumer Research, 35.*

Gollwitzer, P. M. (1999). Implementation intentions: Strong effects of simple plans. *American Psychologist, 54*(7), 493–503.

Head, K. J., Noar, S. M., Iannarino, N. T., & Harrington, N. G. (2013). Efficacy of text messaging-based interventions for health promotion: A meta-analysis. *Social Science and Medicine, 97,* 41–48.

Hotelchatter blog. (2013). "Great Debate: Why Using Your Towel Only Once Kind of Makes Sense." Retrieved from www.hotelchatter.com/story/2013/6/2/193637/3919/hotels/ Great_Debate%3A_Why_Using_Your_Towel_Only_Once_Kind_of_Makes_Sense_

Hussar, W. J., & Bailey, T. M. (2014). *Projections of Education Statistics to 2022.* National Center for Education Statistics.

Karabenick, S. A., & Dembo, M. H. (2011). Understanding and facilitating self-regulated help seeking. *New Directions for Teaching and Learning, Summer, 126,* 33–43.

Knapp, L. G., Kelly-Reid, J. E., & Ginder, S. A. (2012). *Enrollment in Postsecondary Institutions, Fall 2010; Financial Statistics, Fiscal Year 2010; and Graduation Rates, Selected Cohorts, 2002–2007* (NCES 2012–280). U.S. Department of Education. Washington, DC: National Center for Education Statistics. Retrieved from https://nces.ed.gov/ pubs2012/2012280.pdf

Lotkowski, V. A., Robbins, S. B., & Noeth, R. J. (2004). The role of academic and non-academic factors in improving college retention: ACT policy report. Retrieved from http://act.org/research/policymakers/pdf/college_retention.pdf

Milkman, K. L., Beshears, J., Choi, J. J., Laibson, D., & Madrain, B. C. (2011). Using implementation intention prompts to enhance influenza rates. *Proceedings of the National Academy of Sciences, 108*(26), 10415–10420.

Nickerson, D. W., & Rogers, T. (2010). Do you have a voting plan? Implementation intentions, voter turnout, and organic plan making. *Psychological Science, 21,* 194–199.

Pew Research Center. (2014). The rising cost of not going to college. Pew Research Social and Demographic Trends.

Raisman, N. (2013). *The cost of college attrition at four-year colleges and universities.* Economic Policy Institute.

Robbins, S. B., Lauver, K., Le, H., Davis, D., Langley, R., & Carlstrom, A. (2004). Do psychosocial and study skill factors predict college outcomes? A meta-analysis. *Psychological Bulletin, 130*(2), 261–288.

Rozin, P., Scott, S., Dingley, M., Urbanek, J. K., Jiang, H., & Kaltenbach, M. (2011). Nudge to nobesity I: Minor changes in accessibility decrease food intake. *Judgment and Decision Making, 6*(4), 323–332.

Ryan, A. M., Pintrich, P. R., & Midgley, C. (2001). Avoiding seeking help in the classroom: Who and why? *Educational Psychology Review, 13*(2), 93–114.

Schneider, M. (2010). *Finishing the first lap: The cost of first-year student attrition in America's four-year colleges and universities.* American Institutes for Research.

Sherman, D. K., Hartson, K. A., Binning, K. R., Purdie-Vaughns, V., Garcia, J., Taborsky-Barba, S., Tomassetti, S., Nussbaum, A. D., & Cohen, G. L. (2013). Deflecting the trajectory and changing the narrative: How self-affirmation affects academic performance and motivation under identity threat. *Journal of Personality and Social Psychology, 104*(4), 591–618.

Silva, E., & White, T. (2013). *Pathways to improvement: Using psychological strategies to help college students master developmental math.* Carnegie Foundation for the Advancement of Teaching.

Spencer, S. J., Steele, C. M., & Quinn, D. M. (1999). Stereotype threat and women's math performance. *Journal of Experimental Social Psychology, 35,* 4–28.

Steele, C. M., & Aronson, J. (1995). Stereotype threat and the intellectual test performance of African Americans. *Journal of Personal and Social Psychology, 69*(5), 797–811.

Stephens, N. M., Hamedani, M. G., & Destin, M. (2014). Closing the social-class achievement gap: A difference-education intervention improves first-generation students' academic performance and all students' college transition. *Psychological Science, 25*(4), 943–953.

Thaler, R. H., & Sunstein, C. R. (2008). *Nudge: Improving decisions about health, wealth, and happiness.* New Haven, CT: Yale University Press.

U.S. Department of Education, National Center for Education Statistics. (2013). *The Condition of Education 2013* (NCES 2013–037), Institutional Retention and Graduation Rates for Undergraduate Students.

Walton, G. M., & Cohen, G. L. (2007). A question of belonging: Race, social fit, and achievement. *Journal of Personality and Social Psychology, 92*(1), 82–96.

Walton, G. M., & Cohen, G. L. (2011). A brief social-belonging intervention improves academic and health outcomes of minority students. *Science, 331*(6023), 1447–1451.

Walton, G. M., Cohen, G. L, Cwir, D., & Spencer, S. J. (2012). Mere belonging: The power of social connections. *Journal of Personality and Social Psychology, 102*, 513–521.

Wechsler, H., Nelson, T. F., Lee, J. E., Seibring, M., Lewis, C., & Keeling, R. P. (2003). Perception and reality: A national evaluation of social norms marketing interventions to reduce college students' heavy alcohol use. *Journal of Studies on Alcohol, 64*, 484–494.

Wei, J., Hollin, I., & Kachnowski, S. (2011). A review of the use of mobile phone text messaging in clinical and healthy behaviour interventions. *Journal of Telemedicine and Telecare, 17*(1), 41–48.

Yeager, D. S., & Walton, G. M. 2011. Social-psychological interventions in education: They're not magic. *Review of Educational Research, 81*(2), 267–301.

Young, J. R. (2011, April 10). The Netflix effect: When software suggests students' courses. *Chronicle of Higher Education.* Retrieved from http://chronicle.com/article/The-Netflix-Effect-When/127059/

APPENDIX

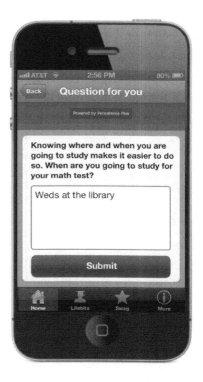

FIGURE 1

In the screen shot at left, students are asked how they are feeling about the upcoming semester and are given tailored encouragement based on their response. In this example, a student who has indicated that they are not doing well (2 stars out of 5) is informed that such feelings are universal, thereby aiming to intercede before doubts about their social belonging may ensue (Walton & Cohen, 2007). The screen shot at right shows a nudge based on the principle of implementation intentions. Before an upcoming exam, Persistence Plus asks students to identify a time and place to prepare for the exam, as committing to a specific time to complete a task significantly increases the likelihood that the task will be completed (Gollwitzer, 1999).

GLOSSARY

The best single source for many of the ideas referenced in this volume is the entertaining and accessible *Thinking, Fast and Slow*, by Daniel Kahneman. Some of the ideas are handled in a more formal way in Eric Angner's textbook *A Course in Behavioral Economics*.

Cognitive overload Especially when confronted by complex and difficult choices, decision-makers can suffer from cognitive overload. For example, a rational choice among the wide range of American postsecondary institutions involves comparing attributes as various as the quality of academic programs, available financial aid, location, and non-academic amenities such as dormitories or athletic teams. When the choice, like that involved choosing a school, involves comparing attributes along many dimensions, the choices are "non-alignable" which can lead to cognitive overload and poor choices (Gourville & Soman, 2005).

Default options Empirical evidence from studies in a number of areas, including retirement savings (Madrian & Shea, 2001; Thaler & Benartzi, 2004) and organ donation (Johnson & Goldstein, 2003) illustrate that the option that takes effect if the decision-maker fails to make an active choice—the default option—has a powerful influence on the ultimate decision. For example, in countries where the default option is to donate one's organs in the event of a fatal car accident, the percentage who "choose" donation is far higher than in countries where the default option is not to donate.

A number of reasons for why the default option is so powerful have been proposed. One reason is a form of loss aversion which makes the status quo appealing because any movement from the status quo (here, the choice not to go along with the default option) is perceived as a loss and is therefore avoided (Samuelson & Zeckhauser, 1988). Another reason is limited cognitive ability, leading people to choose the path of least resistance when faced with complex or worrisome choices, thus limiting the need expend cognitive effort.

Framing   Social psychologists have long known that the way a choice is presented can affect the choice that is made, even when the objective features of the choice are the same. The idea is that the details of the situation are crucial (Ross & Nisbett, 1990). Famously, Tversky and Kahneman (1981) posed questions about a situation in which 600 people were threatened by a deadly disease. They asked one group of people to choose between a treatment that would save 200 of the 600 people with certainty and a treatment what would have a one-third chance of saving everyone and a two-thirds chance of saving none of them. A second group of people we asked to choose between a treatment that would lead to the certain death of 400 of the 600 threatened people and a treatment that had a one-third chance that no-one would die and a two-third chances that everyone would die.

For the first group, the framing was positive with the emphasis on lives being saved. For the second group, the framing was negative, with the emphasis on certain deaths. Choices were very different across the two groups. In the first group, more than 70 percent chose the certain option ("200 are saved") over the risky option. In the second group, less than a quarter chose the certain option ("400 die") over the risky option. But the two groups objectively faced the same choices. The certain option was that 200 would be saved and 400 would die. The risky option was that there was a one-third chance that all 600 would live and a two-thirds chance that all 600 would die.

Loss aversion   No one enjoys losses. The term "loss aversion," as used by behavioral economists and decision theorists, is particular twist on how people view losses. Given a particular starting point, the idea is that a loss of a fixed amount—say, $100—causes a greater reduction in pleasure than a gain of the same amount causes an increase in pleasure. Loss aversion in this sense lies at the heart of the prospect theory developed by Kahneman and Tversky. The starting, or reference point, is very important because choices can vary with the reference point. For example, in a study of merit pay for teachers, Fryer et al. (2012) created one treatment group of teachers who received merit pay at the end of the year, based on the performance of their students. A second treatment group received the merit pay in advance and had to repay it if their students did not perform adequately. The amount of net pay was identical and the only difference was whether the merit pay was seen as a gain or a loss. Because of loss aversion, Fryer et al. (2012) hypothesized that those who receive the upfront payment would work harder to improve student performance. Empirically, the students of those teachers in fact experienced larger increases in achievement.

Narrow bracketing   When facing complex decisions, people tend to break the overall decision into smaller, more manageable pieces. That tendency is called narrow bracketing and can lead to decision-making errors. Considering all of the possibilities together is called broad bracketing. Broad bracketing generally leads to be better decisions but requires far greater cognitive resources. To illustrate the point, Simonson (1990) gave students a choice of six snacks to be eaten in three upcoming weeks. Those who chose all three snacks in advance (broad bracketing) were far more likely to choose a different snack for each week than those who made their choice on the day of the class (narrow bracketing). In an early paper, Kahneman and Tversky (1979) showed that narrow bracketing can lead people to make two sequential choices that are clearly worse than the choice they would have made had they considered the choice together at the same time. Read, Loewenstein, and Rabin (1999), as well as Rabin and Weizsäcker (2009), elaborate on the importance of narrow bracketing.

Salience The likelihood of making a particular choice depends in part on the salience of that choice. If a choice is made to stand out from others—say, by advertisements on public transport advertising a particular proprietary college—it becomes more salient to the decision-maker. Decision-makers tend to focus too much on the choices that are relatively more visible or prominent and ignore choices that might be better for them but which are less visible and therefore less salient.

Time-inconsistency In the economist's standard model of how people decide between options that are available at different times, preferences are consistent. Suppose you are asked whether you'd prefer to have A in 30 days or B in 60 days and you answer that you would prefer B in 60 days. Now suppose you are asked whether you would rather have A right now or B in 30 days. Because the distance in time between A and B is again 30 days, your preferences would be consistent if you say that you would prefer B in 30 days. Your preference would be time-inconsistent if you preferred A right now rather than B in 30. In less abstract terms, most of us have had the experience of promising ourselves in the evening that we will wake up early the next morning rather than sleeping in, only to reverse that choice when the alarm rings.

Chapter 8 of the text by Angner covers the standard model of choices over time. Chapter 9 is an excellent discussion of a newer model that captures time-inconsistency and cites the seminal academic articles on the subject.

References

Fryer, Jr., R. G., Levitt, S. D., List, J., & Sadoff, S. (2012). *Enhancing the efficacy of teacher incentives through loss aversion: A field experiment* (Working Paper No. 18237). National Bureau of Economic Research. Retrieved from www.nber.org/papers/w18237

Gourville, J., & Soman, D. (2005). Overchoice and assortment type: When and why variety backfires. *Marketing Science, 24*(3), 382–395.

Johnson, E. J., & Goldstein, D. (2003). Do defaults save lives? *Science, 302*(5649), 1338–1339.

Kahneman, D., & Tversky, A. (1979). Prospect theory: An analysis of decision under risk. *Econometrica, 47*(2), 263–291. doi:10.2307/1914185

Madrian, B. C., & Shea, D. F. (2001). The power of suggestion: Inertia in 401(k) participation and savings behavior. *The Quarterly Journal of Economics, 116*(4), 1149–1187.

Rabin, M., & Weizsäcker, G. (2009). Narrow bracketing and dominated choices. *The American Economic Review, 99*(4), 1508–1543.

Read, D., Loewenstein, G., & Rabin, M. (1999). Choice bracketing. *Journal of Risk and Uncertainty, 19*(1–3), 171–197. doi:10.1023/A:1007879411489

Ross, L., & Nisbett, R. E. (1990). *The person and the situation: perspectives of social psychology.* London: Pinter & Martin.

Samuelson, W., & Zeckhauser, R. (1988). Status quo bias in decision making. *Journal of Risk and Uncertainty, 1*(1), 7–59.

Simonson, I. (1990). The effect of purchase quantity and timing on variety-seeking behavior. *Journal of Marketing Research, 27*(2), 150–162. doi:10.2307/3172842

Thaler, R. H., & Benartzi, S. (2004). Save More Tomorrow™: Using behavioral economics to increase employee saving. *Journal of Political Economy, 112*(S1), S164–S187. doi:10.1086/380085

Tversky, A., & Kahneman, D. (1981). The framing of decisions and the psychology of choice. *Science, 211*(4481), 453–458.

CONTRIBUTORS

Sandy Baum is Research Professor of Education Policy at George Washington University and a Senior Fellow at the Urban Institute. A higher education economist, she focuses on college prices, student aid, and other aspects of college finance.

Benjamin L. Castleman is an assistant professor of education and public policy at the University of Virginia. His research applies insights from behavioral economics and social psychology to nudge students towards better educational outcomes.

Jill Frankfort is the co-founder of Persistence Plus. Frankfort was previously a Kauffman Foundation Education Ventures Fellow and a director at Jobs for the Future, where she worked with colleges and districts to improve educational outcomes.

Charles Kurose is a Program Associate at the Spencer Foundation. Prior to joining Spencer, he worked as an independent researcher with teams at nonprofit research and advocacy organizations such as the College Board, the Century Foundation, and the Brookings Institute. His research focuses on the economics of higher education and covers topics ranging from student financial aid to institutional finance in higher education.

Ross E. O'Hara is a behavioral researcher at Persistence Plus, where he is focused on improving the educational outcomes of college students. O'Hara received his Ph.D. from Dartmouth College, and completed postdoctoral fellowships at the University of Missouri and the University of Connecticut Medical School.

Joshua A. Price is an Assistant Professor of Economics at Southern Utah University. His research focuses on the economics of education, health, and sports.

Kenneth Salim is the co-founder of Persistence Plus and the Superintendent of Weymouth Public Schools in Massachusetts. The first person in his family to graduate from college, Salim has a doctorate in education from Harvard University.

Saul Schwartz is a professor in the School of Public Policy and Administration. His interests are the economics of education and consumer debt.

Judith Scott-Clayton is an Assistant Professor of Economics and Education at Teachers College, Columbia University, where she teaches courses on labor economics and causal inference. She is also a Senior Research Associate at the Community College Research Center (CCRC), and a Faculty Research Fellow of the National Bureau of Economic Research. She holds a B.A. from Wellesley College and a Ph.D. in Public Policy from Harvard University.

Robert M. Shireman, executive director of California Competes and former U.S. Deputy Undersecretary of Education, has played a leading role in efforts to redesign college accountability systems, financial aid, and repayment of student loans.

Nicole M. Stephens is an Associate Professor of Management and Organizations at Kellogg School of Management. As a social and cultural psychologist, her research explores the ways in which the social world systematically influences how people understand themselves and their actions. Her specific focus is on how social class, race, and gender shape people's everyday life experiences, as well as important life outcomes such as educational attainment and health.

Sarah S.M. Townsend is an assistant professor of management and organization at the Marshall School of Business at the University of Southern California. Her research focuses on how people's social and cultural contexts shape their mindsets. As a social psychologist, she examines how these mindsets, in turn, influence people's ability to thrive in diverse settings, shaping their behavior, emotions, and physiological responses.

INDEX